Instructor's Resource Manual

for

The Speaker's Handbook

Seventh Edition

Jo Sprague

Douglas Stuart

THOMSON

WADSWORTH

Australia • Canada • Mexico • Singapore • Spain • United Kingdom • United States

For more information about our products,
contact us at:
Thomson Learning Academic Resource Center
1-800-423-0563

For permission to use material from this text or
product, submit a request online at
http://www.thomsonrights.com
Any additional requests about permissions can be
submitted by email to
thomsonrights@thomson.com

Thomson Wadsworth
10 Davis Drive
Belmont, CA 94002-3098
USA

Asia
Thomson Learning
5 Shenton Way #01-01
UIC Building
Singapore 068808

Australia/New Zealand
Thomson Learning
102 Dodds Street
Southbank, Victoria 3006
Australia

Canada
Nelson
1120 Birchmount Road
Toronto, Ontario M1K 5G4
Canada

Europe/Middle East/South Africa
Thomson Learning
High Holborn House
50/51 Bedford Row
London WC1R 4LR
United Kingdom

Latin America
Thomson Learning
Seneca, 53
Colonia Polanco
11560 Mexico D.F.
Mexico

Spain/Portugal
Paraninfo
Calle/Magallanes, 25
28015 Madrid, Spain

Contents

Introduction

All teachers are more than dispensers of information, but it seems that the teacher of public speaking wears an exceptional number of instructional hats. You are a coach, a judge, a consultant, an MC, sometimes even an amateur therapist. Above all you are the manager of a very complex system. The nature of the course requires that most of your major pedagogical decisions be made before instruction starts. The scheduling of the class is simply too tight to allow for many modifications during the term. Part I of this instructor's resource manual reviews a number of the preliminary decisions a teacher makes when designing a class.

You have already made one excellent decision. By selecting *The Speaker's Handbook* you have made a choice for flexibility. The Handbook approach allows you to design your class in a modular fashion. You may start anywhere and assign sections as they fit your objectives. Students can be referred to chapters already covered if it is apparent that they need review. Students can also be referred to chapters that have not yet been discussed in class. The sections of the book are written to stand alone and to be used by students without a great deal of guidance. If your course is designed to emphasize theory you can supplement the prescriptive advice with additional readings or with lectures to provide a theoretical context.

Part II of this instructor's resource manual offers you a sampling of course materials that have worked well for us and our colleagues. The syllabi, assignments, and critique forms serve to illustrate only some of the ways that you can adapt materials of your choice to make the most of the Handbook format.

Part III of the manual directly concerns itself with the five large sections of *The Speaker's Handbook*: Foundation, Preparation, Organization, Development, and Presentation, and offers sample activities and assignments for these topics as well as discussing how to use the exercises in the text. For access to the sample speech transcripts and outlines referred to in many of the exercises, please go to Sample Speeches under Book Resources on *The Speaker's Handbook* Web site.

Part IV consists of sample test questions over the material in the Handbook.

Part V, the Resource Integration Guide, is a list, by chapter, of the variety of other resources available to you from Wadsworth/Thomson Learning.

Acknowledgments

We begin by acknowledging three former co-authors of the Instructor's Resource Manual; in the pages that follow, many of their words and ideas are still present: thanks to Gary Ruud for his invaluable assistance with the first three editions, to Mindi Ann Golden for her contribution to the fourth edition, and to Neeley Silberman for her work on the fifth and sixth editions. The Resource Integration Guide that constitutes Part V was put together by Shona Burke of Wadsworth, to whom we are grateful. We are also grateful to several former graduate teaching associates at San Jose State University for offering us class activities and test questions to include in this manual. Specifically, we would like to thank Michelle Waters for her contribution of the "Ethical Quality Scale" exercise (described in Part III of this manual, Chapter 3), and to Shar Gregg and Melody Ross for creating and contributing the "Supporting a Claim Speech" (described in Part II of this manual). It is never possible to acknowledge all the creators of classroom activities, which make the rounds among committed teachers who add their own variations. This collaborative development of pedagogical materials provides an ideal illustration of the socially constructed nature of communication. We thank those who have helped our collective store of teaching activities evolve, and apologize to those we cannot acknowledge by name. Finally, we would like to thank the instructors who use *The Speaker's Handbook* and who continue to provide us with the valuable comments and suggestions that make a revision of this magnitude possible.

Part I
Issues in Teaching Public Speaking

As you begin to design a class, you must recognize the outside forces that limit your options. Public speaking classes are often service courses that are required by programs and departments. Your course objectives must be tailored to the needs of your consumers. A career-oriented public speaking course for business students is very different from a general education course designed to help all students develop intellectual skills they will need for communication as mature learners throughout the rest of a college education. Because speech classes are often multi-section courses, there may also be department standards regarding the number of assignments, the student workload and the evaluation methods. Become aware of the agreements that govern the course you will teach and inform yourself about the reasons behind them. Even with some limitations, there will remain a great number of issues that are left to your discretion.

An instructor must first make some initial decisions about the goals, roles, and norms of public speaking instruction and then give some thought to the implications of teaching speech in an increasingly multicultural society. The specific issues related to grading, evaluating, and managing a public speaking class are complex. Here we highlight some of the major implications of the decisions you will make. We have not attempted to disguise our preferences on some of these topics, but we recognize their complexity. Many outstanding teachers select totally different approaches to classroom management. What is most important is that you give all of these issues thoughtful consideration before you set up your class. Be aware of the impact of your decisions on student learning. Then resolve each issue in a way that is best suited to your teaching style, the characteristics of your students, and the specific objectives of your class.

A. Goals, Roles, and Norms

Before a teacher can set objectives for student learning or select specific speech assignments, it is essential to think about the purposes of the course. One of your authors has delineated four main thrusts of communication instruction: transmitting cultural knowledge, developing students' intellectual skills, providing students with career skills, and reshaping the values of society (Sprague, 1990). Obviously, how a teacher prioritizes these goals will have everything to do with whether students are learning to present technical reports so they can succeed as middle managers, finding their own voices as citizens, or seeking to enter into a long tradition of eloquence.

Springing from these most basic decisions about the purpose of speech education is a series of questions about what role the teacher plays. Is one a transmitter of knowledge, a role model of effective speaking, a moderator of real public interactions among students about real social issues? In the area of criticism, it has been suggested that teachers can function quite differently depending on whether they respond to student speeches as judges, coaches, or articulate audience members (Sprague, 1991).

Finally, once a class has a certain sense of its overall direction, and a feel for what the teachers' role will be in guiding students in that direction, the class will take on a certain ambiance and develop norms of interaction. Some speech classes feel like lecture classes where the topic just happens to be communication, but the usual classroom norms prevail. Others seem like recitation sessions or even take on the aura of speech contests. The norms are those of a performance event with a focus on the "stage." Other classes are best described as workshops or laboratories. The norms are those of collaboration toward skill acquisition. These "workshop" classes are rather informal and speeches are seen more as exercises than real public communicative events; the skills are being mastered now for application in "real" arenas later. Finally, some classes are constituted as "public spaces," with norms being those that are followed for serious public exchange about important topics among members of a community.

Most classes combine a variety of goals, roles, and interactional norms. But teachers who have thought about their educational priorities in terms of how they see their class fitting into broader social contexts tend to provide a more unified educational experience than those who operate only at the level of moving through a set of assignments.

B. Cultural and Gender Issues

The Speaker's Handbook stresses the relationship between speech and social identity. The implication of this for teachers of public speaking is that recommendations about how a person should speak are, in a very real sense, recommendations about who a person should be. As a discipline we are experiencing a heightened awareness of the ways that our taken-for-granted assumptions about classroom practices and about speech effectiveness might inadvertently give privilege to some groups of students and inadvertently exclude or marginalize other groups. This topic is too far-reaching and complex to address in an Instructor's Resource Manual, but we urge you to review all the messages that might be transmitted to students by your instructional choices. All classrooms should be hospitable places. Public speaking classes are special in at least two respects. First, the public nature of the student performances makes it more visible when instructors or students are insensitive to issues of gender and culture. But more important, public speaking classrooms offer opportunities for different groups to find areas of commonality and to bridge their differences through civil, rational, public conversations.

Specifically, the Mosely-Braun speeches and responses provided in Sample Speeches under Book Resources on the *Speaker's Handbook* Web site offer an opportunity for discussion of cultural factors. Have your students read this exchange and initiate a conversation about the ways that each participant was revealing values, historical experiences, and cultural identities both in what they argued and in the ways they chose to frame their arguments and their use of language.

1. What cultural factors influence our understanding of effective public speaking?

The models of public communication taught in the traditional public speaking class, and generally those emphasized in *The Speaker's Handbook*, emphasize clarity and directness. In many cultures this "plain speaking" would not be considered eloquent. In fact the directness and explicitness of messages may appear rude or unpolished to some students. What appears to be a simple requirement of establishing credibility can be seen as forcing a student speaker to brag inappropriately, if he or she comes from a culture that places a high value on humility or has a long tradition of indirectness of expression.

As an instructor, you can never be aware of all of the cultural variations you may encounter, but you can communicate an openness and curiosity about various forms of public speaking. Ask students to share models of what they consider effective speaking. Include sample speech materials from Native American speakers, Mexican American speakers, and African Americans. You can also open discussions of women's experiences as speakers. Are there double standards for speech effectiveness? Are women forced to make choices between their private speaking styles and the prescribed public style that creates special problems for them? A few general readings at the end of this section will suggest ways to integrate these cultural and gender issues into your class.

This edition of the *Handbook* places an even greater emphasis on the strengths of oral communication. The over-reliance on speech formats and styles patterned after written expression has emphasized certain cultural patterns, implicitly suggesting that others are inferior. For many centuries, and in many parts of the world today, oral language has dominated. Some scholars call the mediated communication of our electronic age a second phase of orality. In any case, we cannot be too sure that in the emerging global society the student trained in full sentence outlining and linear propositional reasoning will be the most successful. A student with an ear for the rhythms of rap music or a feel for the subtle nuances of social dynamics may fare just as well.

We are not suggesting that you abandon the prescriptions from the book that we have written and you have selected. Obviously, these ways of speaking are serviceable in contemporary US culture. But we believe it is important that teachers recognize there are alternative forms of eloquence and that they open dialogues with their students about the entire range of human symbolic behavior.

2. What about accents?

An accent is a habit pattern from one language that is carried over into a second or third language. There are two problems with accents. First, speech that is too heavily accented may be incomprehensible and thus the entire point of speaking is lost. Secondly, accents may be judged on sociolinguistic grounds, allowing some listeners to attribute characteristics to speakers based on their national or regional speech patterns.

Both of these problems are problems for listeners as well as speakers. Although the speaker who is unfairly dismissed as inferior is a clear loser, an audience who fails to hear the "truth" of a message because of nonstandard pronunciation or diction loses as well. Meaning is jointly constructed. If your class is a multicultural community, it would be a disservice to treat these topics as problems only of the non-native or nonstandard speaker. Native speakers of English (most of whom are not fluent or even minimally trained in other languages) can come to realize how fortunate they are that so many other speakers have come 90% of the way into their speech communities to make intercultural exchange possible. Their communicative competence in a multicultural world ought to include a willingness to go the remaining 10% of the way and to practice attuning their ear to unfamiliar inflections and minor variations in sounds. US audiences would also benefit from being reminded that American English is only one of the many acceptable Englishes among the world languages. We seem to recognize this when speaking to an Australian or British speaker, but frequently commit the faux pas of treating a Kenyan or a Malaysian as a second language speaker.

The public speaking class can be a place to look for a common language rather than to enforce a standard language. This seems to us to be a particularly important distinction to make at this moment in history.

C. Grading

Problems of grading and evaluation plague all teachers. Public speaking classes are particularly troublesome, however, for several reasons. A student's speech performance is often affected by anxiety beyond the student's control. Because the public disclosure of one's ideas is so closely linked to one's identity, students are highly ego-involved in their presentation. They are much more likely to feel personally diminished by a low grade on a speech than by a low grade on a history exam. The ephemeral nature of the speech act further complicates grading. A teacher must make complex evaluations about a fleeting interaction and record those evaluations while continuing to listen and watch. These factors compound the difficulties inherent in all evaluation, making it especially important that you give careful though to grading decisions like the following:

1. What aspects of the course will be graded and in what relative proportions?

A grading system cannot be selected until you have clearly delineated the course objectives and settled on a basic set of assignments. Then you should consider the relative weighting of the various components of the course. First, consider the ratio of speech performance to cognitive understanding of rhetorical principles. Some classes have a heavy emphasis on theory, while others focus on actual public speaking skills. What balance is appropriate for your course—50/50, 80/20, 40/60? Be sure that the weights you assign to grades for outlines, exams and written projects reflect your conscious choice. Similarly, decide how you want to weight the components within the speech assignments. Is delivery equal in importance to content? Half as important? Twice as important? The way you distribute points or compute total grades makes a philosophical statement to your students.

Mentally run through several scenarios of different types of students to see if the final grade calculation reflects your best intent. What will happen to the very glib and articulate student who does little research? What about the student who excels on exams, outlines, class attendance but gives uninspired speeches? How will a student fare who skips a couple of major assignments altogether but shines on the ones attempted? It's easy to think about grading the consistent student, but consider in advance how you want your grading system to deal with these inconsistent but not uncommon patterns of student performance. The system you devise should work for you; you should not be surprised by what it "makes you do" in any circumstances. Even those of us who have taught for a long time are constantly revising the weighting of our assignments and try to leave a certain margin in our systems for holistic judgments to offset atomistic ones.

2. What general system or grading structure will be used?

There are a number of ways to design an evaluation system, each with its advantages and disadvantages. Select the one, or the combination, that suits your class and your instructional philosophy and the norms of the department in which you teach.

Letter grades on each assignment. These grades are transformed into numerical values (usually A = 4, B = 3, etc.) and then weighted according to a pre-announced system (for example, Speech 1 will count 15 percent of the final grade). This system has the advantage of using symbols familiar to students and in being fairly simple to administer. On the other hand, A, B, C grades on each assignment can sometimes lead to obsessive student concentration on grading. Additionally, the five-point scale, even expanded by pluses and minuses, may not provide enough range for a teacher to express the many degrees of competence observed.

Point systems. The teacher determines a potential number of points for each assignment by assessing its difficulty and its value as a learning assignment. Students receive a point score for each assignment and these are totaled at the end of the class. Final grades are determined by a pre-announced system, most often 90 percent of the possible points qualifies for an A, 80 percent for a B, etc. For instance, if it were possible to earn 300 points in a course, 270–300 would be an A, and 240–269 would be a B. These systems allow teachers to quantify the relative importance of various assignments and of components of assignments. Delivery might be worth five points in a thirty-point speech, for instance. Very fine discriminations are possible on major projects.

One drawback of point systems is that they can trigger sustained discussions about the difference between a "32" and a "33" on a fifty-point speech. Students also sometimes become confused about how the points translate to a final letter grade. The D received by a student who made 60 percent of the possible points on every assignment can come as a sudden shock.

Contract systems. Students can contract for the grade they wish to receive and often can select from among several options to achieve the grade. Explicit criteria are established to define the conditions of the contract. These systems allow students to participate in designing the experiences that will be most meaningful for them. Frequently students are given more than one opportunity to meet the objectives set forth in the contract. This does much to reduce the anxiety surrounding letter grades, since most performances are evaluated as either "acceptable" or "not acceptable yet." Contract grading takes great skill to establish and administer, and despite its compatibility with the behavioral objectives orientation to instruction, is controversial among some administrators. That is, charges of "grade inflation" are leveled because any student can theoretically achieve the top grade. Some people believe that such systems reward quantity rather than quality of student work. It is useful to consider carefully answers to these charges within an institutional context before adopting contract grading.

3. Will the grading system be norm-referenced or criterion-referenced?

Each teacher must decide whether student performance will be evaluated by comparing it to pre-established criteria, or by comparing it to the performance of other students in the class. A now-classic article by Smythe, Kibler and Hutchings (1973) provides an excellent comparison of the benefits of criterion-referenced versus norm-referenced grading systems. It should be acknowledged, though, that no system of competency-based instruction is established without the instructor drawing on normative data. When a teacher gives a student twenty-six out of thirty points or certifies that an objective in a contract has been met, that teacher thinks not just of abstract criteria but of a backlog of experience with similar students in similar courses. Conversely, not even the most entrenched proponent of norm-referenced grading holds, in practice, to strict quotas for each letter grade. These instructors usually recognize that there are exceptional classes where "normal" distributions of final grades would be inappropriate. Philosophically, we prefer the criterion-referenced approaches where every student understands the criteria for success and every student has a chance to receive a final grade based only on his or her own performance. The prescriptive delineation of skills that is the backbone of *The Speaker's Handbook* is well suited to a competency-based, criterion-referenced system.

4. Should grades reflect such factors as effort, improvement, attendance, and attitude?

The basis of all grading systems should be the student's actual performance—written or oral—as measured against relevant and public pre-established criteria. When a teacher assigns a final grade, she or he in effect certifies that a student has a certain skill level. If the grades reflect the instructor's judgments about a student's effort or attitude, they are reporting inferences rather than trained observations. A student can try very hard and still turn in a substandard performance. A student can have a negative attitude toward the class and still show an outstanding grasp of the theories of public speaking. Grading on improvement can lead to highly misleading reports. If a student improves 100 percent from absolutely terrible to just poor, should that student receive an A, while a student who did very good work all term receives a D because there was no improvement? The example is extreme, but it illustrates the difficulty of making and interpreting such judgments. Because the learning curve is negatively accelerated, students who start at the lowest level of competence will probably make the most dramatic improvement. This does not mean that other students are not working as hard.

Finally, grading on attendance does tend to trivialize a course, and is forbidden on some campuses. Students must be present to hear their classmates' speeches. The incentive to do so can take the form of powerful persuasion from the instructor or the requirement of a certain number of written critiques. The learning as an audience member is what is evaluated, not the mere presence of the student.

It cannot be denied that un-objectifiable factors influence an instructor's global evaluation of students. We recommend that you relegate such factors, like *your perceived judgment* of attitude or effort, to a minor role. You may use them to deal with borderline cases in a letter-graded course, or, in a point system, you can assign a relatively small number of points to a factor such as "Participation and Commitment."

Remember that you do not *know* about the private lives and internal states of all of your students, so it is unfair to overemphasize what you happen to know about some or what you may infer about others. We have heard teachers say, "I couldn't help being impressed with the fact that she commuted fifty miles to class and was never late, so I gave her the next higher grade." Perhaps the student next to that one commuted seventy miles but did not happen to talk about it. Better, we think, to show your concern and admiration for students efforts in a supportive style of communication and flexibility and generosity toward the entire class than to let these inferences have much influence on your grading. What you know about for sure, and what you are most trained to assess, is their oral and written performance as speech students.

5. Who should grade?

Some classes include peer grading or self-grading as part of the course. While peer *feedback* and self-*evaluation* are excellent sources of learning for a student, we think that assigning grades is the teacher's responsibility and should not be delegated. In these days of easy access to videotaping, it is even possible to grade your own students when you must miss class. Let the substitute teacher manage the session and give some immediate feedback, but you can view the tape and assign the actual grade.

D. Providing Feedback

While students may gain marginally from the mere experience of giving speeches, the real improvement comes from receiving feedback on aspects of their performance. One of the most important tasks of a public speaking instructor is to structure the course so that the feedback is comprehensive, constructive, and appropriate. Here are some of the issues one must consider:

1. Who should give the feedback?

Presumably you, the instructor are the most qualified to evaluate the speeches and certainly it is a major part of your responsibility to respond in detail to each performance. There can be no justification for substituting peer feedback for instructor feedback. Many courses draw on the impressions of classmates as audience members, though, to supplement instructor comments. This practice has several advantages. The student critics themselves gain in critical listening skills and in understanding of rhetorical principles by being required to make specific and intelligent comments on classroom speeches. The speaker receives a variety of perspectives on the speech. No matter how skilled the instructor, he or she cannot react to every aspect of the speech that is worthy of comment. The more critics responding, the greater number of strengths and weaknesses that are likely to be identified. Also, student comments can serve to reinforce an instructor's comments. The speaker may believe that the teacher is "a nut about organization" and discount a comment on shaky transitions. It is harder to ignore the fact that a dozen classmates state that they also had trouble following the flow of the speech.

In almost direct contrast, another advantage of peer criticism is that it dramatizes to speakers the inconsistency of responses to certain aspects of a speech. The complexity of the speech process and the variety of audience reactions becomes clear when an introductory joke is classified as "a wonderful attention getter," "tacky and tasteless," and "a boring waste of time." The speaker comes to see that audience analysis is indeed an art rather than a science.

There are some risks and limitations to peer criticism that must be considered. Sometimes, reactions do not range across a continuum but present a sharp contrast between the judgment of the majority of the class and the judgment of the instructor. This creates an awkward situation if the student opinion is based on a less-informed understanding of the speech process, for example, if a "halo effect" error is in operation where excellent delivery skills overshadow flimsy content. (An instructor should be open enough to at least entertain the notion that a conclusion wildly at odds with a unanimous audience reaction might reflect some sort of blind spot or reverse halo effect.) A second danger of peer criticism is that student critics may be harsh, tactless or trivial in their comments. A final disadvantage of peer criticism is that students who are acting primarily as critics are not providing the student with a realistic audience situation. It is disconcerting to speak to thirty tops of heads as listeners labor over comments and checklists, and unnerving to have a witty comment greeted not by laughter but by a scramble for pencils to write "good use of humor."

To minimize the risks of peer criticism we suggest these steps:

Train students as critics. Talk to them about the criteria by which speeches are judged and about the techniques of phrasing comments constructively (**2d**).

Structure the peer criticism. Provide checklists or critique forms that focus on important aspects of a speech performance so that presentation does not overshadow substance. If you are using oral peer criticism, control it tightly early in the class. Do not ask, "What did you think of Linda's speech?" Somebody might tell you! Ask, "What did Linda do in her introduction to get your attention?" or "If Linda were to concentrate on improving one aspect of her delivery for her next speech, what would you suggest take priority?"

Limit peer criticism so that the speaker still experiences a relatively spontaneous audience response. Try not to have the entire class serving as critics to all aspects of every speech. There are several ways to preserve a natural speech environment. For instance, allow no writing during the speech and have each student fill out a brief checklist or questionnaire after each speech. Or appoint groups or rows to focus on certain components of the speech and write comments on organization only, delivery only, attention factors only, etc. Or, designate a few students each day to serve as critics, require each student to critique one speech per day or five speeches per round, or in some other way provide for a sampling of audience comments rather than comments for every speaker from every audience member. Oral criticism can likewise be distributed by assigning certain students to talk about particular speeches or about a component of a series of speeches. For instance, at the end of a class period, one student might talk about the introductions she heard that day, another might comment on the use of reasoning, and so on.

2. Should feedback be written or oral?

Technically, the main differences between written and oral feedback are that written feedback takes longer to encode and that it provides the student with a record of comments to which to refer. The controversy over whether teachers should rely on written comments or on oral comments is more accurately an issue of whether feedback should be public or private. Most academic judgments are communicated to students in a confidential manner. Students even rebel against having their grades posted by social security number because some see this as a violation of their right to privacy. Why, then, do speech teachers feel justified in presenting elaborate and detailed public discussions of the strengths and weaknesses of individual student performances, even at the risk of embarrassing the students? To some extent, the psychomotor nature of some of the skills taught encourages speech teachers to draw on a "coaching" model in instruction, correcting errors on the spot as a football coach or music teacher might do. Instructors also like to illustrate important principles to observing students by pointing to immediate models of good and bad speaking.

As a general rule, we believe that feedback to individual students should be private, usually through written comments and checklists. You can save writing time and deal with some of the subtle or complex points by delivering some of your criticism in private or semi-private conferences. Some instructors try to dismiss class a few minutes early and speak individually to the day's speakers, or to meet with them the next class period when returning written critiques. These conferences may be very brief but still add a personal touch to the written critiques, and allow the students to ask questions and clarify points.

When an instructor chooses to make individual public comments they should be brief, supportive, and directed toward impersonal components of communication. Never make public remarks about a speaker's mannerisms or speech habits that reflect on personality. Never tease or imitate a student.

Individual speeches do present wonderful "teaching moments" that provide perfect illustrations of points you want to make. Remember that the student who has just spoken and is still standing at the lectern is not in the best frame of mind to digest a subtle point about credibility. Admit that you are probably choosing to teach the concept to the other students, likely at the expense of the student most involved. If you want to seize a teaching moment, consider waiting until you are back in the instructional role rather than the critic role. After a set of speeches, you can go back to the front of the room and say, "It became clear today that several people are still having trouble with introductions. Now let me remind you . . . ." Use the speeches, as a group, to illustrate some points to the entire class.

3. When should feedback be given?

Learning theory tells us that in order for feedback to be effective, it should occur as close as possible to the behavior that one wants to reinforce or discourage. Yet communication theory tells us that communication channels are often overloaded with psychological noise at moments of high stress and that this is not an optimal time to process complex information. Speech teachers tend to argue these issues vehemently when they compare their timing of giving speech feedback. Some teachers give elaborate individual oral critiques right after each speech and have their comments written, grades recorded, and written comments ready to hand to students as they leave class. Other teachers say a noncommittal "thank you" following each performance and return written comments and grades the next class period or even several days later at the end of a round of speeches. Choices on this issue are largely a matter of teacher style and experience. Beginning teachers find it difficult to write comprehensive and meaningful comments under pressure. Some more experienced teachers report that it adds to their "burnout" factor to rehash entire rounds of speeches outside of class and that they prefer to find efficient ways to communicate their feedback on the spot.

If you grade speech content and organization before or after the performance, primarily on the basis of outlines, then you can jot comments on delivery, audience adaptation and the like during the speech. Developing checklists and critique forms streamlines the process and saves you from writing the same comments again and again. Be sure, though, that student critiques, whether written or oral, never seem to be mass-produced or mechanical. The speaking student has shared some personal ideas in a risky public forum and deserves some individual confirmation and recognition. By this same token, if you do withhold your official comments and grades until a later class period, give each student some immediate and positive reinforcement on the spot. Smile, make eye contact, and say something like, "That was fascinating, Dave. I never knew there were so many kinds of lizards. Your own enthusiasm for the subject showed through with your liveliest delivery so far."

Another issue of feedback timing is whether to discuss each speech immediately after presentation, or to wait until the end of a round of speeches. Questions and discussion of speech content right after the speech enhances the student's experience of speaking as a give-and-take of ideas. Too much immediate focus on the speech *as a speech* can overemphasize the image of the speaker as performer (See **1c** in the *Handbook*). Brief, specific comments on speech effectiveness might be in order but more extended teaching by example should be reserved until the focus is back on the instructor. If you subscribe to the coaching model remember that most coaches do their work in practice sessions, not in public. Build in opportunities for work sessions and support group meetings. If possible, try to arrange a speech lab where students can come by and practice with instructors or tutors. In the presentation of class speeches, we recommend that you follow the norms of an audience setting. Let the students experience being treated as guest speakers, free from interruptions and public correction.

4. What should you say in your criticism of speeches?

Even after the who, how, and when of classroom critique is determined, the teacher is left with the biggest question of *what* to say that will be most helpful. This is a rhetorical task of selection. It is not possible or desirable to communicate all your judgments on every speech. Students will become depressed and discouraged if you overload them with comments, just as they do when the receive a paper so covered with red ink that their own ideas are totally obscured. Yet, they do want to receive a substantial amount of information about your reaction to the speech, and research shows that they are eager to receive suggestions for improvement as well as compliments. The most important thing to bear in mind is that the feedback you give should be tied in to the assignment that was made. The sample critique forms in this *Instructor's Resource Manual* clearly parallel the assignment sheets that the students worked from in preparing for the speech. It is unfair to stress organization and reasoning in making an assignment and then to write most of your comments on the speaker's language and style. Emphasize the points that are most important. When you comment on minor problems, make that clear by putting the comment in parentheses, off in a box in the corner, or by prefacing it with, "This is a small issue but you might also try to work on . . . ."

Critique forms can be set up to indicate the relative importance of components of a speech. Look at your checklists and forms to see what message they are sending to the students. Do they have three sections on content and twelve on delivery? If you do not want to subtly suggest that delivery is four times as important as content, adjust the visual message through indentation, capitalization, and so on.

Remember that students may read your comments over and over and dwell on their recollection of your oral remarks. Take time to phrase tactful and supportive messages. Be sure to comment on positive as well as negative points. Acknowledge apparent effort. Remind the student of your willingness to help. Occasionally, insert a personal comment. This serves to communicate that although you may be interacting primarily as teacher to student you also acknowledge a person to person relationship with each student. Use the students' names; refer to their earlier speeches. You might say, "I'm so pleased with your improvement," or "I'm disappointed in your delivery," or "I loved the opening story," or "Maya Angelou is my favorite, too," or "I know it's discouraging, but keep trying."

E. Classroom Logistics

An effective public speaking teacher needs management skill as well as instructional skill. Beginning speech teachers can be overwhelmed with the demands of scheduling, coordinating, timing speech performances, lectures, exams, critique sessions, and make-up work. Once you have made decisions about the content and evaluation of your course, here are some of the problems you will have to face.

1. Scheduling of speeches

You can pass around a sign-up sheet for each assignment, rotating who has the first options. You can divide students into permanent groups and assign a group for each day, again rotating order so that the same people don't go first each time. Or you can use any of dozens of other logical schemes. What we strongly recommend is that you announce a schedule of speakers, either for the entire term or well in advance of each assignment. Then stick to the schedule! Speech performances are stressful and students deserve to be able to plan for the day of the event. They may want to eat a good breakfast that day or wear their lucky socks. It is disrespectful of their schedules to ask them to be prepared several days in a row.

2. Make-up speeches

By the same token, students should understand the seriousness of their commitment and be prepared to speak at the assigned time. All too often a round of speeches that should take four class periods stretches over six or seven because of students who miss class due to genuine emergencies and students who simply are not prepared to speak at the assigned time. This is perhaps the most universal and frustrating logistic problem teachers face, and we have never encountered a completely satisfactory solution. Here are a few approaches that have been tried:

No penalty for the first miss, regardless of the reason. There would be increasing grade penalties for subsequent misses, regardless of reason. (This is the school of thought that says, "Go to the beach if you want, but you're gambling that you won't get sick on the day of another speech.")

Students who miss speeches must be ready to speak every class period thereafter until a space becomes available. The instructor allocates this available time by drawing lots or by his/her perception of the students' overall attendance and commitment up to that point in the course. No grade penalty is assessed, but the student has the uncertainty of wondering if and when a make-up opportunity will be available and the inconvenience of being prepared each time until a chance is given.

Out of class make-up sessions at the teacher's convenience. Students doing this sort of make-up must assemble an audience of at least twenty people to hear their speeches. For example, if five students were giving speeches they would have to collaborate to draft at least sixteen classmates, roommates, friends, family members and such, to round out an audience.

A system of standby speakers. A student assigned to speak at a future meeting would volunteer to be ready one class earlier in case a scheduled speaker misses class. No one has to do this more than once a term and it helps the class to stay more or less on schedule.

Student groups are allocated "slots" to fill over the entire course. They have about ten percent more speaking slots than they need for their members to do all assignments. They may use the extra slots for make-ups, trade them to other groups or leave them unused. This is a fascinating exercise in group dynamics and some time for planning should be allotted in class. This model works well with a support group approach to the class. The teacher stays completely out of all scheduling issues. She or he just arrives in class and says, "Today I will hear up to five speeches. Group Three, give me a list of who will be speaking."

Have students make-up speeches on videotape or in your office during office hours. Speaking in any setting other than to a live audience is not comparable to the experiences we build speech classes around. This option should be used very sparingly. We would suggest that it never be allowed for more than one speech and then only if an extreme emergency arises too late for a classroom speech to be scheduled. Or if an instructor requires that every speech be given to pass the course and a student misses every reasonable opportunity, this sort of assignment might be substituted but with a severe grade penalty.

3. Timing of speeches

Time limits must be adhered to for a class to stay on schedule. It is a good idea to time question-and-answer periods and critiques, too. A teacher is usually too busy to serve as timekeeper and should use student volunteers. The timekeeper can give signals at a few points during the speech or can go through a set of cards that provides continuous information on the amount of time remaining. Although the latter procedure may not represent conditions in the "real world," it helps beginning students learn to manage their speaking time.

4. Audience demeanor

It may be advisable to discuss your standards for audience behavior. Try to approach this as a discussion of listening techniques and minimizing distractions for the speaker rather than as a diatribe on good manners.

5. Level of formality

Once it was customary to require student speakers to wear business attire when speaking, and in general to simulate a formal speech situation. Today the classroom laboratory generally has a much more casual atmosphere. Still, some teachers are reviving the practice of appointing a different student chairperson to MC each class period—introducing speakers and their topics and moderating the class discussion. Decide whether or not you want to have applause after each speech.

Taken separately, these and related logistic questions can sometimes seem trivial. Yet in combination the decisions you make will set a tone for the class and establish your own image of competence. Once you have decided on the classroom format you want, discuss the ground rules with your students. You might want to go as far as one teacher did in developing a handout to summarize these points, as shown on the next page.

Protocol for Speech Days

Speakers

1. Get to class on time. Preferably a few minutes early.
2. Turn in your outline and critique form to the instructor before speeches begin.
3. Be sure your videotape is advanced to the end of your most recent speech and that your name is on both the tape and the box. Give the tape to the video operator before speeches begin.
4. Be as organized as possible before class begins. Have your presntation aids and equipment organized.
5. Try to treat the entire period as a real audience setting. Talk to the instructor about any problems before or after class. Do not break the mood of a speaking situation with questions, conferences, apologies, etc.

Audience

1. Be there on time. If you are unavoidably late, wait outside the door and enter between speeches.
2. You are required to be courteous; requested to be attentive, responsive, supportive listeners.
3. Fill out the required number of critiques. Do not write during the speeches. During the question/answer period you should have time to write specific, constructive and tactful comments. Be sure your name is on the critiques and hand them to the instructor after class. Your name will be removed before they are passed on to the speakers.
4. Ask penetrating but not hostile questions. This will make the class more interesting for all of us (and it helps your participation grade).

Timekeeper

1. Sit near the center of the room and hold the cards so they are visible.
2. Work down from the maximum time. When the 1/2 minute card is reached, hold it higher.
3. When the stop card is reached, hold it up and turn it so the instructor can see.
4. Record the time of each speaker and turn in the list at the end of class.
5. Thanks for volunteering.

Video Operator

1. Arrive a few minutes early and review the working of the equipment.
2. Collect the videotapes from the speakers and arrange them in order.
3. Insert each tape, adjust the camera to speaker's height, focus; give them a nod to begin.
4. During the speech keep mostly a nearly full figure shot. Zoom in once for a head and shoulders shot for a minute or so. Try to follow the speaker's movement and include presentation aids and demonstrations, but do not make constant adjustments.
5. Tape the question and answer period as well as the speech.
6. Return the tapes to speakers at the end of class.
7. Thanks for volunteering.

F. Fear of Speaking

At least one study has shown that fear of public speaking is the most widely held fear, overshadowing even the fear of death. This complicates speech instruction, as you must deal with the extreme emotional reaction most students experience as they approach the public speech. Your job goes beyond transmitting information and requires you to set a psychological tone that will optimize learning. Since most speech teachers love to talk, they may find it difficult to empathize with the fear and even more generalized anxiety that some students feel. One must recognize that this apprehension is far more debilitating that the mildly uncomfortable twinges of excitement that actually serve to energize experienced speakers.

Begin by becoming familiar with the different types of fear (communication apprehension, stage fright, reticence, shyness), the effects and symptoms of each, the self report and observational instruments used to assess fear, and the various treatment programs available. The literature on this topic is vast. A good summary and synthesis of the key issues is found in a series of articles in *Communication Education* (1997), volume 46(2).

Once you understand the scope and nature of the problem, you can consider ways to structure your classroom experience to minimize the effects of fear of speaking. Some teachers argue that we should not "pamper" students by creating an environment more supportive than they will encounter in the real world. We believe, though, that the classroom is a laboratory—admittedly artificial—which develops students' skills. As those skills develop, advanced students can encounter situations that more accurately simulate real life challenges.

John Daly and Arnold Buss (1984) have developed a model of public speaking anxiety that suggests that the amount of fear experienced is a function of such factors as the level of uncertainty about the task, the level of uncertainty about the speech situation, the novelty of the experience, the size of the audience, the perceived status of the audience, the anticipation of evaluation, and the degree of conspicuousness felt by the speaker. Many of these factors can be minimized by an instructor's decisions. Here are some techniques that teachers have used to reduce fear of speaking.

1. Address the topic directly.

Assign Chapter 4 in *The Speaker's Handbook* early in the class. Engage students in a discussion of their fears about speaking and have them share some of their techniques of coping. You may want to administer one of the common self-report instruments such as the Personal Report of Confidence as a Speaker (PRCS) or the Personal Report of Communication Apprehension (see Part III, chapter 4, of this manual for a copy of this instrument, or go to the *Speaker's Handbook* Web site). This will give you data on the class as a group, help you identify any extremely anxious students who may need special help, and give the students a basis for engaging in the sort of self-analysis recommended in Chapter 4.

2. Create a positive classroom atmosphere.

Spend some time during the first few class periods doing some get-acquainted and ice-breaking exercises. Help the students feel comfortable with each other and with you. When they stand up to give the first speech they should not feel that they are confronting a hostile group of strangers, but a supportive group of friends.

3. Develop support groups among students.

Some instructors assign students to permanent groups which meet in workshop sessions throughout the course. Students can practice speeches in these groups or talk through ideas they are developing. Some teachers recommend using a group speech or a symposium for the first assignment. Being seated with a group of colleagues reduces the conspicuousness a student feels when required to stand alone. Though this method prolongs the total time "on stage," this may actually reduce anxiety for the next speech by eliminating some of the novelty of being in front of the group.

4. Play down evaluation, especially on the early presentations.

Whenever possible try to ease the student into public speaking by making the early assignments fun, manageable, brief, and informal. Several suggestions are given in the next chapter of this instructor's manual. If the first experience is a successful one, the student will be able to concentrate on skill rather than mere survival in later performances. Being in front of an audience is sufficiently threatening for most students without the added anxiety that is attendant to grading. Some teachers don't grade the first speech. Some give very little weight to the first one or two assignments so that the consequences of failure are minor in the greater scheme of course grades. Other teachers throw out the lowest speech grade of the course. Still others make a more general assurance that "if you really blow it on one assignment where your effort is apparent, we'll work out an appropriate chance to make up the grade." What is important is that you find some way to remove some of the pressure toward perfection and show some flexibility—without, of course, lowering your standards or seeming like a pushover.

You should also ensure that students will not be subject to harsh public criticism from instructor or peers. Several of the suggestions in the preceding section on criticism address this issue.

5. Make your expectations clear.

Ambiguity and uncertainty increase fear of speaking. The prescriptive *Handbook* approach and the use of detailed assignment sheets recommended in the next section let the students know what is expected of them. They can put their energy into meeting the requirements of the assignment instead of making themselves anxious trying to figure out what you really want. Go further in defusing anxiety by providing students with information on the mechanics of the speech performances. Tell them just what procedures will be followed in terms of time signals, question and answer periods, videotaping, critiques, and so on. Much of the *Handbook's* advice on presentation and overcoming fear is based on positive and realistic visualization of the speech situation. Remove the ambiguity whenever you can so that students can use these techniques effectively.

G. Videotaping Speeches

Video cassette recorders offer an opportunity for speech students to view and evaluate their own performances. Teachers can use the video record to confirm aspects of their feedback that students may not have understood. Most students enjoy the chance to see themselves on a television screen and to take a somewhat detached look at their behavior. In fact, research shows that attendance is higher in speech classes that use videotaping and that student motivation is somewhat heightened. The research on the effect of videotaping on actual speech improvement is somewhat mixed. Earlier evidence that videotaping seemed to contribute to speech anxiety has not been confirmed. Surely the less obtrusive technology and the widespread experience with taping have served to make the practice less threatening. Still, for students with high communication apprehension, there is the possibility that videotaping may increase their fear of speaking.

Since videotapes are relatively inexpensive, we find it most useful to have each of our students buy one for use throughout the course. Most students enjoy keeping a permanent record of their progress in the class, just as they would keep a notebook for another class. Many campuses have speech laboratories where students can tape rehearsals of their speeches and work with classmates, tutors or teaching assistants on their presentations. Many of our students not only review their videotapes at home, but also have access to cameras for rehearsal.

Here are a few suggestions for the teacher who is just starting to make use of videotape.

1. Create a non threatening climate for taping.

Be sure the students understand the purpose of the taping. Most people feign reluctance to be taped but are actually fascinated with their own image. Consider taping a few practice exercises before the first taped speech so that students can get used to having the equipment in the room and get over the shock of seeing themselves. Usually, they settle into a professional and relaxed attitude toward taping after the initial exposure. Be sure you treat the taping process as an educational tool. Keep the emphasis on communication rather than on performance. Do not let a technician change the tone you have set for your class, much as photographers can tyrannize entire wedding parties.

2. Make sure that you are well prepared for a videotaping session.

You should have access to equipment of good quality, placed inconspicuously in the room, with correct lighting and easily adjustable sound. It must be feasible to get the equipment set up so that your class can start on time and move along at its regular tempo. Either a professional staff member should do the taping, or if the recorder is very uncomplicated, you can ask for a student to volunteer. As the instructor, you have more important things to do during a round of speeches than to focus cameras, keep track of counter numbers, and test microphones.

3. Structure the playback sessions to ensure a positive learning experience.

Since most teachers can barely schedule the required speeches into a term, it is not feasible to use class time to play back and discuss tapes. Certainly, student learning would reach a point of diminishing returns long before they viewed and evaluated each classmate's speech for the *second* time. How viewing is handled is the main determinant of whether videotaping is effective and psychologically safe. Far too many students are turned loose to check out their tapes from a campus audio-visual center and to watch them alone. Under these conditions most students will focus on image and delivery, and those with low self-concepts will focus on their weaknesses rather than their strengths. You must take some steps to ensure a balanced perspective. In descending order of desirability, here are some methods to use:

Ideally, view the tapes with the student yourself. Point out the strengths and weaknesses of several aspects of the speech.

Have the students view the tapes with a trained assistant. This could be a teaching assistant, an advanced student facilitator, or someone else specifically trained to give constructive speech feedback.

Have the student view the tape with a group of classmates or with partners from the class. The groups can look at each other's tapes and assess the performances according to some assigned criteria.

15

If the students must view their tapes alone, they should be trained in what to observe and be provided with structured checklists and critique forms to require them to attend to several dimensions of the speech and to list the speeches' strengths as well as areas for improvement.

H. Speaking Ethics

It is always difficult to introduce beginning speakers to the complex problems of ethics. This problem could be compounded by the handbook approach of this text. We feel strongly about the need for speakers to think about the value implications of their choices and have a chapter in the Handbook on the ethics of speaking, chapter **3**.

What can you do in the classroom to approach these ethical issues? We recommend that you expose students early to the rights and the responsibilities that go along with public speaking, especially in a free society. You may want to distinguish between what speech practices are *effective*, in terms of meeting a speaker's goals, and what are *right*, in terms of the values they tend to perpetuate. Even the simplest discussion of ethics will soon center around the ends/means controversy. Is a speaker justified in using marginally ethical methods if the goal of the speech is a lofty one? Or are some means of communicating, such as quoting out of context, inherently unethical no matter who is using them to what end? Those who lean toward the "ends justify the means" position will soon find themselves pressed to answer the question of who decides on the morality of goals. Surely Hitler believed his goal was noble, as do pro-life and pro-choice advocates, liberals and conservatives.

The proponents of the other point of view, that some techniques of speaking are unethical, are on sounder philosophical ground perhaps. But they rapidly run into problems when pressed to differentiate between specific cases. It is wrong to make up evidence, but is it wrong for a speaker to emphasize evidence that supports his/her thesis? It is wrong to substitute emotional appeals for sound reasoning, but is it wrong to use emotional material to create a sense of urgency in an indifferent audience?

Hance, Ralph, and Wiksell (1975) are among the writers who effectively argue that there is nothing unethical about presenting only one side of an issue, or using emotional appeals or making full use of one's credibility or arranging ideas and material in a sequence designed to secure a certain effect. The *Handbook* also defends a speaker's right to build the best persuasive case possible once one has done sufficient inquiry and as long as one lives within certain guidelines.

These guidelines are most often expressed in terms of perpetuating the values of a free society. Hance, Ralph, and Wiksell suggest four ethical standards based on democratic principles. First, a speaker must be worthy of respect, which means that he or she is well prepared and has carefully thought the topic through. It is unfair to waste the time of an audience. Second, the speaker must present facts and opinions accurately. Either intentional or unintentional distortion is not excusable. Third, the speaker must reveal the sources of the information and the sources of the personal values and opinions as well. Finally, the speaker must welcome dissent, not just tolerate other opinions but value them as a way to test the validity of ideas.

Additional References

Civikly-Powell, J. (1999). Creating a new course. In J. A. Daly, G. W. Friedrich, and A. L. Vangelisti (eds.), *Teaching Communication: Theory, Research and Methods*, 2nd ed. (pp. 61-72). Hillsdale, NJ: Lawrence Erlbaum Associates.

Daly, J. A., & Buss, A. (1984). *Avoiding communication: Communication apprehension, reticence and shyness*, J.A. Daly and J.C. McCroskey (eds.), Beverly Hills, CA: Sage.

Friedrick, G. W., & Cooper, P. (1999). The first day. In J. A. Daly, G. W. Friedrich, and A. L. Vangelisti (eds.), *Teaching Communication: Theory, Research and Methods*, 2nd ed. (pp. 15-30). Hillsdale, NJ: Lawrence Erlbaum Associates.

Gorham, J. (1999). Diversity in classroom dynamics. In J. A. Daly, G. W. Friedrich, and A. L. Vangelisti (eds.), *Teaching Communication: Theory, Research and Methods*, 2nd ed. (pp. 257–268). Hillsdale, NJ: Lawrence Erlbaum Associates.

Hance, K. G., Ralph, D. C., & Wiksell, M.J. (1975). *Principles of speaking*, 3rd ed. Wadsworth.

Jensen, J. V. (1985). Teaching ethics in speech communication. *Communication Education*, October, pp. 324-330.

Powell, R., & Collier, M. (1990). Public speaking instruction and cultural bias. *American Behavioral Scientist*, 34(2), 240-250.

Rubin, R.B. (1999). Evaluating the product. In J. A. Daly, G. W. Friedrich, and A. L. Vangelisti (eds.), *Teaching Communication: Theory, Research and Methods*, 2nd ed. (pp. 425–446). Hillsdale, NJ: Lawrence Erlbaum Associates.

Sprague, J. (1999). The goals of communication education. In J. A. Daly, G. W. Friedrich, and A. L. Vangelisti (eds.), *Teaching Communication: Theory, Research and Methods*, 2nd ed. Hillsdale, NJ: Lawrence Erlbaum Associates.

Sprague, J. (1991). Reading our own speech critiques as texts that reveal educational goals, instructional roles and communicative functions. Basic Communication Course Annual, 3, 179-201.

Vangelisti, A. L. (1999). Evaluating the process. In J. A. Daly, G. W. Friedrich, and A. L. Vangelisti (eds.), *Teaching Communication: Theory, Research and Methods*, 2nd ed. (409–424). Hillsdale, NJ: Lawrence Erlbaum Associates.

Gender Issues in the Communication Classroom is the subject of the entire issue of *Communication Education*, January, 1991. Seven articles.

Multicultural Issues in the Communication Classroom is the subject of the entire issue of *Communication Education*, July, 1991. Five articles.

The few resources listed here are mainly synthesis articles. For topics that you wish to explore more fully, the references in these articles will lead you back to the classic studies. For the most current findings on these topics refer to *Speech Communication Teacher, Communication Education*, and the *Basic Course Annual*. The National Communication Association publishes annotated bibliographies and booklets that translate research findings into concise applications for classroom teachers. The ERIC educational database contains unpublished resources for speech teachers. Address your inquiries about all of these topics to:

Associate Executive Secretary for Education
National Communication Association
www.natcom.org

Part II
Basic Course Materials

A. Sample Course Syllabus

For many students the first few days of a course are accompanied by feelings of uncertainty and apprehension about what is expected of them. During this initial period the instructor can ease the pain somewhat by providing the students with a well thought-out syllabus. This allows the teacher to set the climate of the course and espouse his or her philosophy toward speech as well as giving pertinent information regarding the structure and content of the class. Although syllabi vary greatly, each should include the essential requirements of the course. Students appreciate knowing the textbook(s) to be used, the number and types of assignments and exams, course policies, and the like. The following is just one example of a syllabus used in a basic public speaking course.

Instructor: Neeley Silberman
Public Speaking I
Office Hours: TTh 9:30-10:00 and by appt.

Dept. Office: Saint Mary's, D329
Dept. Phone: 555-4666

REQUIRED TEXT: Sprague and Stuart, *The Speaker's Handbook*

Also required: One VHS video cassette to be brought to class each day you are scheduled to speak.

COURSE OBJECTIVES: This course is designed to provide you with basic theories and skills that are essential to effective public speaking. Topics include audience analysis, organization, persuasion, credibility, and delivery. Ideally, you should be able to apply these skills in a variety of public speaking situations whether in future college courses or in non-academic settings. As a member of the class you will also become an active listener and learn to analyze, critique, and evaluate the speaking of others.

ATTENDANCE: Your attendance and active participation are essential to the success of this class. Your participation in exercises, speech evaluation, and class discussion is encouraged and should make the class more interesting and a better learning experience. As a general rule, make-up speeches will not be allowed. If an extreme emergency arises, and you notify me as soon as humanly possible, we can try to work out an exception to this policy. Except in these very rare cases, there will be a substantial penalty for late work. Your participation in exercises, speech evaluations, class discussion, and question and answer periods is encouraged and rewarded. You are expected to do your own work for the course, to work independently and to give credit for all materials used in your research.

You must complete all assignments/exams to pass the course.
- I.   Speaking Assignments:
  - A. Impromptu   5% of grade
  - B. Mini-speeches   10% of grade
  - C. Informative   15% of grade
  - D. Persuasive   20% of grade

II.   Examinations:
   A. Two multiple choice exams based
       on textbook, lectures, classroom
       activities and discussion   20% of grade
   B. Final: Essay exam (comprehensive)   20% of grade
III. Attendance, participation, completion of
     class exercises and critiques   10% of grade

Since the course syllabus is in effect an informal contract, it is important that students understand and internalize the requirements and ground rules that it spells out. One way to check on this is to develop a quiz on the syllabus. It can be an ungraded early exercise, or it can be graded, giving students some easy points so that the start the class on the upbeat. Of course, this should not be done in a patronizing manner.

B. Sample Course Calendars

A course calendar should be prepared along with the course syllabus. Whether or not you expect to distribute this day-by-day schedule to students, it should be planned before the class starts. Take into account holidays, time needed for students to prepare for each speech, and allow some flexibility. Here are two sample calendars, one for a skills-oriented course, where five presentations are required by departmental policy, and one for an elective class that uses student support groups to unify the course.

1. Skills-Oriented Class (Semester Calendar)

Class Period	Class Activity	Assignment
1.	Introduction to Course Lecture	
2.	Students interview each other /Discuss overcoming fear of speaking	1,4
3.	Lecture/discuss Modes of Delivery, Listening and Planning	2, 5, 24
4.	Speech I—Impromptu or Personal Experience Speeches	
5.	Speech I	
6.	Lecture/discuss Speech Topics & Purposes, Topic Analysis, & Contexts	6, 23
7.	Lecture/discuss Outlining and Selecting Points. Scrambled Outline exercise	11
8.	Lecture/discuss/exercise. Arranging Points and Transitions	9, 10, 12
9.	Lecture/discuss Introductions and Conclusions. Group Exercise	13, 14
10.	Speech II—Demonstration Speeches	
11.	Speech II	
12.	Speech II	
13.	Speech II	
14.	Speech II	

15.	Lecture/discuss/exercise	
	Supporting Materials	15
16.	Lecture/discuss Research, Inform. Strategies.	
	Scavenger Hunt exercise	8, 21
17.	Lecture/discuss Attention and	
	Interest, and Style. Video tape	17, 18
18.	Lecture/discuss Vocal Delivery.	
	Charades exercise	26
19.	Lecture/discuss Physical Delivery.	
	Charades exercise	27
20.	Speech III—Informative Speech	
21.	Speech III	
22.	Speech III	
23.	Speech III	
24.	Speech III	
25.	Midterm	
26.	Lecture/discuss Audience Analysis.	
	Audience Analysis Assignment	7
27.	Lecture/discuss Persuasive	
	Strategies. Group exercise	22
28.	Lecture/discuss Reasoning.	
	Critique sample speech	16
29.	Lecture/discuss Credibility.	
	Famous people exercise	19
30.	Lecture/discuss Ethics	
	Ethical Quality Scale Exercise	3
31.	Speech IV—Problem-Solution Speech	
32.	Speech IV	
33.	Speech IV	
34.	Speech IV	
35.	Speech IV	
36.	Lecture/discuss Motivational	
	Appeals. Advertisement exercise	20
37.	Lecture/discuss Presentation Aids.	
	Videotape of newscasters	28
38.	Lecture/discuss Adapting to	
	Speech Situation	29
39.	Lecture/discuss Answering Questions.	
	Simulation	30
40.	Speech V—Motivated Sequence	
41.	Speech V	
42.	Speech V	
43.	Speech V	
44.	Speech V	
45.	Make-ups/Review for Final	

2. Elective Course Calendar

Class Period	Class Activity	Assignment
1.	Orientation	
2.	Form support groups, get acquainted	FNDTN., PREP. INTRO
3.	Delivery/Confidence	1,4
4.	Speech Ethics. Listening, Assign Speech I	
5.	Speech purposes. Meet in groups	2, 5, 6
6.	Organization	9-12
7.	Introductions and Conclusions	13, 14
8.	Practice in groups, Inform. Strategies	21, 25
9–13.	Group speeches evaluating the ethics of one speech from the Web Site	
14.	Recap Speech I, Assign Speech II	
15.	Research, library tour	8, 21
16.	Supporting Materials	15
17.	Presentation Aids	28
18.	Attention and Interest. Audience Analysis	7, 18
19.	Credibility	19
20.	Practice in groups, Adapting to Contexts and situations	23, 29
21–25.	Informative Speeches	
26.	Assign Speech III, review for midterm	
27.	Midterm examination	
28.	Physical and vocal delivery	24, 26, 27
29.	Style and language	17
30.	Reasoning	16
31.	Discuss audience analysis assignment, assign Speech IV	
32.	Workshop session in groups	
33–36.	Speech defining an abstract concept	
37.	Motivational appeals	20
38.	Persuasive strategies	22
39.	Workshop session in groups & Answering Questions	30
40–44.	Persuasive speeches	
45.	Review for final	Audience analysis papers due

C. Sample Assignment Sheets

Besides the syllabus and calendar, we find it useful to distribute a sheet spelling out the purpose, requirements, and grading criteria for each speaking assignment. Today's students come from varied academic backgrounds. While some are able to respond to a two- or three-minute oral description of an assignment, many need more guidance and detail. Without lowering one's standards or getting into remedial instruction, a teacher can adapt to the needs of many entering students by making criteria explicit and by defining a task as prescriptively as possible. Lower division students especially are learning not only how to give public speeches, they are learning the study skills essential for college. After they have done their preliminary research they should be able to follow the directions on the sheet, referring to the designated sections of *The Speaker's Handbook* when necessary. After the speech is prepared, they should check it against the criteria to be sure it meets all requirements.

These assignment sheets do not spoon feed students. On the contrary, they foster a sense of individual responsibility for insuring that the speech adheres to all the guidelines. The following pages contain examples of assignment sheets for several popular assignments. They are taken from two different instructors to show you how individual styles differ. Notice how these assignment sheets reflect the cumulative nature of most courses. Early in a course only a few basics are required. As the course progresses, more requirements are added and more advanced skills are addressed. While the total demands may increase, the prescriptiveness may decrease in some areas once a student demonstrates mastery of a skill. For instance, you may insist on an explicit preview of points in any early speech, but later just require an effective logical orientation, leaving to the student how best to fulfill that function.

One-Point Speech
Assignment Sheet

Prepare a 3- to 4-minute presentation supporting a specific statement of fact or value. Your outline should be a complete-sentence outline and is due on the day of your speech. Use and label the supporting materials (definitions, examples, statistics, testimony) from Chapter 15. Also use and label at least two of the techniques of clear explanation from Chapter 21 (emphasis cues, signposting, acronym, slogan, or figurative analogy).

The assignment is designed to build speech-making skills rather than represent a complete or typical speech. Below is a brief example of the outline format you will use. Naturally, your outline will include more details and will be of a more serious nature.

Outline

I. Gary Ruud is a lousy teacher.
   A. Gary Ruud doesn't show concern for his students.
      1. Class evaluations indicate 97% of Gary Ruud's students rank him in the bottom 5th percentile in this category. **(Statistic)**
      2. Students have complained to the administration about Gary Ruud's uncaring behavior.
         a. Student Ferd Whitlock said "I went to Mr. Ruud's office to ask for help but all he did was make fun of my name." **(Testimony)**
         b. Student Buck Macho said "I went to Mr. Ruud's office six times during the quarter and I cried each time I left."
      3. Faculty members have made comments about Gary Ruud's uncaring behavior.
         a. Pat Bendigkeit, Mr. Ruud's supervisor, says, "He has about as much compassion for students as this anvil I use for a door-stop." **(Figurative Analogy)**
         b. And so on . . .
   B. Gary Ruud grades unfairly.
      1. Teachers generally use one of two grading systems.
         a. Using a typical curve suggests that there will be a small percentage of As and Fs, a larger percentage of Bs and Ds, and the largest percentage of Cs. **(Definition)**
         b. Using a criterion-based system suggests that any students, no matter how many, who meets established criteria will receive the designated grade.
      2. Mr. Ruud bases his grade on ethnic origin.
         a. Students that are of Italian-Norwegian descent receive As.
            (1) Luigi Magnusson flunked all of his exams and received an A for the course.
            (2) Olaf Mapelli flunked all of his assignments and received an A for the course.
            (Example)
         b. Students that are of Bulgarian-Australian descent receive Fs.
            (1) And so on . . .

Presentation

You are to use one or two 3x5 notecards. Delivery should be **extemporaneous**. Utilize the physical and vocal skills we've worked on in class. Content should be clear, organized. Use supporting materials and cite sources when appropriate. Have fun!!!

Grading

Outline	50%
Presentation	50%

Supporting-a-Claim Speech
Assignment Sheet

Purpose of This Assignment

In persuasive speaking it is essential the speech be made up of claims that support the proposition/thesis. Each of these claims is then supported through the use of evidence and reasoning. For example, the claim that fatty foods cause high cholesterol must be supported by evidence such as statistics, testimonies, and/or examples. Once the evidence is established, the speaker must then use his/her own reasoning skills to inform the audience of the importance of the evidence. In other words, by reasoning, you tell the audience how that evidence supports the claim. For this assignment, you are to give a two-minute speech which establishes one claim, supported by three pieces of evidence as well as one use of reasoning linking each piece of evidence to the claim.

Requirements

1. Create a proposition/thesis. (See example below).
2. Create three main points/claims that support the proposition. [9]
3. Choose one of the claims and then support it using three pieces of evidence. [15a, b, c, d]
4. Connect your evidence to your claim through reasoning [16a].
5. Your speaking exercise should be 2 minutes in length. You *do not need* an introduction or a conclusion.
6. You are required to turn in your completed planner on the day you speak. Your planner should include:
    *   Clearly stated thesis [6]
    *   Provide three main points/claims [9, 16]
    *   Display one main point as the claim to be supported [9].
    *   Three pieces of evidence, taken from *two* different sources [15 a, b, c, d].
    *   Follow the conventional outline format [11].
    *   Include a reference list of at least two sources in correct bibliographic form [8e].
7. Use a conversational and extemporaneous style of speaking. [24]
8. One note card may be used. [25]

Supporting A Claim: Example

Part One:

    Proposition: The US schools system should adopt a school uniform policy.
    Main Point I: Within the last decade there has been an increase in juvenile crimes.
    Main Point II: School uniforms will reduce competition.
    Main Point III: School uniform programs will decrease juvenile crimes.

Part Two:

I.   **(Main Point/Claim):** School uniform programs will decrease juvenile crimes.

    A.   **(Evidence)** Sonoma county school district has seen a 10% reduction in juvenile crimes since implementing their school uniform policy one year ago (Stevens, 1997).
        Statistic

        Reasoning: If one school district has seen a decrease in crimes committed by juveniles then it is probable that others will as well.

    B.   **(Evidence)** Steven, a student at a school that has a uniform policy, stated that before the policy he and his friends had stolen articles of clothing, but since the uniform policy he has not found a need or desire to continue stealing clothing (Brawley, 1996).
        Example

        Reasoning: One student says he has stopped stealing as a result of having to wear a school uniform. There are undoubtedly others we don't know about yet who feel the same way now.

    C.   **(Evidence)** A Professor at the University of California, Berkeley states that her research has found a direct correlation between the need for material possessions and the need to commit crimes (Stevens, 1997).
        Testimony

        Reasoning: This testimony shows that if the materialistic aspects of schooling are decreased, it may lead to a decrease in the students' desire for such items, thus resulting in a decrease in criminal activities.

Tribute Speech
Assignment Sheet

Purpose of This Assignment

One of the forms of public speaking that we do not do enough of is paying tribute to another human being. There are many occasions in our lives for giving a tribute: family gatherings, weddings, graduations, retirements, special birthdays, etc. This presentation will give you an opportunity to practice such a speech. Choose a person who is important to you—who touched your life or impressed you—and share two specific things about this individual. The person you choose must still be alive and could be a family member, friend, teacher, coach, pastor, musician, writer, sports celebrity, etc. You will receive credit for the assignment by completing the exercise planner as well as delivering your presentation to the class.

Requirements

1. You will honor one living individual who has influenced you in a positive way. Share two specific things about this person that made him/her so influential.
2. Your speech should have three parts—an introduction, body, and conclusion [**11, 13, 14**].
3. The introduction should begin with a sentence that gets our attention and previews the two things you will be sharing about the person [**13**].
4. The body should devote one main point to each of the two important things about this person [**9, 10**].
5. The conclusion should summarize your two points and leave the audience with a closing thought about this person [**14**].
6. The speech should be between 3–5 minutes in length.
7. Your outline will be turned in before you speak, and MUST be typed.
8. Use a conversational and extemporaneous style of speaking [**24**]. 3 note cards may be used [**25**].

Criteria for Evaluation

First, you must meet all of the above requirements to receive a passing grade for the assignment. Then, points will be assigned based on how well you carried out each aspect of the assignment. In other words, if each requirement is present, expect to receive about 70% of the possible points in that category (C range). If you fail to meet one of the basic requirements, the grade will be lower on that component. If you not only meet the minimal requirements, but carry them out very well, expect to receive 80-89% (B range) or 90-100% (A range) of the possible points.

Suggestions for Preparation

Choose a person who is important to you—who touched your life or impressed you. Keep in mind the importance of clarity. This is largely achieved through effective organization. Do not have too many main points. Confine your speech to two or three main ideas and group the other points under these. Clarify the relationship between your points. Use clear, explicit *previews, transitions* and *summaries*. Keep your speech moving ahead according to a well-developed plan; do not jump back and forth from one idea to another.

Practice the speech several times but do not memorize it [**24**]. Time your speech when practicing. After you have written your outline, set it aside and practice speaking from brief notes.

Demonstration Speech
Assignment Sheet

Purpose of This Assignment

Informative speeches take many forms, one of which is the demonstration speech. The primary purpose of any speech to inform is to ensure the audience's clear understanding of the ideas presented. This assignment asks you to explain and demonstrate to the audience the steps involved in carrying out a certain task or process.

Requirements

1. The topic should be informative and challenging to this audience.
2. The speech should be four to six minutes in length.
3. The three functional steps of the introduction [**13b,c,d**] and the three functional steps of the conclusion [**14a,b,c**] should be clearly identifiable.
4. There should be a definite, logical transition bridging each component of the speech [**12**].
5. Each main point should be clearly stated and developed [**9, 10, 11**].
6. Delivery is to be in the extemporaneous mode [**24**]. Use only two or three notecards [**25**].
7. You are to use at least one visual presentation aid according to the guidelines presented in the text [**28**].
8. A typed outline, submitted on the day of the speech, should
   — state the specific purpose of your speech [**6**]
   — state your thesis [**6**]
   — follow the correct outline format [**11**]
   — label the three functions of the introduction [**13,b,c,d**]
   — label the three functions of the conclusion [**14**]
   — include a reference list of at least two sources in correct bibliographic form [**8e**]

Criteria for Evaluation

First, you must meet all of the above requirements to receive a passing grade for the assignment. Then, points will be assigned based on how well you carried out each aspect of the assignment. In other words, if each requirement is present, expect to receive about 70% of the possible points in that category (C range). If you fail to meet one of the basic requirements, the grade will be lower on that component. If you not only meet the minimal requirements, but carry them out very well, expect to receive 80-89% (B range) or 90-100% (A range) of the possible points.

Suggestions for Preparation

Select a topic that you are already familiar with and on which you can quickly gather additional information.
Keep in mind the importance of clarity. This is largely achieved through effective organization. Do not have too many main points. Confine your speech to two or three main ideas and group the other points under these. Clarify the relationship between your points. Use clear, explicit *previews, transitions* and *summaries.* Keep your speech moving ahead according to a well-developed plan; do not jump back and forth from one idea to another.

Prepare your visual aids and gather your props and materials at once and practice with them. Practice the speech several times but do not memorize it [**24**]. Time your speech when practicing. After you have written your outline, set it aside and practice speaking from brief notes.

Problem Solution Speech
Assignment Sheet

Purpose of This Assignment

This speech is to introduce you to persuasive speaking by working first on the logical substance, or *logos*, that is the essence of any persuasive effort. If you advocate a change, you should be able to clearly document the existence of some sort of a problem and then explain specifically what course of action is necessary to solve that problem. For this speech, assume that you are speaking to a logical, unbiased audience. You should relate to your audience through effective psychological orientation in the introduction and psychological closure in the conclusion, and through effective use of attention factors. However, the emphasis of this speech is on sound reasoning and solid support for your points.

Requirements

1. The topic should be timely, timeless [6] and controversial. Choose a topic on which you hold strong convictions and upon which you can realistically expect to influence an audience through reasoned argument.
2. The speech should be five to seven minutes in length.
3. The three functional steps of the introduction [13] and the three functional steps of the conclusion [14] should be clearly identifiable.
4. There should be a definite, logical transition bridging each component of the speech [12].
5. The speech should follow the problem-solution format. Main point I should explicate the problem. Main point II should explain the solution [9, 10].
6. Delivery is to be in the extemporaneous mode [24]. Use only two or three notecards [25].
7. You are to use at least three different kinds of supporting material [15].
8. You are to use at least three different attention factors [18].
9. A typed outline, submitted on the day of the speech, should
    — state the specific purpose of your speech [6]
    — state your thesis [6]
    — follow the correct outline format [11]
    — label the three functions of the introduction [13]
    — label the three functions of the conclusion [14]
    — label the three kinds of supporting material [15]
    — label the three kinds of attention factors [18]
    — include a reference list of at least four sources in correct bibliographic form [8e]

Criteria for Evaluation

First, you must meet all of the above requirements to receive a passing grade for the assignment. Then, points will be assigned based on how well you carried out each aspect of the assignment. In other words, if each requirement is present, expect to receive about 70% of the possible points in that category (C range). If you fail to meet one of the basic requirements, the grade will be lower on that component. If you not only meet the minimal requirements, but carry them out very well, expect to receive 80-89% (B range) or 90-100% (A range) of the possible points.

Suggestions for Preparation

Select a topic that you can research readily in the time available. Once again, strong organization is your best ally. Make your main points clear and be very explicit on how the subpoints relate to each other and to the main points. Use summaries and transitions like the following: "I have shown you the economic and social manifestations of the problem. Now let me tell you about its social impact." Do not rush through a long string of facts and statistics. Take time to explain them and to make clear what they mean.

Practice the speech several times but do not memorize it [24]. Time your speech when practicing. It is difficult to keep control of a number of facts and statistics. Students have a tendency to read this speech. To read or memorize it will effect your delivery grade. After you have written your outline, set it aside and practice speaking from *brief notes.* It is a real challenge to be very familiar with your material and still maintain a conversational delivery.

Audience-Analysis Project: Overview
Persuasive Speech

Purpose

The purpose of this assignment is to demonstrate that (a) you understand the theory of audience analysis, and (b) that you can apply this theory by adapting your persuasive speech to this particular audience. There are three parts to this assignment. Parts 1, 2, and 3 are to be turned in along with your outline prior to your speech. All three parts are explained below so that you can see how the assignment as a whole is structured.

Pre-Speech Analysis: Parts 1, 2, and 3

To complete these segments you must participate in the in-class audience analysis project. This means you will type or neatly print your proposition statement (as it was approved) on the pre-speech audience analysis form in the space provided. Make _____ copies of your questionnaire and bring them to class with on the day the data will be collected. DO NOT FORGET! If you miss the chance to collect this pre-speech information, it will affect your grade on the outline and the speech. After you have collected the data from your classmates, review it and write a few paragraphs discussing the next three topics. Turn this write-up in along with your outline.

Part 1: General Audience Analysis

What do you know about the composition of this group offhand? Include audience size, age, sex, etc. Also include the general impressions you have formed about the value orientations of the audience, their intellectual pre-dispositions, and their conduct as an audience from your experiences during the course of this semester (Remember, these are things you could say about this audience regardless of the topic they were listening to). Explain your basis for these statements.

Part 2: Specific Audience Analysis

What have you learned about your audience in terms of their attitudes toward your specific speech topic? What was the average audience score? What was the range of their scores? It is your job to interpret this data in your write-up. For example, is your audience fairly homogenous or heterogeneous in terms of their attitudes? Would you classify them as unfavorable, neutral, favorable, or a combination of these? What additional information did you collect about your audience? Summarize the results and explain why this information is relevant to your speech.

Part 3: Persuasive Strategy

Justify your speech strategy with regards to your audience. What ratio of reasoning, motivational appeals, and credibility do you feel is demanded for this audience on this topic? Should you use counter arguments? Which ones? On what basis do you justify your organizational pattern? On what basis do you justify your introduction and conclusion? How much attention-getting material do you need for this audience? How much background information? These are questions to consider. While I don't expect you to justify your speech sentence by sentence, I do expect you to justify each major decision of persuasive strategy.

Post-Speech Analysis: Parts 4 and 5

Part four is to be turned no later than one class session after you deliver your speech.

After you give your speech, your audience will fill out a Post Speech Analysis Form. They will report their attitudes after the speech and make comments on why they were or were not persuaded. Take this information home, analyze it, and compare it to the Pre-Speech Audience Analysis. Next, write a few paragraphs that covers parts four and five.

Part 4: Comparison of Pre-Speech and Post Speech Results

Report on the shift of attitude, if any. How successful were you? Give specific examples of dramatic shifts in opinion, if any, as well as general description of the audience as a whole. Sometimes a bar graph or table is useful here as well as a comparison of the audience mean attitude scores before and after the speech. Also, summarize the comments made by the audience on why they were or were not persuaded.

Part 5: Analysis of Persuasive Impact

Why do you think some people were persuaded? Why do you think some were not? If you had the entire speech to do over again to an identical audience, what would you do differently both in conducting your speech analysis and in preparing and presenting your speech? Be specific.

*Pre-*Speech Audience Analysis

Write your proposition below and add four more questions that you would like to have answered by your audience as you prepare your persuasive strategy. This is information you will be able to use to reformulate your speech. The questions should be clear, concise, and the entire questionnaire must be possible to complete within 2 minutes. Make _____ copies for the audience and bring them to class on the day scheduled for the data collection.

Questionnaire
1. What is your attitude toward this statement?

   Speaker's Proposition:

   _____

Strongly Disagree	Moderately Disagree	Slightly Disagree	Neither Agree nor Disagree	Slightly Agree	Moderately Agree	Strongly Agree
1	2	3	4	5	6	7

Category Two: Factual

2.

3.

4.

Category Three: Open-Ended

5.

Sample Pre-Speech Audience Analysis

Questionnaire
1. What is your attitude toward this statement?

   Speaker's Proposition: "School uniforms should be required in all public schools for grades K-8."

Strongly Disagree	Moderately Disagree	Slightly Disagree	Neither Agree nor Disagree	Slightly Agree	Moderately Agree	Strongly Agree
1	2	3	4	5	6	7

Category Two: Factual
2. Do you have children? Yes or No
3. Would you feel differently about this issue if you were a parent? Yes or No
4. Have you ever attended a school that required uniforms? Yes or No

Category Three: Open-Ended
What would be the advantages and disadvantages of requiring school uniforms in public schools for grades K though 8?

Post-Speech Audience Analysis

Speaker's Name:

Instructions:
Put your name and proposition, exactly as it was phrased on the Pre-Speech Audience Analysis Questionnaire, on this sheet and make _____ copies for your audience. Bring these to class with you on the day of your final speech.

Speaker's Proposition:
_____

(Indicate your attitude *after the speech* by circling one of the following)

Strongly Disagree	Moderately Disagree	Slightly Disagree	Neither Agree nor Disagree	Slightly Agree	Moderately Agree	Strongly Agree
1	2	3	4	5	6	7

Comments on why your attitude did or did not change:

Comments on the speech: Content, organization, delivery, etc.

D. Short Speech Assignment Ideas

1. The speech of introduction

This popular assignment takes many forms. A student may introduce herself or himself, highlighting certain features that have been specified. In addition to the obvious demographic and biographical factors—major, hometown, interests—a person could be asked to address some topics like "how communication skills will fit into my career goals."

A variation on this assignment that facilitates group interaction and reduces self-consciousness is to have students introduce a classmate.

2. The personal experience speech

This speech is a good early assignment that introduces students to each other. The narrative nature of the content helps students organize their points and tends to hold audience attention. The assignment can be as general as "tell about a significant experience that you will never forget," or it can be focused toward more specific experiences such as:

My most embarrassing moment

My first date

My worst date

An experience that changed my life

My greatest triumph

The biggest mistake I ever made

Variations:

The culture shock speech. The student tells about an experience where he or she became starkly aware of being in an unfamiliar cultural situation and discusses how communication came into play. In one class of all international students these were some of the shocks students received about US culture: people sunbathing on campus to try to get a tan, people spending money and lavishing attention on dogs and cats, people expecting you to help yourself to food or drink in their homes rather than serving you directly, students challenging their teacher's authority or opinions, students laughing and seeking help after failing an exam instead of being ashamed, people staying in their homes on holidays instead of going to public places to celebrate as a community. All of these points help US students to see that their cultural patterns are arbitrary rather than "natural." The exercise gives international students a chance to be experts and to excel on an early assignment. At the same time, most US students can identify some culture shock experience, either through travel experiences or hosting of international visitors. As necessary, culture can be defined more broadly to include any experience where one moved into a setting where the values and norms that were taken for granted were unknown to the individual. The very issue of whether moving from the South to the West, or going to work in a high tech company after previously working in retail is really a "culture shock" makes for an interesting discussion.

A speech that analyzes a personal decision. The student tells about a decision such as where to go to college, what car to buy, what to major in, and discusses the *process* of the decision making. Who were the key sources consulted? How credible were they? How did logic and emotion enter into the decision making?

A speech about a person. The most unforgettable character the student ever met, the student who has influenced you the most, the person admired the most, the favorite/least favorite teacher, the most credible speaker you ever heard, the strongest leader you know, etc.

The day you were born. This is an interesting way for students to learn to use library resources and to know a little about history. They can describe what was happening politically, what songs were popular, what sports teams were doing, etc.

A speech on a speech experience. My worst speech, my best speech, how I handled fear of speaking, how I used persuasion on my job, how I lost/gained credibility, how I learned the importance of audience analysis, and so on.

Analysis of a communication breakdown. If a communication model is presented early in the course, students can provide examples of breakdowns they have witnessed, analyze the causes of the breakdown and suggest ways it could have been averted.

3. Television advertisement speech

Assigning this speech at the beginning of your discussion on persuasion helps students understand the function of Monroe's Motivated Sequence as a persuasive organizational pattern. Students should develop a 1- to 1-1/2-minute advertisement in which they try to persuade the class to buy some product or use some service. Because this speech is designed as a television advertisement, students should be creative and use visual materials during their presentation.

4. The group speech

To ease speech anxiety and to emphasize the macrostructure of an organized speech some instructors have students give their first speech in a group. Speaker One of the group presents the introduction, consisting of an attention getter, psychological orientation, and a logical orientation (preview), and then makes a transition to the first main point. Speaker Two states, develops, and summarizes the first main idea and then makes a transition to the next speaker's point. After two, three, or four speakers present the remaining main points, the final speaker concludes the speech with logical closure (a summary), psychological closure, and a clincher. Students have the opportunity to work together on the overall division and organization of the topic and they have the moral support of speaking with a group of colleagues. In addition to the chapters of *The Speaker's Handbook* dealing with organization (9-14), you might refer students to Chapter 23.

5. The demonstration speech

This is a popular and effective assignment to use early in a course to break the ice and help students learn about their classmates' interests and talents; the heavy, intellectual topics can come later in the term. For this assignment encourage students to explain a process with which they are very familiar. They will be less self-conscious when the focus is on an activity like serving a tennis ball, washing a dog or making a Caesar salad. The process to be explained can often be easily organized into natural steps. If the body of the speech organizes itself in this manner, a novice speaker can concentrate on clearly structuring the introduction, transitions, and conclusion.

Variations:

A presentation aid speech using charts, models, etc. See **28**.

A process speech that requires explaining more complex and difficult material. Such topics would be the process of photosynthesis, how an employee orientation program is established, or how to analyze a poem.

Reminder: If you have not taught before, beware of the range of student creativity on this assignment. You may want to give a humorous disclaimer that there should not be any dangerous or illegal materials brought to class, or you may want to have students clear topics in advance. A favorite subject of conversation among veteran speech teachers centers on the theme: The day one of my students let a king snake get away in the classroom; caused a chemical explosion; drew the university police by firing a gun with blank bullets; changed his sister's diapers; pierced her roommate's ears; brought a razor blade, mirror, and some flour to show us how to cut a line of cocaine; put a condom on a cucumber, etc. Think through your boundaries in terms of safety, legality and good taste, and then communicate these to your students.

6. The "what I believe" speech

This is another good first or second assignment. The goal is to communicate a belief, and three reasons for that belief, so clearly that the entire audience understands the speaker's point of view. The goal is not to persuade listeners to agree. The main criterion for the supporting reasons is that they are in fact separate and roughly equivalent reasons for the stated conclusions. The reasons need not be factually supported or fully defended. This is an excellent chance for students to air their pet peeves, religious convictions, and other passions that may not be suited to other speeches. The emphasis should be on clear organization and explicit previews, transitions, and summaries.

7. The impromptu speech

The instructor prepares a list of topics which are placed in a hat (envelope, bowl, whatever). Just as it is his or her turn to speak each student draws three slips, selects one, returns the others and has one minute to prepare a two- to three-minute speech.

Here is a list of words that can be used for impromptu topics:

Hot Tubs	On-line Dating	Espresso Bars	Exercise	Traveling
Insomnia	Color	Junk Food	Parking Meters	Divorce
Hangovers	Teachers	Dentists	Dormitories	Marriage
Pets	Nightmares	Surprise Parties	Vegetarianism	Roommates
Commercials	Reality TV			

Add local and current topics, names of entertainers, politicians, etc.

Persuasive Impromptu Topics:

Select something you have in your possession or on your person. Convince us why we need one too.

We want to take a trip during our summer vacation. Convince us where we should go.

We want to take a friend out to dinner for his or her birthday. Convince us where we should go.

We want to rent a movie or go to a movie this weekend. Convince us what we should see or rent. (You may also convince us to read a book or watch a particular television show.)

Select a course in your major. Convince us why we should take it.

We want to get involved in a club or organization. Select a club or organization and convince us to join.

We are in the market for a new car or truck. Select a model and convince us why we should buy it.

We want to get a pet. Select an animal and convince us that it should be our choice.

We know exercise is important. We want to take up a sport or activity, but can't decide among all the options. Select a sport or healthful activity and convince us to take it up.

We win some money in the lottery. We decide to use some of the money to make a donation. Select a charity and convince us why we should donate money to that organization.

We want to buy a computer. Macintosh or Windows? Convince us which one to buy.

Informative Impromptu Topics:

Tell us about a tradition you have in your family.

Share an experience you have had with another culture.

Tell us about your best or worst date.

Tell us about a hobby you have or an activity you are involved in.

Tell us about a dream you hope to realize or goal you hope to achieve.

Tell us about a unique job you have or had.

Variations:

Use proverbs, provocative questions or phrases as topics. One teacher brought a bag of fortune cookies to her early morning class. Those who drew one of those inscrutable quotations to discuss were rewarded with a snack.

Have students turn in three of four topics each and use these for the impromptu speeches. If your students fill out an information card at the beginning of the course listing hobbies and interests, you can give each student a personally selected topic you are sure she or he can talk about.

Vary the preparation and speaking time. One popular format is to let a speaker draw a topic just as the preceding speaker is ready to begin and to step outside the classroom to prepare in private during that speech. (Surprisingly few students disappear!)

Instead of scheduling the assignment as a complete round of speeches, use it as a filler throughout the course. Whenever there is some time left at the end of a class period, take volunteers for impromptu speeches. This will use time efficiently when lectures run short or scheduled speakers are absent. Also, the use of volunteers tends to encourage the more confident and experienced speakers to speak early. The more reticent can wait until later in the course and the additional speech experience often serves to reinforce their newly-developed skills.

8. The rhetorical analysis speech

In this speech the student gives a speech about a speech, analyzing its effectiveness in terms of rhetorical criteria. Speeches may be drawn from anthologies, *Vital Speeches*, or published transcripts of current speeches. Require that a copy of the speech be turned in along with the speech outline so that you can evaluate the student's analysis. One format for a speech of this type might be:

Introduction
    Include a description of the occasion, setting, audience, speaker, etc.
I.   Designate and justify what you think are the three most important criteria for speech effectiveness.
    A.   First Criterion
           Justification
    B.   Second Criterion
           Justification
    C.   Third Criterion
           Justification
II.   Compare the speech to those criteria.
    A.   How the speech compares to the first criterion
           Examples and quotations to justify
    B.   How the speech compares to the second criterion
           Examples and quotations to justify
    C.   How the speech compares to the third criterion
           Examples and quotations to justify
Conclusion
    Synthesis of points, leading to an overall evaluation of the effectiveness of the speech

Variations:

Cross-cultural speech analysis. If you or your students are able to locate speeches by men and women of various ethnic and cultural backgrounds, it would be very effective to use this speech to lead into a discussion of how the nature of eloquence varies across groups. The criteria for effectiveness will certainly vary and students can identify ways that public speaking both reflects and shapes social life. In your discussion, take note of how both gender and culture come into play for both speakers and audiences.

The ethics speech. Assign students to evaluate speeches of their choice according to standards of ethical communication. Guidelines can be drawn from chapter **3** of the *Handbook* and supplemented in lecture or through additional readings such as those mentioned in Part I of this instructor's resource manual.

Combine the group speech and the rhetorical analysis speech. One group of students might present a symposium/panel on each speech from the Sample Speeches Web Site for *The Speaker's Handbook* or on another speech of their choice. Individual speakers could address issues of organization, reasoning, motivational appeals, and so forth. Or a group of students could address a common rhetorical concept such as credibility and each speaker could discuss the application of that concept in a different speech.

9. The speech on an abstract concept

For this assignment the student is to select an abstract term of concept such as love, leadership, commitment, productivity, or peace. The goal of the speech is to make the speaker's understanding of that concept clear to the audience. (They need not agree, but they should have a very concrete image of the term.) The speaker is required to use a variety of techniques from **21, 15, 18,** and **13.**

E. Speech Outlines

You will notice that the treatment of organization in the *Handbook* separates the marshalling of ideas from the preparation of the outline. In the former process, it seems to be pedagogically sound to encourage experimentation and to discourage premature moves toward locking into a set of main points and a specific phrasing. Students need to have disposable drafts at this stage. The later process of refining a set of points into a final outline requires quite a different set of skills and tools.

The virtually universal practice of teachers requiring speech outlines has persisted for several reasons. Outlines give the teacher a chance—away from the distractions of the classroom—to analyze the structure of the student's speech and the depth of her or his analysis. Outlines provide an impetus for students to prepare thoroughly. Although students complain about them throughout the course, at the end they are almost unanimous in their comment that the discipline of outlining was useful. They do not recommend depriving their successors of this learning experience.

Though nearly every teacher requires some sort of outlines, the uses vary widely. At one extreme is the instructor who is primarily concerned with the actual oral presentation of the speech, conceiving of the outline only as a helpful organizational tool or as a way to force students to prepare their speeches before the last minute. Outlines are not optional in their classes, but they are typically given very little weight in grading, or perhaps just given a ✓ , ✓ +, or ✓ -. The rationale given for this approach is that in the real world, outlines are not essential; what is said is what matters, not what a speaker plans to say. At the other extreme is the teacher who views preparation of a detailed outline as an integral part of each speech assignment and weights it heavily in evaluating content and organization. This approach holds that in the classroom laboratory the *preparation* of a good speech is one of the most teachable skills. Inexperience or fear may cause a student to botch part of an oral performance, but given solid skills in developing speech content, smooth delivery will come along in time. Thus, a student should be rewarded for producing a coherent, logical, well-supported outline.

Teachers also divide along lines of how much detail they want included in their outlines. Some want a spartan, logical plan in propositional language. The points must clearly stand out as separate from the proof or development of them. The outline of the McNeil speech in Sample Speeches under Book Resources on *The Speaker's Handbook* Web Site leans toward this approach. The defenders of this position argue that students should never come close to writing a manuscript. More-elaborate outlines too often merge transitional language and even, heaven forbid, evidence, into the phrasing of main points. Subpoints often turn out to be more than a sentence long if they are statements of the evidence as it will be used. The reader of the outline loses the ability to visually scan the basic relationships of points. The student is tempted to read from the outline or to memorize points as phrased. The phrasing of points in delivered speech should be created during oral practice and not resemble writing.

Those who prefer a more detailed outline argue that an instructor cannot really evaluate how a student has put a speech together without a look at the substance of the speech. An outline that contains more fully stated points and completely cited evidence is more like a legal brief. The student is forced to lay out the points as they actually will be delivered. The issue of how to get students to lay the outline aside and present the speech in an oral and conversational manner is a different one altogether. It is secondary to the important skills of speech preparation which are developed through outlining.

Outlines primarily serve to organize ideas. Additionally, many instructors use the outline assignment to direct their students' attention to the choices they make in designing a speech. This is achieved by calling for marginal notations to label required speech elements and rhetorical devices. The composition of the notations would vary according to the type of speech. One speech type might highlight organization issues. another attention factors, or reasoning. A few specific expectations for notation should be spelled out in each written assignment with the goal of making students conscious of what they are doing, and inducing them to use a variety of elements. And beyond this, students need to be reminded that every speech has a psychological as well as a logical structure. While a formalized content outline helps crystallize the relationships between propositions and support, the student can also use the outline to chart the relationships between speaker and audience. Handbook chapters 15–22 explain how to use many speech elements and rhetorical devices to enhance the speech. If the students make marginal notations on their outlines, showing where these elements and devices are to be used, it will help them o see what they are doing so they can improve the audience appeal of their speeches, if necessary. Is all the humor clustered at the beginning and end of an hour-long lecture? Perhaps some humor can be shifted to the middle. Does a student support every main point with a fact followed by a hypothetical example? Perhaps he or she can vary the forms of support. An example of a notated outline (McNeil) can be found in Sample Speeches under Book Resources on the *Speaker's Handbook* Web Site.

Decide how you see the role of outlines in your class. Are they rough strategic plans for you to respond to as you coach students before the speech? Or are they to serve as a reflection of the final speech content? Clarifying these issues will help you decide when to collect outlines and how to evaluate them. Some teachers have outlines due at least two class periods before the scheduled speech date so they can return them with feedback that the student can incorporate into the finished product. Others require the outlines the class period before the speech, evaluate their content and organization outside of class, and focus on evaluating delivery, adaptation, and oral style during the speech. Still others have outlines turned in at the time of the speech, and evaluate and return them later.

The generic outline checklist inside the back of *The Speaker's Handbook* will save you time in checking outline format and will tell students where to find guidelines for correcting their errors. The example on the facing page shows how easily that checklist can be tailored to a particular assignment by substituting specific criteria for the topic selection and for the labeling of whatever rhetorical devices are being highlighted in that speech.

Outline Checklist—Problem-Solution Speech

Topic
    Significant, challenging and controversial
    Timely and timeless   **6a.3**
    Sufficiently narrowed   **6b**
    Lends itself to reasoned argument

Purpose
    Specific Purpose identified   **6c.2**

Thesis
    Single declarative sentence   **6d.1**
    Reflects the major ideas of the speech   **6d.1**

Main Points
    Phrased as single declarative sentences   **11b**
    All directly related to thesis sentence   **9c**
    Arranged in logical order   **10**
    Appropriate number   **9**
    Mutually exclusive   **9d**
    Equal in importance   **9f**
    Phrased in concise parallel language   **11d**

Outline Format
    Typed (spelling, punctuation correct, typos neatly corrected)
    Consistent and correct use of symbols   **11a.1**
    Indentation reflects relationships   **11a.2**
    Two or more points at each level of subordination   **11a.3**
    No more than one sentence per symbol   **11a.4**
    Label three parts of introduction   **13b,c,d**
    Label three parts of conclusion   **14a,b,c**
    Label three different kinds of supporting material   **15**
    Label three attention factors   **18**
    Label three kinds of reasoning   **16**
    Reference list appended   **8e**
        Minimum of four published sources
        Correct bibliographic form

F. Critique Forms

On the next few pages are a number of sample critique forms. The first is a comprehensive checklist, followed by two instructor critique checklists that were developed to go along with the informative and problem-solution speeches described in Part II of this instructor's resource manual. You will find it easy to devise your own forms by shortening and adapting the comprehensive checklist (also available on the Web site). Make the chapter references on the form as specific as possible. Then, when you use the forms during speeches you may want to become even more specific, for instance indicating which introduction pitfall was fallen into. You can spread these categories out, leaving ample white space for comments, or keep the checklist compact and append comments on another sheet.

We find it useful to distribute the critique forms with the speech assignment sheets to show students exactly how they will be evaluated. In the spirit of conserving paper, they are requested to return the critique form to the instructor on the day they speak. They may provide certain information such as their name and speech topic. It is sometimes effective to ask the student to designate a couple of categories where they have set special goals and are focusing on being consciously competent. These designations invite the instructor to provide special feedback on the targeted areas for improvement.

Following the instructor's checklists are sample critique forms for self-evaluation, peer evaluation and peer shift of opinion.

Sample Evaluation Checklist

(Select those categories relevant and appropriate to the kind of speech being evaluated.)

ORGANIZATION

Introduction
Attention getter needed **13b**
Psychological orientation
    Establish relationship **13c.1**
    Relate topic to audience **13c.2**
Logical orientation
    Establish a context **13d.1**
    Orient audience **13d.2**
Avoid introduction pitfalls **13f**

Main Points
Improve overall pattern **10a**
State clearly **11d**

Transitions
Express logical relationships **12a**
Employ internal previews and summaries **12b**

Conclusion
Logical closure
    Summarize main points **14a.1**
    Connect with larger context **14a.2**
Psychological closure
    Relate back to audience **14b.1**
    Make an appeal **14b.2**
Clincher needed **14c**
Avoid conclusion pitfalls **14d**

DEVELOPMENT

Reasoning
Invalid inductive patterns **16b**
Invalid deductive patterns **16c**
Invalid causal reasoning **16d**
Invalid reasoning from analogy **16e**
Avoid fallacies **16f**

Supporting Materials
Clarify explanations **21b**
Improve definitions **15a**
Improve use of examples **15b**
Improve statistical evidence **15c**
Improve use of testimony **15d**
Use variety of supporting materials **15**
Cite sources **15e.1; 8e**
Weave support smoothly into speech **15e.2**

Motivational Appeals
Relate to needs and values of listeners **20b, c**
Avoid misuse of emotional appeals **20d**

Attention and Interest
Use concrete and familiar materials **18a.1**
Involve audience **18a.2**
Variety and movement needed **18a.3**
Inappropriate humor **18c**

Language and Style
Employ oral style **17a**
Strive for clarity **17b**
Use appropriate language **17c**
Use vivid, varied language **17d**

Credibility
Establish competence **19a.1; 19c.1, 2, 3**
Establish concern **19a.2; 19c.5**
Establish trustworthiness **19a.3; 19c.4**
Establish dynamism **19a.4; 19d**

PRESENTATION
Study extemporaneous mode **24a**
More practice needed **25b**
Work on confidence, poise **4**

Vocal Delivery
Eliminate distracting characteristics **26d**
Speak loud enough **26a.1**
Speak at appropriate rate **26a.2**
Enunciate clearly, naturally **26a.3**
Strive for vocal variety **26b**
Use acceptable pronunciation **26c**

Physical Delivery
Be conscious of your appearance **27a**
Eliminate distracting mannerisms **27b**
Improve posture **27c**
Employ purposeful movements **27d**
Gesture naturally **27e**
Maintain eye contact **27f**
Control your facial expression **27g**

Presentation Aids
Needed/not needed **28a**
Make clear and manageable **28b**
Use more effectively **28c**

GENERAL
Select appropriate topic **6a**
Conform to time limit **6b.1; 25d**
Sources cited appropriately **8e**
Learn to handle distractions **29b, c**
Be responsive to audience questions **30**

Persuasive Strategies
Adjust to audience attitude **22c**
Use psychological pattern of organization **22d.1**
Arrange main points for max. persuasive impact **22e**
Answer appropriate counterarguments **22f**

Informative Speech: Evaluation Form

Instructions

Fill in your name and roll number and hand in this form, with your outline attached, on the day that you speak. After it is returned to you with comments, keep it until the course is over. The ratings on the sub-categories stand for Excellent, Good, Average, Fair, and Needs Improvement.

Speech Element	Rating					Comments
Speech Topic						
Topic Meets Requirements [6a, b]	EX	GD	AV	FR	NI	_____

Organization

Introduction						
Attention Getter [13b]	EX	GD	AV	FR	NI	_____
Psychological Orientation [13c]	EX	GD	AV	FR	NI	_____
Logical Orientation [13d]	EX	GD	AV	FR	NI	_____
Avoids introduction pitfalls [13f]	EX	GD	AV	FR	NI	_____
Body						
Main points stated declaratively [11d]	EX	GD	AV	FR	NI	_____
Use of supporting material [15]	EX	GD	AV	FR	NI	_____
Organizational pattern [10a]	EX	GD	AV	FR	NI	_____
Transitions between points [12a, b]	EX	GD	AV	FR	NI	_____
Conclusion						
Logical Closure [14a]	EX	GD	AV	FR	NI	_____
Psychological Closure [14b]	EX	GD	AV	FR	NI	_____
Clincher [14c]	EX	GD	AV	FR	NI	_____
Avoids conclusion pitfalls [14d]	EX	GD	AV	FR	NI	_____

Content

Points clearly developed [21]	EX	GD	AV	FR	NI	_____
Defined terms as needed [15]	EX	GD	AV	FR	NI	_____
Sufficient information presented	EX	GD	AV	FR	NI	_____

Delivery

Vocal Delivery [26]	EX	GD	AV	FR	NI	_____
Physical Delivery [27]	EX	GD	AV	FR	NI	_____
Use of Note cards [25]	EX	GD	AV	FR	NI	_____
Use of Presentation Aids [28]	EX	GD	AV	FR	NI	_____
Speech Overall	**EX**	**GD**	**AV**	**FR**	**NI**	_____
Appropriate Speech Length	**EX**	**GD**	**AV**	**FR**	**NI**	_____

SPEECH GRADE: **COMMENTS:**

Persuasive Speech: Evaluation Form

Instructions

Fill in your name and hand in this form, with your outline attached, on the day that you speak. After it is returned to you with comments, keep it until the course is over. The ratings on the sub-categories stand for Excellent, Good, Average, Fair, and Needs Improvement.

Speech Element	Rating					Comments
Speech Topic						
Topic Meets Requirements [6a, b]	EX	GD	AV	FR	NI	_____

Organization

Introduction						
Attention Getter [13b]	EX	GD	AV	FR	NI	_____
Psychological Orientation [13c]	EX	GD	AV	FR	NI	_____
Logical Orientation [13d]	EX	GD	AV	FR	NI	_____
Avoids introduction pitfalls [13f]	EX	GD	AV	FR	NI	_____
Body						
Main points stated declaratively [11d]	EX	GD	AV	FR	NI	_____
Use of supporting material [15]	EX	GD	AV	FR	NI	_____
Organizational pattern [10a]	EX	GD	AV	FR	NI	_____
Transitions between points [12a, b]	EX	GD	AV	FR	NI	_____
Clear and sound reasoning [16]	EX	GD	AV	FR	NI	_____
Sources cited [8e, 15]	EX	GD	AV	FR	NI	_____
Conclusion						
Logical Closure [14a]	EX	GD	AV	FR	NI	_____
Psychological Closure [14b]	EX	GD	AV	FR	NI	_____
Clincher [14c]	EX	GD	AV	FR	NI	_____
Avoids conclusion pitfalls [14d]	EX	GD	AV	FR	NI	_____

Content

Supporting materials [15]	EX	GD	AV	FR	NI	_____
Sufficient information presented	EX	GD	AV	FR	NI	_____
Sufficient support presented	EX	GD	AV	FR	NI	_____
Attention factors [18]	EX	GD	AV	FR	NI	_____

Delivery

Vocal Delivery [26]	EX	GD	AV	FR	NI	_____
Physical Delivery [27]	EX	GD	AV	FR	NI	_____
Use of Note cards [25]	EX	GD	AV	FR	NI	_____
Use of Presentation Aids [28]	EX	GD	AV	FR	NI	_____
						_____
Overall Speaking Improvement	**EX**	**GD**	**AV**	**FR**	**NI**	_____

SPEECH GRADE: **COMMENTS:**

Self-Evaluation Form

1. How well do you think you achieved your purpose?

2. Which of your main ideas seemed to be accepted best?

3. Which of your main ideas seemed to be least acceptable?

4. How comfortable and confident did you feel during the speech?

5. What types of questions were asked by the audience? (Requests for information? Requests for clarification? Questions about relevance of information? Challenges of your reasoning? Other?)

6. Do the kinds of questions asked indicate anything to you about your preparation?

7. If you had it to do over again, what changes would you make in preparation, support, organization, or delivery?

8. What one goal do you have for improving content in your next speech?

9. What one goal do you have for improving delivery in your next speech?

Peer Critique Form

1. What was the specific purpose of this speech?

2. Was the introduction effective? Why or why not?

3. Was the body clearly organized?

4. What were the main points? List them.

5. Were the main points supported? How?

6. Was the conclusion effective? Why or why not?

7. Did the speaker make adequate eye contact?

8. Were vocal characteristics (articulation, volume, rate, and variety) effective?

9. Were body movements appropriate?

10. What was your overall impression of the speaker?

G. End of Class Awards

To culminate a term, it is fun to give awards to speakers in various categories. In one class they were called the Emenemmies Awards (the prizes were M&Ms) and students voted before the final exam; ballots were tallied during the exam and awards were given at a class party immediately following. The teacher made sure that every member of the class won some award. There were several ties and she created a few new categories herself to make it come out that way. Variations might be to have the class make nominations for the "big" awards, best speaker, best delivery, etc., and actually vote for finalists during one of the last few classes. A committee could meet with the teacher to devise special awards. One recent class awarded the *introduction pitfalls* award to a student who began her final speech by asking the camera operator, "does my hair look OK?" and the *handling distractions with aplomb* award to a student who out shouted construction noises in the hallway. Here are a few categories to consider. You and your students can make up others.

Most improved speaker	Most credible image	Best visual aids
Best delivery	Most expressive face	Best gestures
Most sincere speaker	Best use of pathos	Most poised
Most relaxed speaker	Most humorous speaker	Most organized
Ms./Mr. Congeniality	Most unusual topic	Most creative
Most enthusiastic speaker	Clearest explanations	Best evidence
Most penetrating questions by an audience member	Most supportive audience member	Best overall speaker

Part III
Teaching the Chapters

A. Introduction

Part III of the *Instructor's Resource Manual* is designed to assist with the teaching of each chapter in the *Speaker's Handbook*. To help instructors quickly and easily organize their lessons, the material for each chapter is organized into three sections: Chapter Exercises, Class Activities, and Additional Resources.

The first of these sections discusses the exercises from the *Handbook*. There are two types of exercises in the seventh edition: exercises that relate to the video speeches and speech clips accessible through Speech Interactive on the Speaker's Handbook CD-ROM, and exercises that relate to the printed content of the handbook (see the table on the following page). Exercises of this second, "book content" type can be assigned as homework to check individual student's understanding of the principles delineated in the text. Note, however, that for the exercises that deal with the videos on Speech Interactive, the student can access "authors' comments" on the CD-ROM that repeat what we say in our discussions in this part of the instructor's manual. It is important that students generate their own answers to these exercises first, before checking our comments. (There is no particular value in having them just copy or paraphrase the available answers, so either make this a purely self check-up assignment or ask students to comment on how their first responses agreed with or differed from those provided.)

Many of the "book content" exercises, can also be used as assignments for extended papers or as essay questions on examinations. These exercises from the *Handbook* are designed to give students an opportunity to express their opinions on a variety of topics related to public speaking, so the answers to many of the exercises are not necessarily a question of right or wrong. Students are encouraged to think about their options, make intelligent choices, and explain their rationale for doing so. You can prepare for class discussions by making sure you are comfortable explaining the rationale for those exercises that have "right" answers and by preparing some examples of your own answers to the more open-ended questions. The exercises can also form the basis for in-class exercises and discussion by being used in one of the following ways.

1. Have each student respond to an exercise out of class and then have them meet in groups to discuss and compare their answers. If you want to ensure that students have thought about the preassigned exercises in advance, either have them write out their answers or email them to you by a prescribed time before the class meeting. Such assignments are best graded credit/no credit or accumulated as part of a broader participation segment of the grade.

2. Have groups work together to respond to the same exercise. Then call on a spokesperson to present and, if necessary, defend the group's answer.

3. Assign a different exercise or part of an exercise to each group. Then have spokespersons report to the entire class. For instance, ask students to identify a component in a speech from the Sample Speeches on the Web, assigning one speech to each group. Some of the exercises incorporate several examples to evaluate, in which case you can have each group take just one or two of the examples.

4. You can move through several topics in a class period by using these exercises. Leave students seated in their groups while you briefly highlight the main ideas of each subsection, assign a set of exercises to the groups for five minutes of discussion, spend five minutes having each group report, and then move on to another subsection.

Ch.	Book Content Exercises	Speech Interactive Exercises	Ch.	Book Content Exercises	Speech Interactive Exercises	Ch.	Book Content Exercises	Speech Interactive Exercises
1	1, 3–7	2	11	1–3	4	21	1, 2	3
2	2, 3	1	12	1, 2	—	22	1–6	—
3	1–4	—	13	2, 4, 6–8	1, 3, 5	23	1–5	—
4	1, 2	—	14	1–3, 5	4	24	—	1
5	—	—	15	1, 4–6, 10	2, 3, 7–9	25	—	—
6	1–15	—	16	1–3, 5–10, 13, 15, 16	4, 11, 12, 14	26	—	1, 2
7	1	2	17	1–4, 6	5	27	—	1
8	—	—	18	1, 3–5	2, 6	28	1	2
9	1	—	19	1–4, 6, 7	5	29	—	—
10	1, 4	2, 3	20	1, 2, 4–7	3	30	—	—

The Class Activities section offers several in-class activities you can use to supplement lecture and discussion. While some activities can be completed quickly, others may require several class sessions to complete. Instructors should be prepared to adjust the activities to fit the individual needs and time constraints of their classes.

The Additional Resources section offers a sampling of additional resources, usually in print, related to the individual chapter and which may assist with other pedagogical and instructional choices. Also look at Part V, Resource Integration Guide, for a variety of material made available through Wadsworth/Thomson Learning.

B. Teaching Chapters 1–4: Foundation

1. Chapter 1: Understanding Speaking

Chapter Exercises

Exercise 1. Share some of the resources you draw upon as a public speaker. For example, one colleague draws upon her high school drama experience to manage nervousness. Her heart used to pound whenever she stepped onto the stage. Her anxiety did not last, however, because once she spoke her first few lines, she knew her preparation was not going to fail her. She draws on this experience because she knows that she will be nervous when she stands in front of an audience as a speaker, but reminding herself that she is prepared and that is her best defense against anxiety. Although her drama experience is a rich resource, it is also an area from which she may draw too much. As a speaker she cannot let adequate preparation slide into memorization.

Exercise 2. Richard Rodriguez, as a professional writer, made extensive use of his skill with language. Obviously, it took a great deal of careful preparation to craft phrases and to create images that were vivid and effective. He also made use of the conversational resource in his low key delivery style and his informal and even humorous speech pattern. His references to sitting in his hotel room early that morning and hearing students out partying in the street created an impression of spontaneity and that at least part of his speech was not fully prepared but was being composed as he spoke. He made little use of the performative resource in any traditional sense, yet he did hold the audience's attention and have a good sense of timing. His personality, albeit a rather reserved one, was authentically projected to the audience. Norman Mineta also made substantial use of the resource of writing by carefully preparing his remarks. It was clear that many phrases were planned to have emotional impact on the audience. He also had a strong command of the facts and statistics he used, which undoubtedly reflected that these had been reduced to a written manuscript. However, Mineta relied on the resource of performance in that he spoke with the cadence and pauses of a political speech and had taken the time to become very familiar with his speech so that he did not stumble over phrases at any point. He also used the resource of conversation in that he was relaxed and personal, mentioning people in the audience. Though his was a formal speech, Mineta has a very conversational style of speaking. The differences in the two may be attributed somewhat to the different occasions since Commencement speeches are typically more "eloquent" than business speeches, with the expectation of an inspirational use of language and imagery. Nonetheless, Mineta was speaking of a matter of life and death and Rodriquez was speaking about how one feels about the quality of life over time, so the topics had different levels of intensity. Both of these speakers had rather low key conversational speaking styles compared to many other Commencement speakers and political leaders, but the difference between the writer and the administrator probably had the greatest impact on how they used the three kinds of resources available to them as speakers.

Exercise 3. Try to give examples that are not speech related. You may describe what it was like to learn how to play golf or learn how to drive a car. You may find that your examples are parallel to what your students are experiencing in your public speaking class. That is, your examples may illustrate what it feels like to move through the four stages or to be "stuck" in one of the stages (conscious competence/incompetence?).

Exercise 4. You may relate a particular experience where skill was secondary to your increased awareness of other factors. Dancing seems to require a certain amount of skill but just knowing the steps may not be enough. I, for example, know the steps to many dances. However, I used to have the nasty habit of looking at my feet constantly as I proceeded to do a waltz. As a result, many of my partners left me in the middle of what I thought was a rather masterful performance. I have since learned to be aware of other things—my partner, the rest of my body, the music.

Exercise 5. Focus on particular areas of public speaking and use as a basis for goal-setting. Each student should try to identify her or his strengths and weaknesses and concentrate on establishing a program to enhance public speaking skills. Rather than taking a broad approach, select a few areas where improvements can be made, and monitor the progress.

Exercise 6. There are many misconceptions in addition to the ones listed in this text. For example, students may think speaking ability is necessarily related to intelligence. While there may be a correlation, there are cases where people of average intelligence are effective speakers and conversely many examples of intelligent people who are average in speaking ability. Another misconception is that effective speakers aren't apprehensive. Chapter 4 indicates that it is normal to have some degree of speaker apprehension. A common misconception is that public speaking consists of "tricks." This misconception is often a result of supermarket books that offer shortcuts to effective public speaking. One popular notion instructs the speaker to picture the audience in the nude to reduce anxiety—although one would think that this might tend to increase anxiety in many people! While these types of "tricks" may be useful at times they may also oversimplify the often complex task of effective public speaking.

Exercise 7. Have students share their responses in class and conduct a discussion on the importance of public speaking in their own professions.

Class Activities

The following are community building exercises.

The name game
Nearly every communication teacher has some version of this game. Learning classmates' names early sets an informal and supportive tone and is the first step toward audience analysis. The most common version of the game is a variation of the old add-on memory games played as kids, "I'm going to my grandmother's house and I'm taking . . ." The class sits in a circle and the first person says, "My name is Bob." The second says "I'm Carol and this is Bob." The third says, "I'm Ted and this is Carol and this is Bob." Then Alice states the cumulative list. It's amazing how successfully a group can learn about twenty-five names, and the teacher can introduce the classical canon of *Memoria* and invite a brief discussion of mnemonics. A variation on this game is to offer a adjective that describes you and will help people remember your name (Jolly Jo and Dignified Doug) or a phrase like I'm Susan who likes to surf, and this is Frank from Fresno, and this is Mike who rides a motorcycle.

Uncommon commonalties
There are several variations on this activity as well. We find that it is a nice way to introduce the importance of finding common ground with an audience. Students can mill around the room with a note card in hand and find four people with whom they have something in common. It is more entertaining to require them to search for "uncommon commonalties." Return to a circle and report what you found. A variation is to have groups of six or so try to find one or more uncommon commonalties. A spokesperson can introduce the entire group and tell the near-misses as well as the one commonality discovered. "Four of the six of us were born in the South. Another four of the six of us work more than twenty hours a week," etc.

Circle of diversity

In addition to the preceding activities, this activity can be adapted to fit the needs of most classes. Have students form a double circle in the middle of the classroom. The Dyads should face each other and take turns introducing each other. After the introductions, the students take turns answering specific questions. However, when the student in the inner circle is speaking the outer student should be silent, and vice versa. Allow approximately one minute for each question. Next, have the outer students rotate clockwise and begin the process again. The following questions can be adapted to fit the individual needs of any instructor, course, or time limit. This activity works especially well in the beginning of the semester as it helps foster a supportive climate while also allowing students get to know each other in a non-threatening way. For variations to this assignment see: Using the Howard University Moorland-Spingarn Research Center to Study African-American Communication. http://cctr.umkc.edu/user/jaitken/index.html

Potential questions:
- Describe one goal you have for this course. How do you plan to accomplish this goal?
- What is your greatest fear about public speaking? How might you overcome this fear?
- Who do you believe is an excellent public speaker? What qualities does this person possess?
- Describe a class you've taken where you felt very supported by your fellow classmates. What was it about that class that stands out in your mind?
- Why is it important to learn how to become an effective public speaker?
- Tell your partner what accomplishment you feel most proud. Why?
- Describe a speaking situation when you wished you could have been more articulate—or that your ideas could have been more organized.
- What do you enjoy doing in your free time?
- What do you perceive as being the most difficult part about/of public speaking?
- What irritates you the most about this world?
- What would be the title of a book about your life story?
- Which food best describes your personality? Why?
- If you had to lose one of your 5 senses, which one would you choose?
- What is your nationality, ethnic background or group identification? (You may define "group" any way you like)
- Was your "group" in the majority or minority where you grew up? Were ethnic traditions maintained in your neighborhood?
- Who has been the most influential person in your life? What qualities does that person possess?
- What are some perceptions you think members of the opposite sex have of you?
- What sort of prejudice or bias have you experienced in your personal life and in the workplace?
- What are the stereotypes others form about you?
- Describe an embarrassing moment you've had that was witnessed by someone else. Why were you embarrassed? How did you overcome the embarrassment?
- If you could change either your race, gender, sexual orientation, or political view, which would you choose? Why?
- What does a grade of A mean to you?
- What grade you hope to earn in this course this term? How do you plan to accomplish this goal?

What is public speaking like?

This is a good exercise to do the first or second day of class. In some ways, it is most successful even before the students read Chapter 1. It can serve as one of your community building activities because students are engaged in discussing course related materials, but can draw on their general experiences. Prepare six note cards or sheets of paper each of which contains one of the following statements:

a. Giving a public speech is like acting in a play
b. Giving a public speech is different from acting in a play
c. Giving a public speech is like writing a paper or article
d. Giving a public speech is different from writing a paper or article
e. Giving a public speech is like engaging in an interpersonal conversation
f. Giving a public speech is different from engaging in an interpersonal conversation

Divide the class into six groups and give one statement to each group. Give the students about ten minutes to list as many reasons as they can think of to support the statement. This works best if the groups are not informed about the topics assigned to other groups. They can concentrate on their own statement without thinking comparatively.

Have spokespersons report out for each group. Either they or the instructor can write the points on the board for discussion. The discussion following this activity usually reveals that there are some similarities to each other area. For example, public speaking is like acting in that the communicator must project a message, sometimes through exaggerated physical and vocal expression. Also, a speaker, like an actor must be able to recapture a sense of "newness" with each audience, even if the words have been spoken before. Public speaking is like writing in that much attention must be paid to organization, research, and careful selection of language. It is like conversation in that communicators are adapting on the spot to the feedback that they receive from listeners. Yet, there are clear and dramatic differences between public speaking and each of these other communicative forms. The activity makes it possible to emphasize these from the first: speakers are being themselves, not playing a role, and they are always speaking their own words (unless they give credit). Speakers do not write their speeches out word for word because, unlike writers, they are addressing specific audiences, not general audiences. They can use their full physical and vocal resources, so their words, though important, do not have to "work as hard" as do those of writers. Although the interpersonal conversational model is favored over the other two, students should be aware that a public speech is not merely chatting. Messages are more carefully planned and the floor is not shared as freely.

Identifying these issues early in the class seems to provide a common frame of reference throughout a course. For instance, students can receive feedback that they need to be a little less like an actor, or a writer, or one who is just shooting the breeze. Or, they can be told that in a certain situation they could draw on some of the skills of the actor—projecting emotion, commanding attention; or of the writer—having points carefully arranged, using words precisely or vividly; or of the conversationalist—seeming informal and relaxed, responding to listener response.

Additional Resources

Chism, N., Menges, R., Svinicki, M., & Weinstein, C.E. (1994). *Teaching tips: Strategies, research, and theory for college and university teachers.* Lexington Massachusetts: D.C. Heath and Company.

Fraleigh, D.M., & Tuman, J.S. (1997). *Freedom of speech in the marketplace of ideas.* New York, New York. St. Martins Press.

Olson, L.C. (1997). On the margins of rhetoric: Andre Lorde transforming silence into language and action. *The Quarterly Journal of Speech*, 83(1), 49–71.

2. Chapter 2: Listening

Chapter Exercises

Exercise 1. *Erian* has a very animated and compelling manner of delivery. However, some listeners may be distracted by his colorful clothes, especially the stars and stripes tie, and by his highly rehearsed gestures and movement that might seem unnatural or overly dramatic. As a listener, one must take steps to note these factors, put them in perspective, then set them aside and pull one's attention back to the carefully crafted persuasive message of the speech.

Exercise 2. This is a good exercise for students to complete early in the semester before the first round of speeches begins. There are many ways to revise the statements so they better adhere to the principles of constructive feedback. For example, instead of responding with "Your tone is too dogmatic," a statement that is a bit vague and which could elicit defensiveness in the speaker, an audience member could say, "I find myself most interested in what you are saying when you vary the volume, pitch and tone of your voice." Instead of, "Your speech was interesting," the critic could say, "I found your specific examples on how to create a web page most interesting." And so on. The objective of this exercise is to illustrate the importance of specific and clear critiques.

Exercise 3. Students will find a variety of listening tips as they search the *InfoTrac College Edition*. As a class, discuss the most effective and least effective tips and the way each relates to the public speaking contexts.

Class Activities

Listening Critiques
Have students practice the principles of constructive feedback (as presented in the text) by providing an oral critique of one of their peers at the conclusion of the informative and/or persuasive speeches. Requiring students to provide a critique of their peers will help them practice good listening techniques, avoid listening pitfalls during the speeches, and increase their own critical thinking skills.

Listening Strengths and Weaknesses
Have students analyze their own listening habits to identify their strengths and weaknesses as an audience member. Ask them to create strategies to minimize the "pitfalls" they might encounter while listening to a speech.

Practicing Paraphrasing
Students often experience difficulty with paraphrasing. Frequently, students think repeating verbatim what another has said is effective paraphrasing. In dyads or triads, students can practice this skill by discussing a controversial topic. Have the first student offer his/her opinion on the topic. The second student is then responsible for paraphrasing the first student's opinion. The third student can practice paraphrasing the second student's opinion, etc. This exercise also helps students practice being open to another's point of view, while at the same time critically assessing the speaker's claims.

Asking Questions
Require your students to ask the speakers questions about their speeches. Asking good questions requires good listening. A student who has not listened well will not be able to ask genuine questions.

The Clash
See section E-8 on chapter **22** in this part of the instructor's manual

Additional Resources

Brownell, J. (1996). *Listening: Attitudes, Principles and Skills.* Allyn & Bacon. Boston, Massachusetts.

Deavere, A. (2000). *Talk to me : Listening between the lines.* Random House, New York.

Forestieri, M.C. (1992). Listening Instruction. In Stephen E. Lucas (Ed.), *Selections from the Speech Communication Teacher, 1986-1991* (p. 44). New York: McGraw-Hill.

Portnoy, E. (1992). Activities to promote Students' speaking and listening abilities. In Stephen E. Lucas (Ed.), *Selections from the Speech Communication Teacher, 1986-1991* (p. 45). New York: McGraw-Hill.

Ross, R. (1992). What is in the shoe box. In Stephen E. Lucas (Ed.), *Selections from the Speech Communication Teacher, 1986-1991* (p. 47). New York: McGraw-Hill.

Rubin, D.L., Hafer, T., & Arata, K. (2000). Reading and listening to oral-based versus literate-based discourse. *Communication Education,* v49, p121(13) .

Schneider, V.L. (1992). A three-step process for better speaking and listening. In Stephen E. Lucas (Ed.), *Selections from the Speech Communication Teacher, 1986-1991* (p. 47). New York: McGraw-Hill.

Wolvin, A., Coakley, C.G. (1996). *Listening,* 5th ed. McGraw Hill, Boston, Massachusetts.

3. Chapter 3: Speaking Ethics

Chapter Exercises

Exercise 1. Public speakers face many issues in trying to be ethical and fair. Have students discuss what problems they foresee in being ethical and fair, as well as their perceptions of these cliches and what they say about our culture. Ask some of your non-native English speaking students to share cliches from their cultures that also relate to ethics and public speaking.

Exercise 2. Although the types of "amendments" your students will pose could be endless, in the past, students have made some of the following suggestions: We agree to never omit or distort pertinent information; We agree to use appropriate emotional appeals; We agree to never plagiarize or be unprepared, etc. Have your students discuss, develop, and vote on an "audience bill of rights" that reflects the interests and personalities of the class members.

Exercise 3.
"If you can pinch . . ." Principle #1
"We need the Strategic Defense Initiative . . ." Principle #4
"If I don't raise . . ." Principle #1
"I know how shocked . . ." Principle #2
"You can make $50,000 . . ." Principle #3

Exercise 4. Cheating has become a significant issue. For this reason, many colleges have created academic honesty codes. Have students focus their *Infotrac* search on the ways colleges have begun to tackle the issue of cheating; discuss the ramifications of their findings.

Class Activities

Ethical quality scale
J. Vernon Jensen (1985) urges that students be trained to think of individual speech behaviors as laid along a continuum from highly ethical to highly unethical. This is seen as more productive and more realistic than the black and white labeling of acts as ethical and unethical. Even more important is that we not label individuals as ethical or unethical on the basis of a single speaking decision. In introductory classes we often place constraints on students that make it difficult to live up to the high standards cited above. They must squeeze their preparation into a couple of weeks and their ideas into a few minutes. It is important that they view the class as a laboratory where they can learn processes for application to longer speeches outside the academic environment. Many of the ethical questions students raise can only be answered, "it depends." A student might have to settle for just one example of a key point in a six-minute speech, but he or she should have more examples in reserve for the question-and-answer period. Sometimes less-than-perfect evidence must be used to support a minor point. What is important is for the students to recognize that if they can find only shaky evidence on a key point, perhaps their inquiry has serious flaws.

After an opening discussion of ethical positions, make use of the following exercise to help students better understand the role ethics plays in public speaking. The goal is not for students to agree or even for individual students to come to definite answers, but rather for the students thinking on these issues to become increasingly sophisticated as the course progresses.

Directions: Place students in groups of 3–5 and distribute one of the following "ethical dilemmas" to each group. Ask the students to read and discuss the scenario they receive. After several minutes have students rate the ethical quality of their decisions, encouraging consensus when possible. Once the groups have completed the activity, hold a large class discussion. Encourage the students to lead the discussion, interjecting with probing questions where you see fit. Students usually enjoy this activity as it allows them to think critically about their own code of ethics.

Ethical Dilemma 1

The Situation

You are giving a persuasive speech on the legalization of marijuana and you have found some excellent supporting materials (statistics and studies) in a pro-marijuana flyer you picked up at a downtown rally. The flyer is not professionally made and no sources for the information are listed, still the material is too good to ignore. You decide to go ahead and include the information in your speech even though you cannot validate its authenticity. What is the ethical quality of this situation?

Ethical Quality Scale

Highly Unethical	Moderately	Slightly	Neutral	Slightly	Moderately	Highly Ethical
1	2	3	4	5	6	7

Would your EQ rating vary depending on the following variables?

EQ: _____ The audience will never know.

EQ: _____ It is only a brief part of your argument.

EQ: _____ Your friend who is knowledgeable about the issue assures you the information is legitimate even though he can't trace the source.

Ethical Dilemma 2

The Situation

You are scheduled to give a speech in Comm. 20 tomorrow but unfortunately your recent chemistry final absorbed all of your energy, leaving you with little time to prepare your speech. Your helpful roommate saves the day and offers you her B+ speech from last semester. After contemplating your situation, you decide to deliver your roommate's speech. What is the ethical quality of this situation?

Ethical Quality Scale

Highly Unethical	Moderately	Slightly	Neutral	Slightly	Moderately	Highly Ethical
1	2	3	4	5	6	7

Would your EQ rating vary depending on the following variables?

EQ: _____ You changed the introduction and made minor adaptations through the body of the speech so it isn't copied word-for-word.

EQ: _____ You're typically a great student and clearly understand the principles of research and outlining so you probably would have done just as well, if not better, on you own if you had had the time!

EQ: _____ You are a graduating senior and can't afford to get anything less than a C in the class.

EQ: _____ You dislike the instructor.

Ethical Dilemma 3

The Situation

You are delivering a speech on wilderness safety and you wish to incorporate a great attention-getting story you heard about a man who had been chased up a tree by a moose in Montana. To add to the story's impact you decide to say that the situation actually happened to you, even though it didn't. What is the ethical quality of this situation?

Ethical Quality Scale

Highly Unethical	Moderately	Slightly	Neutral	Slightly	Moderately	Highly Ethical
1	2	3	4	5	6	7

Would your EQ rating vary depending on the following variables?

EQ: _____ No one will ever know.

EQ: _____ Something similar happened to you once.

EQ: _____ Your speech teacher emphasizes the importance of attention-getting strategies.

Ethical Dilemma 4

The Situation

The speech on abortion you will be delivering is in two days, but you have not had as much time to research this topic. The library is closed so it will be impossible for you to get secondary sources. You hear that a friend in your dormitory has had an abortion, though, and you decide to interview her. Although your speech is supportive of the pro-life position, you tell your friend that you believe in a woman's right to choose. Basically, you tell your friend that you would like to know about the procedure and promise to keep her name confidential. While delivering your speech you violate this woman's privacy by divulging her name. What is the ethical quality of this situation?

Ethical Quality Scale

Highly Unethical	Moderately	Slightly	Neutral	Slightly	Moderately	Highly Ethical
1	2	3	4	5	6	7

How would your EQ rating vary depending on the following variables?

EQ: _____ Most of the students in your speech class live off campus and do not know this woman.

EQ: _____ You are a serious pro-life advocate, and disrespect this woman for having had an abortion.

Ethical Dilemma 5

The Situation

When listening to an informative speech by one of your classmates, you realize that much of it is plagiarized from a magazine article you read a couple of weeks ago. After class you confront the student and tell him/her that you know what he/she has done. The student tries to convince you that it is no big deal and no one will know anyway because the article was not in a popular magazine. What is the ethical quality of this situation?

Ethical Quality Scale

Highly Unethical	Moderately	Slightly	Neutral	Slightly	Moderately	Highly Ethical
1	2	3	4	5	6	7

How would your EQ rating vary depending on the following variables?

EQ:_____ You dislike the student who is delivering the speech.

EQ:_____ The student is someone you have wanted to go out with all semester.

EQ:_____ At the beginning of the semester your teacher promised a monetary reward to anyone who reported the name(s) of any student(s) suspicious of plagiarism and/or cheating.

Ethical Dilemma 6

The Situation
In order to bolster your own credibility you try the following strategies. What is the Ethical Quality of each situation?

Ethical Quality Scale

Highly Unethical	Moderately	Slightly	Neutral	Slightly	Moderately	Highly Ethical
1	2	3	4	5	6	7

EQ: _____ To establish competence you tell you audience that you have had an avid interest in your topic for the past year when in fact you have only studied it for the last month.

EQ: _____ Though you are typically a quiet and calm person, you intentionally act as though you have extremely high energy in order to appear dynamic.

EQ: _____ Your motives for speaking are really based on self interest, although you disguise them as concern for your audience's well being. For example, you try to convince your audience that earthquake insurance is essential. Mainly this is because you sell it and will profit from the business, yet you act as if the reason you really want them to buy it is so they will be protected in event of an earthquake.

Speech class bill of rights

Have your public speaking classes develop an "Audience Bill of Rights" that reflects the interests and personalities of the class members. (See exercise 2 on p. 56.) This activity usually encourages students to think about issues of ethics in their lives as well as in the classroom. Having the class develop its own bill of rights will increase the likelihood that the students will follow their guidelines.

"Ghostwriting"

If they haven't done so already, students in your basic public speaking course will inevitably raise questions about the ethical nature of ghostwriting during your ethics discussion. The amount of research on this topic is great, both in breadth and depth. While it is a generally acceptable for politicians to deliver ghostwritten speeches, you might ask your students to consider the ethical implications of this practice.

Ethics worksheet

To help promote a quality discussion on ethics, have students answer the list of questions on the next page. You may wish to assign this for homework or have students complete it in class.

Ethics and Your Role as a Public Speaker

Directions: Write one or two sentences expressing your thoughts on the following questions. Be prepared to discuss these questions in class.

1. In your own words, define ethics.

2. What does it mean to be ethical or unethical?

3. Briefly describe a situation when you felt your ethics were challenged.

4. What are your ethical obligations as a public speaker?

5. Do these ethical obligations (from Q4) vary based on your value system? How about social expectations? Are values or societal expectations important for considering ethics in public speaking?

6. What is plagiarism? Are there degrees/types of plagiarism that are worse than other types of plagiarism? Why or why not?

7. What do you think the college's policy on plagiarism/cheating should be?

Additional Resources

Brown, P. E., & Mausehund, J. (1997). Integrating managerial ethics into the business communication curriculum. *Business Communication Quarterly*, 60(1), 77–92.

Christians, C., & Traber, M. (eds.) (1997). *Communication ethics and universal values.* Thousand Oaks, California: Sage.

Cooper, T. W. (1989). *Communication ethics and global change.* White Plains, NY: Longman.

Jensen, J. V. (1985). Teaching ethics in speech communication. *Communication Education*, 30, 324.

Johnston, J. P. (1998). Value added: A communications assignment that develops ethical perception. *Business Communication Quarterly*, 61(i4), 121-124.

Penner, K. (1995, 1 Jan.). Teaching critical thinking (on-line). Available: http://www.mla.org/main_stl.htm

Reeves, M. F. (1990). An application of Bloom's Taxonomy to the teaching of business ethics. *The Journal of Business Ethics*, 2, 609–616.

Smith, D. L. (1998). A time before deception: Truth in communication, culture, and ethics (book reviews). *Communication Theory*, 8(1), 105–110.

4. Chapter 4: Overcoming Fear of Speaking

Chapter Exercises

Exercise 1. Have students prepare their own version of Table 4-1 before class. During class, have students share, individually or in groups, the positive statements they wrote to counter their negative beliefs.

Exercise 2. Have students share the tips they found to reduce communication apprehension. As a class, discuss the relevance of each suggestion. As an alternate assignment, have students present their findings in a fun, 1- to 2-minute group speaking exercise.

Class Activities

Supportive environment
Any class activity which promotes a supportive classroom environment will help ease some of the anxiety students feel. You may also want to suggest specific breathing, relaxation, and visualization techniques as another way to reduce fear.

Specific fears
As an in-class exercise or as a take-home assignment, have students write down their top five specific fears about public speaking. Once students have written down their fears, have them brainstorm solutions. For example, "I am afraid my visual aids will be ineffective." The solution is of course to check the clarity of your visual aids (28). Save their "fears and solutions" until the last week of class. By the end of the term students have usually forgotten what they wrote. The students typically get a good laugh when they reflect on the fears they wrote down during the first week of class. This exercise not only helps them to reflect on the progress they have made throughout the course, but also on the areas they still need to address.

Administer the PRCA (McCroskey, 1970) to your students at the beginning of the term
This instrument is an effective way to measure the apprehension of your students. Students often find that they are not as nervous as they thought they were; this realization often gives them the confidence to complete the course. (Note: there is an alternative version of the PRCA accessible on the *Speaker's Handbook* Web site.)

PRCA: Personal Report Of Communication Apprehension

McCroskey, J.C. (1970). "Measures of communication bound anxiety." *Speech Monographs,* 37, 269-279.

This instrument is composed of twenty-five statements concerning feelings about communicating with other people in public speaking situations. Please indicate the degree to which each statement applies to you by marking whether you (1) strongly agree, (2) agree, (3) are undecided, (4) disagree, or (5) strongly disagree with each statement. Please just record your first impression. Again, the scale is:

(1) = strongly agree   (2) = agree   (3) = undecided   (4) = disagree   (5) = strongly disagree

*_____ 1. While participating in a conversation with a new acquaintance I feel very nervous.

_____ 2. I have no fear of facing an audience.

*_____ 3. I talk less because I am shy.

_____ 4. I look forward to expressing my opinions at meetings.

*_____ 5. I am afraid to express myself in a group.

_____ 6. I look forward to an opportunity to speak in public.

_____ 7. I find the prospect of speaking mildly pleasant.

*_____ 8. When communicating, my posture feels strained and unnatural.

*_____ 9. I am tense and nervous while participating in group discussions.

*_____ 10. Although I talk fluently with friends I am at loss for words on the platform.

_____ 11. I have no fear about expressing myself in a group.

*_____ 12. My hands tremble when I try to handle objects on the platform.

*_____ 13. I always avoid speaking in public if possible.

_____ 14. I feel that I am more fluent when talking to people than most other people.

*_____ 15. I am fearful and tense all the while I am speaking before a group of people.

*_____ 16. My thoughts become confused and jumbled when I speak before an audience.

_____ 17. I like to get involved in group discussions.

_____ 18. Although I am nervous just before getting up, I soon forget my fears and enjoy the experience.

*_____ 19. Conversing with people who hold positions of authority causes me to be fearful and tense.

*_____ 20. I dislike to use my body and voice expressively.

_____ 21. I feel relaxed and comfortable while speaking.

*_____ 22. I feel self-conscious when I am called upon to answer a question or give an opinion in front of my co-workers.

_____ 23. I face the prospect of making a speech with complete confidence.

*_____ 24. I am afraid to speak up in conversations.

_____ 25. I would enjoy presenting a speech on a local television show.

Scoring The PRCA:

1. Add up your scores for all of the questions with stars next to them.
2. Add up your scores for the remaining questions.
3. Complete the following formula:

84 − _____ (total from step 1) **+** _____ (total from step 2) **=** _____ (PRCA score)

0-24	**Lowest level of apprehension**
25-50	**Low level of apprehension**
51-79	**Normal level of apprehension**
80-125	**Extremely high level of apprehension**

Additional Resources

Ayres, J. (1997). Reducing public speaking apprehension through speech preparation. *Speech Communication Teacher*, 11, 6–7.

Beatty, M. J., McCroskey, J. C., & Heisel, A. D. (1998). *Communication Monographs*, 65(3), 197–220.

Beatty, Michael J. (1987). Communication Apprehension as a Determinant of Avoidance, Withdrawal, and Performance Anxiety. *Communication Quarterly*, 35(2), 202–217.

Booth-Butterfield, Steven, & Cottone, R. R. (1991). Ethical issues in the treatment of communication apprehension and avoidance. *Communication Education*, 40, 172–179.

Brownell, W. W., & Katula, R. A. (1984). The communication anxiety graph: A classroom tool for managing speech anxiety. *Communication Quarterly*, 32, 243–249.

Daly, J. A., Bippus, A. M. (1999). What do people think causes stage fright?: Native attributions about the reason for public speaking anxiety. *Communication Education*, 48(i1), 63.

Dobos, J. A. (1996). Collaborative learning: Effects of student expectations and communication apprehension on student motivation. *Communication Education*, 45(2), 118–136.

Fordham, D. R., & Gabbin, A. L. (1996). Skills versus apprehension: Empirical evidence on oral communication. *Business Communication Quarterly*, 59(3), 88–99.

MacIntyre, P. D., & MacDonald, R. J. (1998). Public speaking anxiety: Perceived competence and audience congeniality. *Communication Education*, 47(4), 359–366.

Motley, M. T. (1995). *Overcoming your fear of public speaking—A proven method*. New York, NY: McGraw-Hill.

Robinson, T. E. (1997). Communication apprehension and the basic public speaking course: A national survey of in-class treatment techniques. *Communication Education*, 46(3), 188–198.

Rolls, J. A. (1998). Facing the fears associated with professional speaking. *Business Communication Quarterly*, 61(2), 103-107.

Rubin, R. B., Rubin, A. M., & Jordan, F. F. (1997). Effects on instruction on communication apprehension and communication competence. *Communication Education*, 46(2), 104–115.

Vessup, A. (1995). *You can control speech anxiety*. Dubuque, Iowa: Brown & Benchmark.

C. Teaching Chapters 5–8: Preparation

1. Chapter 5: Planning

Chapter Exercises

There are no exercises in this chapter.

Class Activities

Planning exercise
This activity can be used as part of each assignment or in conjunction with a single assignment. This assignment must not be seen as policing the student but as a way of making the planning process conscious, and of thinking about the decisions of how to spend one's time. It will also serve to make you, the instructor, assign the speeches with sufficient lead time.

The sheet on the following page suggests one format that you can modify to fit your needs. Fill in the dates that you are imposing, such as assignment, outline due, and speech to be presented. Also designate which steps need to be verified and by whom. The student fills in the intermediate dates and obtains necessary signatures as the process moves along.

This approach is especially effective when someone other than the instructor is involved in the verification of completing steps. If there is a speech laboratory staffed with tutors, or if you are fortunate enough to have teaching assistants for the course, these people can initial the final column of the sheet. If you are using a support group approach to the course, members of the student's support group can collaborate on planning and practice. Or students can work with a different partner in preparing each assignment.

Additional Resources

Luotto, J. A., & Stoll, E. L. (1995). *Communication skills for collaborative learning.* (pp. 165). Dubuque, Iowa, Kendall/Hunt Publishing.

Planning Schedule

Task	Target Date	Date Actually Completed	Verified By:
Speech assignment	10/5		
Select topic			(Instructor approval)
Narrow topic, Select thesis			(Member of support group)
Research completed, Select main Points			(Member of support group)
First draft of outline			(Member of support group)
Typed outline			(Received by instructor)
Developmental practice, Speech notes prepared			
Feedback practice sessions Practice with classmate			(Member of support group)
Refinement practice sessions			
Present the speech	10/20		
Review videotape			(Member of support group)
Turn in post-speech analysis and this planning sheet			(Instructor approval)

Analysis of Planning

In a paragraph or so, address these questions. Given the time available, how successfully did you manage your preparation? Were the interim targets realistic? Why or why not? Did you meet most of the target dates? Why or why not? What have you learned about speech preparation by being conscious of your planning decisions?

2. Chapter 6: Topic Selection and Analysis

Chapter Exercises

Exercise 1. Depending on the focus, each topic may be appropriate to more than one type of audience. Perhaps more important, some topics may be inappropriate to a given audience. Neighborhood youth groups are probably not interested in the litigation/mediation question. On the other hand, discussing the martial arts or the problems of our Social Security System would be good topics for a speech class as long as the student met the designated criteria (factual and statistical evidence, several sources, etc.).

Exercise 2. The way to respond to the "timely" portion of this question, of course, shifts constantly. Any timely example listed here would be out of date before this manual was printed, and would probably look a little quaint. By its nature, however, the "timeless" aspect of each topic should be of enduring interest. There are many "timeless" tacks to take with each topic, so these examples are not exhaustive: for martial arts, what really constitutes self-defense, what justifies self-defense? for mediation, are long or short term goals more important, are economic or just/moral values more important; for Social Security, the role of government in "promoting the general welfare;" for television commercials, the ethical responsibilities of a vendor to its customers; for Islam one might look at the life of its prophet Muhammad, the precepts of the religion, or look at the influence of regional traditional values on the practice of religion.

It should not be hard to come up with timely concerns. If, for instance, it is around election time, the speech on how television commercials are made can focus on current political ads (timely) and perhaps deal with the question of how an informed electorate should react to manipulation of national symbols (timeless).

Exercise 3. 2900 words divided by 125 (average speaking rate per minute) is approximately 23 minutes. So, depending on his/her rate of speaking the speech might take between 20 and 25 minutes to deliver.

Exercise 4. When deciding how to limit a speech, be cautious not to water down the material or resort to superficial means. Instead, the speaker should limit the number of points she can cover and narrow her focus.

Exercise 5. A general approach to limiting the topic would be to cut out the technical material for novices and minimize the obvious for comic book aficionados. One possibility would be to eliminate main point III for those who have a beginning interest in comic books. The option of elaborating on the other main points would depend on the time constraints. For a relatively "sophisticated" audience, main point II might contain material they already know. This audience might be more interested in how comic books have "transcended the static nature of the panel format . . . ." For the speech dealing with women in the labor force, discuss the possibilities available when deciding to limit the topic. You may find that students will make different choices depending on their interests, background, etc. Make sure that the students justify their decisions.

Exercise 6. An informative speech on trains could take several forms. A student could discuss trains from a historical perspective (chronological pattern) or describe different kinds of trains (topical) and so on. A speaker might try to persuade his/her audience to travel across country by train rather than by plane, car, hot air balloon . . . . Or, audiences might be persuaded to support government subsidies of railroads similar to subsidies of airlines.

As you might suspect, the previous examples may also provide material for a speech to evoke. Speakers might also touch upon the romantic notion of train travel—meeting new people, enjoying the vastness of our country, a renewed appreciation our heritage. Discuss the other topics as they relate to each purpose and note the variety of approaches.

Exercise 7. Although each speech has some secondary purposes, *Spencer's* main purpose is to evoke, specifically to honor his sister Princess Diana and to provide comfort to those who grieve her loss. *Wong's* purpose is to inform his audience about the effects that noise has on hearing and to explain the kinds of hearing loss that can result from loud noise. *McNeil's* purpose is to persuade her audience that the tropical rainforests are important to the world in many ways, that they are being threatened with destruction and that people in the United States have a responsibility to protect them.

Exercise 8. Contributing audience outcomes for genetic engineering might include:
   I want my audience to *understand* the basic concepts.
   I want my audience to *appreciate* the potential benefits.
   I want my audience to *be aware* of the potential problems/abuses.

Try to encourage students to employ a variety of different outcomes for the other two topics. Point out that speakers should have a clear idea of specific outcomes prior to giving their speech.

Exercise 9. *Poulakos*— "Despite its central role in human affairs, speech communication has been marginalized in the school curriculum, and speech educators must resolve to restore it to its rightful place." *Wong*— "Sustained exposure to high levels of noise can affect hearing." *McNeil*— "The continuing and accelerating destruction of the tropical rainforests, due largely to the policies of industrialized nations, poses a serious threat to the global environment and community—a threat that must be met by immediate action from concerned individuals." *Pham*— "Major Nguyen Quy An deserves U.S. State Department Orderly Departure Program eligibility." *Smith*— "Censoring the Internet threatens civility." *Erian*— "The health problems that many Americans have as a result of misconceptions about the effect of too much sugar in their diets can be alleviated by taking action at the national level and on a personal level." *Harikul*— "The eye chip is a newly developed technology that can help thousands of visually impaired persons who have certain kinds of retinal disease." *Mineta*— "The Department of Transportation has been involved in missions involving security from international threats, but must now return to its important goal of reducing death and injuries from highway accidents by pursuing ways to increase the use of seatbelts and reducing the number of impaired drivers."

Exercise 10. There are several problems with the following thesis statements. However, you may find that there are several "correct" ways to phrase a thesis statement about a particular subject. Naturally, it depends on the content of the speech and the focus of the speaker. The first example illustrates what is wrong with the statement and a possible alternative. The remaining examples point out the flaws in phrasing. Have your students write thesis statements that adhere to the principles of this section and note the different but "correct" ways to phrase a thesis statement.

What shall we do about the problems of the cities? A thesis statement should be a declarative sentence, not phrased as a question. An alternative might be: The crime, traffic, and overcrowding problems of our cities must be addressed by a coalition of local, state, and federal government.

Cambodia's history, its people, and its problems will be the topic I will cover today. A thesis statement should not make you, the speaker, the subject of a sentence.

We need mandatory drug testing for athletes! This appears to be an adequate thesis statement—specific, clear, declarative sentence.

Taxpayers should not have to subsidize art that is pornographic or unpatriotic. This appears to be an adequate thesis statement—specific, clear, declarative sentence.

Here's how to make a Caesar salad. This is not very specific in relating the steps to making a Caesar salad.

There are three causes of congressional gridlock. As a thesis statement, this should be more specific (and definitive) regarding the causes of gridlock.

Exercise 11. *Poulakos*—Is speech central to human existence? Has it been marginalized in the school curriculum? Why? *Wong*—Are everyday sounds harmful to our ears? How much noise must one encounter for how long before there is danger to hearing? How does noise affect the ear? *McNeil*—Are rainforests being destroyed? Is the global environment threatened by rainforest destruction? How? Are the policies of the industrialized nations responsible? What can individuals and groups do to stop this destruction? *Pham*—What is the U.S. State Department Orderly Departure Program? Is Major Nguyen Quy An eligible for the program? Does Major An deserve program eligibility? *Smith*—How does censorship threaten civility? Should internet access be treated differently than other media? Is freedom the only way to combat the threat of civility? *Erian*—Do Americans have serious health problems that stem from too much sugar consumption? Can these problems be effectively addressed by the proposed national actions? Can these problems be effectively addressed by the proposed personal actions? *Harikul*—How does the eye chip work? How was it developed? Does it improve the sight of visually impaired persons? *Mineta*—Are deaths and injuries from highway accidents a serious national problem? Will these deaths and injuries be reduced by increasing the use of seatbelts? Will these deaths and injuries be reduced by reducing the number of drivers who drive while impaired? Can the Department of Transportation take action to solve this problem?

Exercise 12. Is the curve inaccurate? Is it unfair? Is it elitist? —Is a cruise relaxing? Can you make friends on a cruise? Can you see the world on a cruise? —Are property taxes regressive? Are property taxes an uncertain source of revenue? Are they an inequitable source of revenue for cities?

Exercise 13. *Erian's* title "No More Sugar" is concise but does not truly capture his meaning since he makes it clear that some sugar consumption is acceptable as long as it is not excessive. *Wong's* title effectively sets the tone and previews the subject. *McNeil's* title does not really allude to the ideas of the threat to the planet due to deforestation. *Smith's* title is catchy and effective. It previews the subject and sets the mood.

Exercise 14. Have students brainstorm creative titles for the speeches. As a group, discuss the merits and potential drawbacks each title presents.

Exercise 15.
1. General Topic: Cardiopulmonary resuscitation (CPR) (d)
2. Narrowed Topic: The value of learning CPR (i)
3. General Purpose: To persuade (h)
4. Specific Purpose: To convince the audience that the greater the number of people who know CPR, the better the chance of more lives being saved every day. (b),
5. Primary Audience Outcome: I want my audience to actively work toward increasing the number of people who know CPR. (e)
6. Contributing Audience Outcome: Encourage friends to take a class in CPR. (c)

7.   Thesis Statement: As many people as possible should learn CPR to increase the probability that a person trained in this life-saving technique will be available in the event of a heart attack or similar medical emergency. (g)
8.   Analysis Question: Have more lives been saved when a CPR-trained person has been present? (a)
9.   Title: Learn CPR and Make the World a Safer Place. (f).

Class Activities

Topic selection interview

Divide students into groups of five or six. In each group have Student A interview Student B about background, hobbies, interests, major, etc. After four or five minutes, have the other students in the group brainstorm to produce a list of possible speech topics for Student B. Then repeat the exercise with B interviewing C, C interviewing D, and so on.

Group outline

This exercise spans several topics. Students should form small groups of four or five people. These groups will remain the same throughout this exercise. Beginning on the day topic selection is covered, give each group a different section of a recent newspaper. Ask each group to scan the articles and discuss the timely and timeless aspects of the various stories. The groups should then select a topic from the articles they have discussed and talk about the types of information which would be needed if a speech was to be given on this topic. The next step in this exercise is for group members to each bring one piece of evidence relating to this topic to class. Assuming an informative presentation on their topic is to be given, students can begin phrasing a specific purpose, primary audience outcome, and a working thesis statement. As subsequent chapters are covered in class, students can form main points for their "speech," outline their main points, and create an introduction and conclusion.

Writing purpose statements

Ask students to share their responses to any of the exercises in this chapter. Compare the similarities and differences in responses. As a class, re-write the less effective purpose statements.

Additional Resources

Glaser, H.F. (1998). Focusing the students on three speech topics. *The Speech Communication Teacher,* 12(4), p10.

Woodside, D. (1992). Choosing topics for speeches: A breath of fresh air (Earth, Water, and Fire). *Speech Communication Teacher,* 7(1), 1–2.

3. Chapter 7: Audience Analysis

Chapter Exercises

Exercise 1. This exercise might be utilized as a homework assignment. If your students are using their class as the audience, compare the audience profiles and note how different they are.

Exercise 2. Forensics tournaments are showcases for speakers to show that they can adhere to some very technical requirements of particular speech genres, while still creating an original and believable presentation. Obviously, speakers are making assumptions about the expectations and requirements of the judges. (Other contestants and observers may be present, but for competitors the primary audience is always the judge.) They believe that these audience members are well educated, able to follow a rapid fire and densely documented speech, and willing to become interested in a wide range of topics. If *Erian* were to present "No More Sugar" to a group of parents interested in their children's diets or to a group of high school principals interested in whether to limit the offerings in school vending machines, he might keep the basic argument he is developing and the sound information he has gathered but might consider some of the following changes: A slower, less dramatic, more conversational style of delivery. Less explicit transitions, still leading the listener from point to point but more subtly. He would still want to document his sources, but probably not by laying out the full details of each source. He might say, "a recent study reported in the New York Times," holding in reserve the other information about the source. Most importantly, he would need to bring in several specific references to the particular audience such as noting that Arnell Scott is probably like some of your children or like the students at this school, etc. If *Harikul* were to present "Eye Chip" to a group of senior citizens, for example, she might assume a somewhat slower more conversational style of delivery. The references to Star Trek might be replaced with some other theme. She would still want to document her sources, but probably not by laying out the full details of each source. Most importantly, she would need to bring in several specific references to the particular audience such as commenting on how they may have felt their own vision becoming more fuzzy with age.

Class Activities

Audience analysis
Divide the class into groups of three or four. Give each group the name of an organization (National Rifle Association, Young Democrats, Girl Scouts of America, National Education Association, etc.). Students should compile an audience profile, both demographic and attitudinal, of their organization. They would augment this written report with an oral summary to the rest of the class. A discussion should follow on how the diversity of each group would play a part in preparing a speech for that audience, and why. This exercise, particularly the gathering of information about the organizations, can be used in conjunction with the previous exercise or any other activity stressing research methods.

Audience analysis project
A more elaborate audience analysis assignment can be found in part IV of this instructor's manual under the heading of Persuasive Strategy Project.

Using reasonable assumptions and intelligent inferences to analyze an audience
Divide the class into groups of 3–4. For the greatest impact, give each group a different popular culture magazine (*Cosmopolitan, Sunset, People, PC Gamer, Men's Health, Popular Science, Ebony, Auto Week,* etc.) Tell the groups that they will be delivering a speech to a group of individuals in 3 weeks. Unfortunately,

the only information you can give them, is that the individuals read "X" magazine. With the limited information, have the group compile an analysis which includes pertinent demographic and attitudinal information. Although many men and women in the class will ask for specific magazines they are familiar with, it is interesting to distribute the magazines to groups who may think they are uninterested in the specific theme of the magazine.

You may also want to have the groups suggest 2 or 3 speech topics they would consider developing for this audience. While this activity can also be used in conjunction with the outlining chapters, it is particularly useful in demonstrating the effectiveness of making reasonable assumptions and intelligent inferences about a particular audience. Students are also reminded to think about communication as the joint creation of meaning, and the importance of considering their audience when selecting a speech topic and when developing the content of their speech (i.e., the articles in the magazine). After comparing the observations of each group, you may wish to emphasize the impact the audience analysis would have on the group's choice of topic(s).

Have students analyze a speech
Ask the students to identify how the speaker(s) adapts his/her speech to the audience.

Additional Resources

Canary, D.J., and Hause, K.S. (1993). Is there any reason to research sex differences in communication? *Communication Quarterly,* 41, 129–144.

Hanna, M.S. (1998). Audience Analysis (book reviews). *The Southern Communication Journal,* 63(3), 266–269.

Neumann, D. (1992). Selecting messages: An exercise in audience analysis. In Stephen E. Lucas (Ed.), *Selections from the Speech Communication Teacher, 1986-1991* (p. 14). New York: McGraw-Hill.

Young, K.S. (1997). An alternative to demographic audience analysis. *Speech Communication Teacher,* 11(4), 10–11.

4. Chapter 8: Research

Chapter Exercises

There are no exercises in this chapter.

Class Activities

Library resource search
Divide the class into pairs or groups and give each one or more of the items listed on this quiz.
  a. Book entries in the card catalog are generally divided into _____, _____, and _____.
  b. List the four major international newspapers.
  c. List up to ten important regional newspapers.
  d. List three General Social Science Periodical Indexes.
  e. List at least one Periodical Index for the following areas: Political Science, Business, Medicine, Law and Education.
  f. What are the three levels of the Federal Court System?
  g. Explain the citation, "Escobedo V. Illinois 378 U.S. 478."
  h. U.S. Government statutes are found in _____.
  i. U.S. Government Agency Regulations are found in _____.
  j. The two major indexes to Government Documents are _____.
  k. List at least two major sources for national statistical data. (The U.S. Census is not acceptable.)
  l. List at least two major sources that provide author qualifications.
  m. Name two periodicals that are devoted to nonpartisan analysis of government (U.S. and State/Local) policies.

Have the students bring their answers to the following class meeting. Each group should explain not only the correct answer but the means they used to find the answer, as well as the problems they encountered along the way. A class discussion should reveal the multitude of sources available in the library and ways of finding information expeditiously.

Information treasure hunt
A variation of the preceding exercise would be to have students (as individuals or teams) locate bits of trivia using whatever source (library, interviews, Internet, etc.) they find appropriate. For example: Who was the mayor of Cleveland in 1906? What was the background of novelist Kingsley Amis? How many books has Sue Grafton written? In what states can you find muledeer in their natural habitat? What college did Bill Gates attend? What are the various types of counseling available on campus and where it is available? Who holds the current land speed record? Who were the winners of the silver medal for ice dancing in the last Olympics? What football team has played in the Super Bowl most frequently? Who was the playwright of *Starlight Express* and in what year and country in was it first produced? Who was the original author of "Ask not what your country can do. . .?" As in the previous exercise, students should be able to elaborate on their sources as well as explain difficulties and share helpful hints on finding their answers.

Group outline exercise

See section D-3 in this instructor's manual, on chapter 11.

Supporting main points

After a discussion on conducting research and the use of supporting material, divide the class into groups of 3–5. Give each group one main point of an informative or persuasive speech. The group is then required to go to the library and obtain credible supporting material that supports their main point. Once the groups have reconvened and supported their main point, have one member deliver the main point to the class. After all the groups have delivered their presentations, you can emphasize and discuss the following questions: Does the evidence support the main point? Is the evidence credible? Was the supporting material cited properly within the presentation and the outline? What types of research have the most impact? etc. You may also want to consider using this activity in conjunction with several other chapters (**9, 10, 11 or 15**).

Additional Resources

Schlein, A. M. (2002). *Find it online: the complete guide to online research, 3rd ed.*. Tempe, AZ: Facts On Demand Press.

Hock, R. (2004). *The extreme searcher's Internet handbook.* Medford, NJ: Cyberage Books.

http://www.policy.com/issues/ (This Web site will help students locate issues of policy to research further.)

http://www.mcli.dist.maricopa.edu/tl/ (This site discusses issues related to teaching and learning on the www.)

The following Web sites might be useful to students. At the date of publication, the addresses are:

US House of Representatives Home Page:	http://www.house.gov
White House:	http://www.whitehouse.gov
Library of Congress:	http://lcweb.loc.gov
CNN Interactive:	http://www.cnn.com

D. Teaching Chapters 9–14: Organization

1. Chapter 9: Transforming Ideas into Speech Points

Chapter Exercises

Exercise 1

Thesis: Cats make better pets than dogs.

   Point III does not support the thesis statement.

   Point IV should state that cats are more loyal and affectionate than dogs.

Thesis: A four-day work week would be beneficial to our company.

   None of these points support the thesis statement unless you argue that increased employee morale as a result of these points will be beneficial to a company.

Thesis: Skateboarders are discriminated against wherever they ride.

   Point III does not support the thesis statement.

Class Activities

Andy Rooney exercise

Present students with a totally jumbled set of objects. You might empty your purse or briefcase on a table, or bring a bag containing items from your glove compartment or a junk drawer. Have the students gather around and each silently make an outline that classifies all the objects. Then compare the different classification schemes chosen. Some may organize the items by function, by shape, cost, etc. The exercise illustrates the concepts of subordination, coordination, and mutually exclusive categories.

Planning a party

This exercise works well in either a class discussion or small group format. Tell your students that you want them to plan an end of the semester class party. They may have any kind of party they want, provided they present you with a clearly organized outline of what they will need. Students should begin by brainstorming everything they want or need for their party. Students usually begin with the obvious categories of "food," "music," etc. Challenge them to get as specific as possible. What kind of food do they want, main dishes or desserts? What kinds of desserts? What kinds of music? What types of decorations? After about 5–7 minutes, students will have brainstormed a lot of (seemingly) random ideas. Next, the students should coordinate their information into several distinct categories. While this exercise also illustrates the concepts of subordination, coordination, and mutually exclusive categories, it can also be used in conjunction with the topic selection and outlining chapters. A useful follow up exercise on this activity is to have students take their topical outlines and create a full sentence outline, including purpose statements, an introduction, and a conclusion, as if they were going to give a speech on "the three most important elements to any successful party." Students usually report the "planning a party" exercise as one of their most favorite activities of the semester.

Additional Resources

Ensign, R. L. (1993). The arrow through ass' ribs outline: A teaching aid for the basic course. *Speech Communication Teacher*, 4, 10–11.

Huffman, M. (1985). The maze as an instrument for public speaking. *Communication Education*, 34, 63–68.

2. Chapter 10: Arranging Points

Chapter Exercises

Exercise 1. There are many possibilities for each topic. For example, you might arrange the topic of National Parks as follows.
Chronological
  I.   Public interest in saving our national resources was first apparent in the 1920s.
  II.   The National Park System was established in the 1930s.
  III. The first park lands were brought into the system in 1935.

Problem-Solution
  I.   Rare and fragile natural environmental areas were being threatened by destruction/development.
  II.   To save these lands they must be reserved for specific uses.

Cause-Effect
  I.   The National Park System reserves specified lands for recreational use and preservation.
  II.   (As a result) Rare and fragile environmental areas have preserved natural flora, fauna, and topographical integrity.

Exercise 2. *Erian*—Generally, Erian's speech follows a problem–solution format. It is possible to see the first two points as cause–effect so that the entire speech reflects this pattern. Main Point I (misconceptions) is a *cause* that leads to Main Point II (unhealthy level of sugar consumption), an *effect*, which in turn constitutes a *problem*, that leads to Main Point III (reducing sugar consumption), which is a *solution*. *Harikul*—This speech follows a topical organization. *Mineta*—He used a problem–solution sequence for the speech, first describing the seriousness of the problem of highway deaths and injuries and then talking about ways the Department of Transportation could help reduce highway accidents.

Exercise 3. Rodriguez's speech did not follow any standard organizational pattern. Instead, it reflects the kind of coherence and unity that one finds in some poetry and fictional writings. That is, Rodriguez weaves several strands together into a complex tapestry that has an overall artistic effect. He picks up a thread such as the green eyes of the woman in the wheelchair, Oprah Winfrey, the Kenyon College students who were killed before they could graduate, his own graduation speaker, his parents' aging, his own youth. He elaborates on the theme in an evocative way, seems to drop it, and later picks it up again. By the end of the speech there is a feeling of unity and wholeness, achieved by this shifting and changing or topics. The speech illustrates two important things about speech organization: 1) there is no best way to organize a speech and unique formats can be designed depending on the occasion, and 2) the tapestry (sometimes called string of pearls) style of organization is not effective for beginners; it requires tremendous skill in the use of language and in selecting impactful ways to juxtapose ideas.

Exercise 4. Have students share the results of their *InfoTrac* searches and discuss the effectiveness of the organizational patterns they found.

Class Activities

Classification comparison
Have students share their responses to the chapter exercises and compare the different classification schemes chosen.

Organization choices
Ask students what other organizational patterns the creators could have chosen for the speeches in the Sample Speeches on the Web?

Party outline organization pattern
Have students select an organizational pattern for the "planing a party" speech outline they wrote after the chapter 9 classroom activity.

Main point organization
Ask students to identify the organizational method used in a series of main points.

Additional Resources

See Part V, Resource Integration Guide.

3. Chapter 11: Outlining

Chapter Exercises

Exercise 1. Here is one possible outline for the Poulakos speech:

Attention Getter: When I first came to this country . . . [stories about difficulty in mastering the English language.]

Psychological Orientation & Logical Orientation: Today, I find myself committed to two paradoxical tasks . . .

I. Oral Communication Instruction does not hold a place at the center of the K-12 Curriculum.
    A. As a society, we are ambivalent about speech
        1. We glorify rhetoric but are afraid of its power.
        2. We envy good speakers but also distrust them.
    B. Speaking and listening are taken for granted.
        1. Children can already speak when they start school.
        2. We think the curriculum should focus on more "useful" skills.
    C. Oral communication is "messy" to teach.
        1. Classes are noisy and interactive.
        2. Speech skill is hard to measure objectively.
    D. Oral communication education makes students better critical thinkers.
        1. Skilled speakers often want to reform society and make it better.
        2. They are critical of the status quo and thus threaten those in power.

Transition: This ambivalence has existed since classical time, but instruction in speech has persisted because it is so important. (Isocrates quotation)

II. The importance of Oral Communication has lasted for centuries.
    A. Communication is an essential part of literacy.
        1. Speakers are not born, they are made through their interaction with others.
        2. Students are empowered when they learn to speak and claim a voice in the world.
    B. Speech is essential to democracy.
        1. Freedom of speech is meaningless if people do not have the skill to use it.
        2. The point of speech education is not to make everyone eloquent, but for people to explore their interdepence as citizens.

III. Action is needed to ensure oral communication a central place in the school curriculum
    A. A number of experts and commissions have issued statements in support of oral communication instruction
        1. A Nation at Risk
        2. Task Force on Education for Academic Growth
        3. Boyer's *High School*
    B. The calls for inclusion are not effective unless individuals take action to advocate for oral communication instruction.
        1. Speech educators are the ones who must advocate for speech in the curriculum.
        2. Examples of cooperative action can be found in Pennsylvania.

Psychological Closure: We have come to the "show me" state to show you.

Logical Closure & Clincher. Well, we have come, and we have given you the word. We now hope that you will pass it on. Clearly ladies and gentlemen, I am happy to be here tonight.

Exercise 2. Continue through the main points and show how the full-sentence outline is much more clear and comprehensive than the topic outline. For example, main point I of the topic outline mentions increased industrialization but does not include, as the full-sentence outline does, the rather critical statement that increased industrialization led to increased exploitation of women workers.

Exercise 3.

Thesis: The United Nations is essential to world peace and harmony.
  I.   The United Nations provides countries with a forum for airing their grievances.
  II. The United Nations provides an opportunity for countries to focus their energies toward a common goal.
  III. The United Nations provides an opportunity for all countries to belong to one "family."

Thesis: Advertisers use a variety of techniques to influence consumers.
  I.   Advertisers establish tone and mood through color.
  II. Advertisers use symbols to attain their goals.
  III. Advertisers manipulate shapes for visual impact.

Exercise 4. One possible outline:

Attention Getter: Geordie LaForge reference
Psychological Orientation: Millions of people may be helped by a new technology known as the eye chip.
Logical Orientation: Overview of three points
  I. The eye chip was developed to try to reverse blindness.
      A. In the long history of trying to improve vision, the quest to actually restore vision to blind persons has become the "Holy Grail."
      B. The team of Drs Humayun and de Juan pioneered a technology that bypasses retinal disease.
      C. The retina, which comes between the lens and the optic nerve, proved to be the most promising for a technological breakthrough.
  II. The eye chip is effective in alleviating two kinds of retinal disease.
      A. Retinitus Pigmentosa
          1. Affects the rods
          2. Symptoms are tunnel vision and poor night vision.
      B. Age Related Macular Degeneration
          1. Affects the surface of the retina
          2. Symptoms are blurred and distorted vision.
  III. The eye chip works by bypassing the damaged portions of the retina.
      A. A small camera is mounted in the glasses.
      B. This transfers information to a chip implanted inside the eye.
      C. Although imperfect compared to natural vision, the sight enabled by the eye chip makes a great improvement in the lives of formerly blind persons.
Logical and Psychological Closure: Recap of main points and reference that there is much more research to be done.
Clincher: In the words of Captain Picard, "Make it so."

Class Activities

Viewing informative speeches

This activity requires that you have a videotape of an informative speech. In addition to providing students with a sample presentation, this activity gives them an opportunity to practice their critiquing skills. Divide students into four groups and assign each group one area of responsibility. After the videotaped speech is viewed, give groups time to discuss their area. Each group should then report its assessment to the class.

Group 1: Introductions and Conclusions
Were the three parts of the introduction (attention getter; psychological orientation; logical orientation) identifiable?
Were the three parts of the introduction effective?
—Did the attention getter grab your attention?
—Did the psychological orientation connect the topic to the audience?
—Were the speaker's thesis and preview clear?
Were the three parts of the conclusion (logical closure; psychological closure; clincher) identifiable?
Were the three parts of the conclusion effective?
—Were the thesis and a review of main points provided?
—Did the speaker reconnect the topic to the audience?
—Did the speaker end with a bang, not a whimper?

Group 2: Organization
Were the main points clearly stated?
Were the main points mutually exclusive?
Did the main points develop the thesis statement?
Did the main points follow a logical pattern of organization?
Were transitions used between main points?

Group 3: Content
Did the speaker cite his or her sources?
Was all speech content relevant to the main points and thesis?
Was the information presented clear and understandable?
Were statistics, examples, testimony, and/or definitions used effectively?
Were attention factors used? Did the speaker hold your attention?
If visual aids were used, were they appropriate and effective?

Group 4: Delivery
Did the speaker speak in the extemporaneous mode?
Was the speaker's vocal delivery effective?
—Did the speaker maintain appropriate volume?
—Did the speaker maintain appropriate rate?
—Was the speaker's vocal delivery varied?
Was the speaker's physical delivery effective?
—Did the speaker avoid distracting mannerisms?
—Was the speaker's facial expression appropriate?
—Did the speaker gesture naturally?

—Did the speaker make and maintain eye contact with the audience?

—Did the speaker use his or her visual aid(s) effectively?

Scrambled outline

This classic exercise has students, as individuals or in groups, try to unscramble an outline and discover the relationships among ideas. One such example to use is printed on the following pages. You may design your own, or have students scramble one of their own for another group to untangle, structuring a competitive activity. Note that, as with the example given here, there is usually more than one logical and acceptable way to organize the same material. Discussion of these alternatives is part of the learning experience of this activity.

Additional Resources

Mino, M. (1992). Structuring: An alternate approach for developing clear organization. In Stephen E.Lucas (Ed.), *Selections from the Speech Communication Teacher, 1986-1991*, (pp. 55–56). New York: McGraw-Hill.

Scrambled Outline

Dioxin is more toxic than many well-known substances.

Dioxin has been spread throughout our environment in many ways.

10,000 times more toxic than cyanide

Animal studies show Dioxin produces many adverse reactions even in very small doses.

Dioxin is one of the most toxic substances known.

Lack of clear standards had led to long delays in cleanups while studies were conducted.

Times Beach, Missouri

22 micrograms per kilogram of body weight is lethal for rats.

Cleansing agents

A correlation has been shown between Dioxin and human health problems.

500 times more toxic than strychnine

Liver damage, tumors, and damage to the immune system of animals have been documented.

Choracne and damage to the immune system have occurred in workers accidentally exposed to Dioxin.

It is used in many common substances.

The hazards of Dioxin must be dealt with by both sort-term and long-term solutions.

100 million times more toxic than DDT

Herbicides

An E.P.A. study showed an increase in infant mortality and birth defects in mice exposed to mere trace amounts of Dioxin.

Italy, 1976

Improper disposal of chemical waste has contaminated many areas.

Lumber preservatives

2,4,5-T can be replaced with Krenite.

Miscarriages rose from 6% to 10% in an Oregon city following spraying of a herbicide containing Dioxin.

Industrial accidents have released Dioxin into the environment.

Holland, 1963

Hexachlorophene can be replaced with chlorhexidrene.

Setting clear cleanup standards would allow the E.P.A. to remove dangers in a more timely and consistent manner.

Political considerations often mean that contamination is not handled in the same way in each case.

Banning sources of Dioxin can prevent future contamination.

Love Canal

Unscrambled Outline

I. Dioxin is one of the most toxic substances known.

    A. Dioxin is more toxic than many well-known substances.

        1. 100 million times more toxic than DDT

        2. 500 times more toxic than strychnine

        3. 10,000 times more toxic than cyanide

    B. Animal studies show Dioxin produces many adverse reactions even in very small doses.

        1. 22 micrograms per kilogram of body weight is lethal for rats.

        2. An E.P.A. study showed an increase in infant mortality and birth defects in mice exposed to mere trace amounts of Dioxin.

        3. Liver damage, tumors, and damage to the immune system of animals have been documented.

    C. A correlation has been shown between Dioxin and human health problems.

        1. Miscarriages rose from 6% to 10% in an Oregon city following spraying of a herbicide containing Dioxin.

        2. Choracne and damage to the immune system have occurred in workers accidentally exposed to Dioxin.

II. Dioxin has been spread throughout our environment in many ways.

    A. It is used in many common substances.

        1. Herbicides

        2. Cleansing agents

        3. Lumber preservatives

    B. Industrial accidents have released Dioxin into the environment.

        1. Holland, 1963

        2. Italy, 1976

    C. Improper disposal of chemical waste has contaminated many areas.

        1. Love Canal

        2. Times Beach, Missouri

III. The hazards of Dioxin must be dealt with by both short-term and long-term solutions.

    A. Setting clear cleanup standards would allow the E.P.A. to remove dangers in a more timely and consistent manner.

        1. Lack of clear standards has lead to long delays in cleanups while studies were conducted.

        2. Political considerations often mean that contamination is not handled in the same way in each case.

    B. Banning sources of Dioxin can prevent future contamination.

        1. Hexachlorophene can be replaced with chlorhexidrene.

        2. 2,4,5-T can be replaced with Krenite.

Adapted from a speech by Jeffrey M. Blank.

4. Chapter 12: Transitions

Chapter Exercises

Exercise 1. Many people don't give much thought to transitions when planning their speech. As a result, a speech may lack continuity and coherence. Using appropriate transitions should provide logical links between main points and enable the audience to follow along with minimal effort. In the women workers outline, the transition "however" or "but" puts in perspective the connection between the last sentence of point I and point II. Experiment with different transitions in several areas of each speech outline and notice if the meaning changes.

Exercise 2. Here is one example, from *Poulakos*: Transitions can be found in the 8th and 12th sentences of paragraph 1; 1st sentence of paragraph 2; 2nd sentence of paragraph 3; 2nd sentence of paragraph 4; 1st sentence of paragraphs 5 and 6; 1st and 8th sentences of paragraph 7; 1st sentences of paragraphs 8 and 9; 1st sentence in paragraph 11; 5th sentence of paragraph 12; 1st and 6th sentences of paragraph 13; 1st, 4th, 5th, 6th, 7th, and 8th sentences of paragraph 14; 1st, 5th, and 6th sentences of paragraph 15; 1st and 13th sentence of paragraph 16.

Students will be surprised to observe what a large proportion of a speech like this one consists of transitional sentences and how many sentences contain transitional words. They should be able to identify all of the above transitions as well as internal previews and summaries.

Class Activities

Transition exercise
Prepare slips of paper containing unrelated words, one word per slip, such as elephant, light bulb, spaghetti, Julius Caesar, bicycles, etc. Divide the students into groups and give one set of terms to each. The first student blindly picks two slips and must draw a plausible transition between them. "I've just explained to you how elephants live, but perhaps you do not know that elephants can also be used for transportation. Another method of transportation—one that is lighter and cheaper to maintain—is the bicycle." The next student draws another word and must make a transition from bicycles to say, light bulbs. This can be turned into a competitive exercise by having each group's transitions evaluated by judges.

Writing transitional sentences
Individually or in groups, have students write transitions for the speech they unscrambled in chapter 11. Compare and discuss the different ways students bridge one main point to the next.

Identifying transitional phrases
Have students read the speeches on the Web site. Discuss and critique the transitional words and phrases each of the speakers uses.

Additional Resources

See Part V, Resource Integration Guide.

5. Chapter 13: Introductions

Chapter Exercises

Exercise 1. *Erian* used an engaging story of Arnell Scott. *Harikul* begins the speech with a reference to Geordie La Forge from Star Trek: The Next Generation. *Rodriguez* abandoned his opening sentence about a woman with green eyes without explanation, leaving the audience almost wondering if they had heard him right. This worked to create curiosity (and a certain thrill of recognition when the woman with green eyes was reintroduced later).

Exercise 2. There are a number of way of creating an engaging attention-getter for this speech. One is the Surprising Historical Fact: Colonial women were often autonomous farm managers (point IB2). This fact jostles the standard view of colonial life as totally male-dominated, and an attention-getter developed from this fact could play with the anachronistic thought that in some ways our supposedly traditional forebears could be more pragmatic and "modern" about sex roles than some current spokespersons. Another attention getter might be more personal. For instance, a speaker could relate her shock when she discovered that her grandmother, whom she had seen only as a happy housewife, had been Personnel Manager for a steel company during World War II, but had given it up when the soldiers came home. This outline can engender a variety of attention-getting responses—emotional, political, or sociological.

Exercise 3. Mineta establishes a relationship with his audience and also flatters them by commending them for the heroic work they have done in response to the "call of history" that thrust upon them unexpected demands during the terrorist attacks of 9/11/01, the war in Afghanistan, and the war in Iraq. He establishes common ground by referring to the shared mission they all feel to serve the public. He refers to the setting by thanking the other administrators who are on the dais with him and by defining the nature of an All Hands meeting.

Exercise 4. While you should always avoid stereotypes, knowing your audience and their relationship to the topic should help you when thinking of a creative, relevant psychological orientation. Try to involve the audience—keeping in mind their attitudes, values, and beliefs towards your topic.
   a. Civic organizations are often concerned with social matters so you could appeal to their interests in community/business as well as personal benefits: better health and reduced time off from work; better personal health from reduced smog. Also, fewer auto accidents and a reduced injury/death rate would be important.
   b. Firefighters frequently speak to children and civic groups, provide CPR training classes, and educate the public about fire prevention.
   c. Many college students are interested in fitness and the most effective equipment for exercise.

Exercise 5. *Harikul* defines the term intraocular retinal prosthesis and then previews the three main points she will cover. *Erian* sets a framework by establishing the scope of the problem and then specifically previewing the three points he would be covering: misconceptions, what they lead to, and ways to control sugar consumption. *Gilderhus* gives a specific overview of the topics each group member would cover in the presentation.

Exercise 6. There are many options available for your logical orientation. You could describe your topic from a historical framework, provide definitions, etc. A possibility for the women in the labor force (**11b**) would be to provide an analogy.

"Many of you may think of minorities as being the only group that has been exploited as a cheap and expendable source of labor in our country. Obviously, this type of exploitation is unacceptable in a country that espouses justice, freedom, fairness, equality. It doesn't seem fair then, that women should play a secondary role in the work place. In the work place, women are a minority and like other minorities have been treated rather shabbily throughout the years. Today, I would like to give you a brief historical account of American women in the labor force. I would like to begin with the preindustrial colonial period and then describe three other periods that have had a significant impact on the women's labor force: the period between the Revolution and Civil War, the years between the Civil War and World War II, and finally, ending with the World War II era."

The last sentence gives a specific preview to your main points. A more general preview might just include "Today, I would like to give you a historical account . . ."

Exercise 7. *Poulakos* had an attention getter and then seemed to blend the psychological orientation and the logical orientation by giving an overview of the topic and its importance. He did not specifically preview his points, but forecast them more indirectly by alluding to his two paradoxical tasks. *Pham* does not really partition out the sections of the introduction, but rather begins with a narrative that leads her audience into the topic. It should be noted first that this is a very brief speech, and second, that this manuscript is actually a composite of a short presentation she gave many times, and in most cases the purpose of her speech would have already been made known to the audience. *Smith's* introduction contains all three elements. As is common in a formal speech, he begins with acknowledging the introduction and expressing his pleasure at being present. Though he might not need a formal attention getter, the reference to the cartoon was engaging. It led into a paragraph about the significance and timeliness of his topic. He then presented a brief preview of what he would cover.

Exercise 8. Ask students to evaluate one or two speeches from *Vital Speeches*. What, if any, pitfalls can they identify? This can be a fun exercise and will help students refine their rhetorical analysis skills.

Class Activities

Introductions
After your students have unscrambled the outline (Class Activity from the previous section, Arranging Points), have each group design a introduction for the speech, and then share their creations with the entire class. Or, assign each group a hypothetical audience and have them adapt their introductions accordingly.

Critiquing introductions
Provide a sampling of introductions that contain at least one flaw from student speeches you've listened to. Ask students to volunteer to deliver the introductions to the class. The class should critique the introductions in terms of the criteria specified in chapter **13**. Questions to guide their analyses: What does the speaker do to gain the audience's attention? How are the functions of the logical and psychological orientation fulfilled? What would strengthen the introduction?

Writing introductions competitively
Give the class a topic, thesis, and the main points for a hypothetical speech. Have each group write and deliver their own introduction. After all of the introductions have been read, ask the class to discuss the effectiveness of the introductions.

Viewing informative speeches
See also Class Activities, section D-3 of this instructor's manual, on chapter 11.

Additional Resources

Cox, F. (1998). Introductions: Tips on how to introduce people in public. *PSA Journal*, 64(4), 40.

6. Chapter 14: Conclusions

Chapter Exercises

Exercise 1. *Poulakos* does not really have a logical closure step. He finishes the final point on what has been done in his home state and then concludes quite abruptly, "Well, we have come and we have given you the word. We now hope you will pass it on." Since he had used internal summaries throughout the speech, this may well have been adequate without returning to summarize each main point. *Pham* uses only two sentences to recap her points, but given that it was a short speech and the points were quite evident, this may have been adequate. *Erian* used an explicit but concise summary of his main points as a logical orientation, "Today we've looked at the misconceptions about sugar, where these misconceptions lead, and have found some solutions to our sugar addiction."

Exercise 2. Your logical closure can provide an explicit restatement of your thesis and main points or you may choose to paraphrase. For example, the conclusion to the women in the labor force speech might begin as follows.

"As you can see, the four periods I have described—the colonial settings, the period between the Revolution and Civil War, the years between the Civil War and World War II, and finally the World War II era—have illustrated the systematic exploitation of women in the work place."

Exercise 3. *McNeil* makes an appeal to think beyond the local or national level and take a global perspective. *Wong* refers to the risk to individuals' hearing and to his own slight hearing loss to bring his topic back to the self interest of his audience. *Spencer* brings his speech to an emotional ending by thanking God for his mercy by taking Diana at her most beautiful and radiant when she was filled with joy. This seems rather odd as a way of comforting the listeners.

Exercise 4. *Dawson* encapsulated his main idea using the phrase, "if you only remember one thing from this speech . . ." and then used the familiar and unifying technique of returning to his introduction with another quotation from the same author. The clincher was a single word: "Don't." *Harikul* ends her speech by returning to the Star Trek example and saying:"Make it so," a signature line for Star Trek's Captain Picard. *Mineta* uses a powerful and inspiring final sentence: "I know that with your commitment and energy you will not let this great nation down."

Exercise 5. The important thing to remember when planning your clincher is to avoid the conclusion pitfalls and to make sure your audience knows you are finished. A clincher to the comic book speech (11) might relate back to the attention getter.

"Collecting comic books may not be as lucrative for you as it was for John Snyder but you might be able to pick up a few bucks while enjoying the escapades of Mr. Fudd and the rest of the comic book gang."

Class Activities

Conclusions
After your students have unscrambled the outline from the Arranging Points class activities, have each group design a conclusion for the speech, and then share their creations with the entire class. Or, assign each group a hypothetical audience and have them adapt their conclusions accordingly.

Critiquing conclusions

Collect several conclusions from previous informative and/or persuasive speeches you've listened to. Ask students to volunteer to deliver the conclusions to the class. The class should critique the conclusions in terms of the criteria specified in chapter **14**. Questions to guide their analyses: How effective is the clincher? How are the functions of the logical and psychological closure fulfilled? What would strengthen the conclusion?

Writing conclusions competitively

Give the class a topic, thesis, and the main points for a hypothetical speech. Have each group write and deliver their own conclusion. After all of the conclusions have been read, ask the class to discuss the effectiveness of the conclusions.

Viewing informative speeches

See also Class Activities, section D-3 of this instructor's manual, on chapter **11**.

Additional Resources

See Part V, Resource Integration Guide.

E. Teaching Chapters 15–23: Development

1. Chapter 15: Supporting Materials

Chapter Exercises

Exercise 1.
Cross training:
    a.   This is when Jerry Rice goes out and plays basketball twice a week (Example).
    b.   According to sports physiologist Dr. Bubba Holistic, cross training requires intensive involvement in a sport that requires substantially different patterns of exertion and works different muscle groups than the primary sport (Authority).

Love:
    a.   An intense, affectionate concern for another person (Logical/dictionary).
    b.   The convicted mass murderer had no feelings of remorse, even for his own parents and family; there were no feelings of love within him (Negation).

Collective bargaining:
    a.   Entails sitting down with representatives of each side of a controversy and negotiating a mutually acceptable agreement (Operational).
    b.   Instead of each worker having to be at the mercy of the employer, early unions discovered that they had power collectively to withhold their labor and that when they threatened to use this power they were then in a position to *bargain* with management over wages and working conditions (Historical and Negation).

A tachometer:
    a.   Comes from the Greek *takhos,* meaning "speed," and *metron,* meaning "to measure" (Etymological).
    b.   Is an instrument used in cars to measure the revolutions per minute made by the engine (Operational).

Sibling rivalry:
    a.   Pursuit of the same object or objective by offspring of the same parents (Logical/dictionary).
    b.   Both children clamored for the favor of their mother; each wanted the one remaining piece of pie (Example).

Exercise 2. Harikul offers a logical definition of the eye chip by explaining it as an intraocular retinal prosthesis. She operationally defines the retinal surface by explaining how it works. She also defines retinitus pigmentosa and macular degeneration by references to authorities who explain these two diseases. The optic nerve is defined operationally by explaining that it functions like a bridge between the eye and the brain.

Exercise 3: Fiorina made use of several examples. She used extended factual examples related to Mary Alexander, Belle Otis, Hewlett Packard's Smart Office Initiative and its Business Matchmaking project. She used brief factual examples in mentioning the successes of the Small Business Association, the credentials of the administrators of the SBA, the beginnings of Hewlett Packard in a garage and of Compaq in a pie shop.

Exercise 4: For the topic teenage suicide, a **brief factual** example might simply state that there were four teenage suicides reported in Oxnard, California in 2003. **Extended factual**—You could extend this example by reporting their names, age, background, and elaborating on the circumstances surrounding their deaths. **Brief**

hypothetical— "Try to imagine your son or daughter in a situation where they contemplated suicide," and so on. **Extended hypothetical**— "Try to picture the conditions that might pressure your son or daughter into thinking about suicide. They could be involved with drugs, doing poorly in school, or they may resent being unpopular with other kids," and so on.

Exercise 5: Remember that induction uses specific cases that lead to a probable conclusion. For example, during the last decade there were 800 kidney transplants and 75% of those were successful. It is likely then that this decade will produce similar results.

Exercise 6: For the first example apply the tests of who, why, when, how. Were the studies conducted by competent researchers? Was this data collected in an objective manner or were the researchers possibly trying to use this data for personal gain? Are these recent studies or were they conducted prior to more recent studies that may have different results? Were the studies conducted in a scientific manner? Additionally, you would want to find the base that makes up "total meaning." If you have a large base, two-thirds becomes more significant.

Exercise 7: *Mineta* uses statistics to show the scope of the problem of highway deaths and injuries. He notes that there are 1000 car crashes a day in the country resulting in 40,000 deaths annually. He makes the statistics clear and vivid by stating that the deaths are the equivalent of a Boeing 737 airliner crashing every day or a small city being wiped out every year. He does not cite the exact source of these statistics and he obviously has rounded them off. For this particular audience, agency leaders in the Department of Transportation, it would be unnecessary and probably seem odd to cite the sources of studies so well known to all of them as part of their daily work. For other audiences, it might be more effective to tell a little more about how the statistics were collected. *Erian* makes extensive use of statistics. The following are used to clarify the extent of the problem of sugar consumption and the seriousness of related health problems: the percentage of calories that come from sugar, the amount of sugar consumed annually per capita, the increase of soda consumption, the amount of soda consumption per capita, the mortality rate of pancreatic cancer, the increase in percentage of overweight adults and children, the predictions of future cases of diabetes. Only one statistic is used to support a claim: the percentage increase of likelihood of pancreatic cancer for obese people. He makes statistics easier to understand by using the per capita rates, such as 125 to 150 pounds of sugar per year and 555 cans of soda per year. *Frankel* uses statistical evidence such as the percentage of drivers in accidents who are fatigued, the number of hours truckers drive per week, the amount of campaign contributions made by lobbyists. Most of this evidence is used to bolster controversial claims in her speech.

Exercise 8: Erian's most credible sources in terms of having access to information, qualifications to interpret it, expertise, and freedom from bias are Dr. Linder of the National Institute of Diabetes and Digestion and Kidney Diseases, Kelly Brownell, director of Yale University's Eating and Weight Disorders, author Dr. Ralph Gowen, and the World Health Organization. There may not be sufficient information to fully assess his other sources such as Georgetown University, the New York Times, Newsday, Consumer Reports on Health, and the San Jose Mercury News, but all appear to be credible and fair sources.

Exercise 9: Consistent with the norms of forensics tournaments, *Harikul* gives quite a bit of detail on each source that she uses. This could be seen as over-introducing the evidence, and in another context she might be somewhat more general as long as she had the full information on the study at hand in case there were questions. Although the lead-ins to quotations were detailed, she seemed to do a good job of weaving these in smoothly without losing the conversational flow of her delivery. *Frankel* uses a great deal of evidence from a wide range of sources such as the National Transportation Review Board. She introduces it in enough detail to establish credibility for her claims. Of course, she would need to have at hand additional detail about the qualifications of the experts, the dates of the publications, and the research design of the studies she cites in case she would be questioned about this. But, for the purposes of the speech she seems to weave the citations in smoothly without disrupting the flow of her points.

Exercise 10. Have your students notice that examples are used most extensively in the informative speech. The use of supporting materials in the Sample Speeches on the Web site include, but are not limited to, the following: *Poulakos*—This evocative speech favored testimony and explanation for its purposes. **Explanation:** He explained several things including why his two tasks were paradoxical. **Definition:** The current state of speech education is given an operational definition; he tells how it is being addressed and why. **Examples:** Topics which receive priority treatment over speech education are listed. **Statistics:** (Essentially non-existent). **Testimony:** A significant basis for the speech, testimony included Isocrates and an unidentified Greek, a reputable author on education, as well as quotes and summaries of current reports and proposals. *Wong*—This speech uses each type of supporting material with an emphasis on examples and statistics. **Explanation:** He explains how sound waves affect the inner ear and are transmitted to the brain. **Definition:** Decibels are units of noise level. **Examples:** Ears sometimes ring for days after a concert. **Statistics:** He provides a statistical chart listing the decibel level of several types of sounds. **Testimony:** Information from Dr. Maurice Miller of Lenox Hill Hospital was provided. *Smith*—Smith also uses a variety of supporting material in his speech. Some examples include: **Testimony:** Smith relies heavily on testimonials in this speech including: Justice Gabriel Bach (Israel), the Supreme Court, Reporter for the Boston Globe, Columnist from Miami Herald, An internet user, Cyber Guru Peter Huber, and several other testimonials. **Definition:** Operational definitions are provided for the internet, cyberhate, etc. **Statistics:** (Essentially non-existent). **Examples:** Smith describes a childhood experiences; references the role his company (Bell Atlantic) takes in providing the community with internet access; Describes and relates the controversy that surrounded the first public phone companies to the internet; and finally, cites a specific Web site (National Forum on People's Differences) that follow discussions on sensitive topics. **Explanation:** He explains what options are available to combat cyberhate that don't endanger first amendment rights.

Class Activities

Supporting main points
This activity expands several concepts. After a discussion on using supporting material, divide the class into groups of 3–5. Give each group one main point of an informative or persuasive speech. The group is then required to go to the library and obtain credible supporting material that supports their main point. Once the groups have reconvened and supported their main point, have one member deliver the main point to the class. Have the rest of the class identify the type(s) and effectiveness of each supporting material the speaker used. This is also a useful time to ask students if the supporting material is cited properly within the presentation and the outline. What types of research has the most impact? etc. You may also want to consider using this activity in conjunction with several other chapters (**9, 10, 11**, etc).

Watch informative/persuasive speech
Have students watch sample speeches and identify the type(s) and effectiveness of each supporting material the speaker used.

Evaluating supporting material
Have students read one or more of the speeches in Sample Speeches under Book Resources on the *Speaker's Handbook* Web site and critique the use of supporting material.

Flawed supporting material

Students can often tell you that a certain use of supporting material is NOT effective, but they have a more difficult time telling you WHY it is not effective. Collect several examples of supporting material that has one or more errors. In groups, have students identify the type of supporting material illustrated AND why it is NOT effective. For example: "According to Barbara Walters, learning Kick-boxing is more challenging than learning Chinese." Obviously, this use of testimony in a speech on the Chinese language would not be effective. First, Barbara Walters does not speak Chinese; second, Barbara Walters, while considered an expert in the media, is not a known expert on the Chinese language or on Martial Arts. "A random poll of 50 students at San Jose State University showed 55% of those interviewed oppose funding a manned mission to Mars." Clearly, a random poll of this size is not representative of the opinion of the majority of students or the general public. Provide students with a variety of examples of supporting material that challenges the guidelines presented in chapter 15.

Additional Resources

Baesler, E.J. (1997). Persuasive effects of story and statistical evidence. *Argumentation and Advocacy*, 33(4), 170–176.

Herzog, R.L. (1996). Library research assignment. *Speech Communication Teacher*, 10(4), 7–8.

Hugenberg, L.W., & O'Neill, D.J. (1991). Researching national issues forum topics. In Stephen E. Lucas (Ed.), *Selections from the Speech Communication Teacher, 1991-1994* (pp. 47–48). New York: McGraw-Hill.

Kaufman, James. (1992). Collecting and evaluating evidence. *Speech Communication Teacher*, (3), 12.

Kazoleas, D.C. (1993). A comparison of the persuasive effectiveness of qualitative versus quantitative evidence: A test of explanatory hypothesis. *Communication Quarterly*, 41, 40–50.

Reinard, J.C. (1998). The empirical study of the persuasive effects of evidence: The status after fifty years of research. *Human Communication Research*, 15, 3–59.

Stuckey, M.E. (1992). Anecdotes and conversations: The narration and dialogic styles of modern presidential communication. *Communication Quarterly*, 40, 45–55.

2. Chapter 16: Reasoning

Chapter Exercises

Exercise 1. A variety of evidence could support each claim. For example, "Smoking should be banned in all indoor public places" could be supported with the following evidence: 1) There is no effective means of ventilating cigar, cigarette, and pipe smoke in an indoor, public place; 2) Low birth weight babies are born to mothers who work in indoor public places where smoking is permitted; 3) Smoke accumulating in indoor public places puts non-smokers at risk for heart and lung disease. The first piece of evidence tells us that smoking indoors leads to the accumulation of smoke. Points 2 and 3 indicate the hazards of this accumulation. Taken together, this evidence supports the need for a ban on smoking in indoor public places because something that is known to be hazardous to human health should be banned. Have students evaluate the articles and research they find using their *InfoTrac College Edition.*

Exercise 2.
Example A—Evidence: The form of government in the U.S. has existed for over 200 years.
> Claim 1: We should maintain our present form of government. Link or Reasoning: Our form of government has stood the test of time. It has worked in the past and continues to work today.
> Claim 2: We should change our present form of government. Link or Reasoning: Our form of government was created in and for a different era. Times have changed and our form of government must change with it.

Example B—Evidence: Deaths from firearms have increased in the past few years.
> Claim 1: We need even stronger gun control laws than the ones we have. Link or Reasoning: If we are to control gun crimes, we have to control guns.
> Claim 2: We should get rid of gun control laws. Link or Reasoning: We have passed gun control legislation and the increase in gun related crime illustrates the ineffectiveness of such laws.

Exercise 3. For the school bus example you might want to minimize the cost of installing seat belts in each bus. If the taxpayers perceive the cost to be exorbitant they might reject the proposition. On the other hand, you would probably try to maximize the safety aspect, lower death rates, or fewer injuries.

Exercise 4. Erian establishes that there is great confusion about the definitions of different kinds of sugars that may be identified on labels. He then gives very specific examples of labels from familiar foods that we assume to be healthy, but that actually contain high amounts of sugar.

Exercise 5. The unstated assumption can usually be stated as a major premise. For example, Anyone who hasn't been fired must be doing a good job. The most important thing about housing is low cost. Either management wins or labor wins. Anyone on welfare lacks self-respect.

Exercise 6.
Senator Helms.
Major premise: The Senate should not do anything that causes pain to any group of citizens or that is divisive.
Minor premise: Failure to renew the imprimatur to the confederate flag and is a rebuke to the members of the United Daughters of the Confederacy and thus will cause them pain and will be seen as divisive among Southerners.

Conclusion: The amendment should be passed and the imprimatur granted.

Senator Mosely-Braun.
Major premise: The Senate should not do anything that causes pain to any group of citizens or that is divisive.
Minor premise: Renewing the imprimatur to the confederate flag reopens the wounds of slavery and will cause pain to the descendants of slavery and thus it will be seen as divisive by all those who oppose racism.
Conclusion: The amendment should be defeated and the imprimatur not renewed.

Senator Mosely-Braun.
Major premise: I would not be confrontational or emotional in the Senate unless a matter of absolute importance was at stake and there were no alternative ways to address it.
Minor premise. I have been laid back and congenial on many other topics and have tried to handle this issue in a non-confrontational way but those on the other side did not accept the committee's deletion of the renewal, but rather "sneaked" the issue back into via an apparently unrelated amendment. The symbolism of the confederate flag is of tremendous significance to African Americans.
Conclusion: The intensity of this debate is not caused by my choices but by those who left me no alternative.

Exercise 7. For the natural childbirth example you could use an inductive method by citing studies or testimony to support this conclusion. Study 1 supports natural childbirth, study 2 supports natural childbirth, study *n* supports natural childbirth, therefore natural childbirth is probably best. A deductive argument might state something like: Medical procedures without drugs are beneficial to patients. Natural childbirth does not use drugs. Therefore natural childbirth is beneficial to patients.

Exercise 8. *Poulakos*—This speech demonstrates both types of reasoning. Deductive: Orality is indispensable to literacy. (Implied: Literacy is essential to a participatory democracy.) Democracy is a goal of this country. Therefore: In order to maintain a democracy, we must maintain orality within our population. Inductive: Several cultural sayings devalue the worth of speech: "Talk is cheap," "Actions speak louder than words," "Speaking is silver but silence is golden." Speaking is not highly valued by our culture. *Wong*—There isn't much reasoning in speeches to inform, so this is not a strong hunting ground for examples. *McNeil's* speech uses both deductive and inductive reasoning. A deductive argument is shown in the following example: Loss of our rainforests through deforestation poses serious economical, cultural, and ecological problems. These rainforests, which cannot be replaced, are being destroyed at approximately 100 acres per minute. Therefore, we are rapidly developing serious economical, cultural, and ecological problems through deforestation. Induction: Several respected organizations support environmental protection. Greenpeace, a grassroots organization of private citizens, supports environmental protection. Ben and Jerry's, a corporation, supports environmental protection. The World Wildlife Fund/Conservation Foundation supports environmental protection. It is good for everyone to protect the environment. *Pham*—makes a deductive argument: Individuals displaying heroism should be appropriately rewarded. Major Nguyen Quy An displayed heroism in the Vietnam War. Major An should be appropriately rewarded (eligibility for the Orderly Departure Program would be appropriate). *Smith's* speech uses both deductive and inductive reasoning. A deductive argument is shown in the following example: all forms of free speech should be protected. Cyberhate is a form of free speech. Therefore, cyberhate should be protected and not censored. An inductive argument is shown in the following example: Journalist Peter Huber says we should not censor internet filth; The Supreme Court opposes the restriction of indecent material online; A columnist from the *Miami Herald* believes that censoring internet sites will only lead to more ignorance and fear; An internet user says that the freedom to express oneself on the internet should be supported. It is therefore beneficial to keep the Internet censor free. *Mineta*—Causal reasoning was the primary form of reasoning used by Secretary Mineta. He. states quite clearly that two things will result in lower rates of death and injury from traffic accidents: increasing the number of people who wear seat belts and decreasing the number of people who drive impaired. In this primarily inspirational speech to a highly informed audience, his assertion of these causal claims was appropriate. For a less informed audience a speaker would want to give some statistical evidence of how many serious injuries and deaths have been directly linked to failure to buckle up and also to show how many accidents have been attributed to drivers who were impaired by alcohol, recreational drugs, prescription drugs and fatigue. He could show that when these alleged causes (failure to use seat belts, impairment) and the alleged effects (death and injury) were present and vice versa. For a less informed audience, it might also bolster the causal claim to show how the cause-effect chain actually functioned: how do seat belts reduce injury? How does impairment reduce reaction time and judgment? Again, this level of detail would not be appropriate for the specific audience of the speech who were experts on the topic and highly favorable to the point being made. They might even be insulted by such basic explanations. Another line of causal reasoning was present when Mineta referred to the steps he wanted the agencies to pursue to reach the goal of reducing death and injury: passing laws, enforcing existing laws, educating drivers, and advancing engineering solutions. This was a quick gloss on policy issues that were well known to his audience and would certainly be expanded on throughout the agencies that were responsible for implementing them. For a general audience, even for policy makers outside the Department of Transportation, it would be essential to elaborate on how each of these efforts would cause a reduction in death and injury. *Erian* makes use of causal reasoning when he links sugar consumption to obesity and obesity to diabetes and cancer. This works as a chain of causation. He does not go into the physiological mechanism of how sugar causes these health problems but relies on expert testimony to establish the causal links. Although he does not elaborate on the studies, it is likely that these scientists used controlled experiments with control groups, thus tracking that the alleged effect (cancer or diabetes) was present when the alleged cause (sugar or obesity) was present and vice versa. The time limits of the speech may have restricted Erian from explaining these relationships, but it is to be hoped that he was familiar with the research the experts had conducted and could explain it upon request.

Exercise 9. It could be argued that strokes are not caused by stress by applying the following tests: 1) Do the alleged cause (stress) and alleged effect (stroke) always occur together? No. Presenting examples of individuals with high levels of stress who have not suffered a stroke could disprove this relationship. Scientific studies which fail to link stress and stroke could also be presented. 2) Do the alleged cause and alleged effect vary together? Again, you could provide evidence that shows individuals with high stress levels do not suffer strokes and individuals with low stress levels do suffer strokes.

Exercise 10. Strokes may be a result of several contributing causes of which stress may be one. Other causes could include genetic predisposition, poor diet, and lack of exercise.

Exercise 11. Frankel starts this section of her speech by making the causal claim that the large number of trucking accidents is caused primarily by driver fatigue. She establishes this claim by quoting an expert who says that 30% of all are directly attributable to fatigue. She cites evidence that truckers are driving more than 60 hours a week. Second, she establishes a causal claim between the political strength of the trucking industry and the failure of Congress to pass meaningful legislation. She cites Ralph Nader's finding that the American Trucking Association contributed $14 million to two senators who sponsored the watered-down legislation. Another causal relationship is posited when she ways that the proposed legislation will not cause a reduction in trucking accidents because it fails to address the pay system that is the real cause of the accidents. She makes yet another causal argument in discussing the fact that trucking companies are not making use of the new technologies that would help decrease accidents. She says that the cause of their refusal to adopt these improvements is their unwillingness to spend the money needed.

Frankel summarizes this entire main point with a causal claim: the attitudes and policies of the trucking companies and the government are the cause of the unacceptable high level of trucking accidents. At the end of the clip, she is moving to her next point, the solution of the problem. Here, again, Frankel is claiming that new regulations and better enforcement of existing regulations will *cause* a decrease in trucking accidents.

This brief segment was chosen to show how in every persuasive speech, causal reasoning is ubiquitous. Speakers need to establish what is causing the problems they address and they need to show how their proposed solutions will cause things to be better. It is essential, therefore, that persuasive speakers become very familiar with the principles of causal reasoning and that critical listeners are able to analyze and evaluate the many causal claims they hear.

Exercise 12. Mineta states quite clearly that two things will result in lower rates of death and injury from traffic accidents: increasing the number of people who wear seat belts and decreasing the number of people who drive impaired. In this primarily inspirational speech to a highly informed audience, his assertion of these causal claims was appropriate. For a less informed audience a speaker would want to give some statistical evidence of how many serious injuries and deaths have been directly linked to failure to buckle up and also to show how many accidents have been attributed to drivers who were impaired by alcohol, recreational drugs, prescription drugs and fatigue. He could show that when these alleged causes (failure to use seat belts, impairment) were present, the alleged effects (death and injury) were present and vice versa. For a less informed audience, it might also bolster the causal claim to show how the cause–effect chain actually functioned: how do seat belts reduce injury? How does impairment reduce reaction time and judgment? Again, this level of detail would not be appropriate for the specific audience of the speech, who were experts on the topic and highly favorable to the point being made. They might even be insulted by such basic explanations.

Another line of causal reasoning was present when Mineta referred to the steps he wanted the agencies to pursue to reach the goal of reducing death and injury: passing laws, enforcing existing laws, educating drivers, and advancing engineering solutions. This was a quick gloss on policy issues that were well known to his audience and would certainly be expanded on throughout the agencies that were responsible for implementing them. For a general audience, even for policy makers outside the Department of Transportation, it would be essential to elaborate on how each of these efforts would cause a reduction in death and injury.

Exercise 13.
A football game and a war:
   Similarities include: highly competitive, goal oriented, primarily waged by men.
   Differences include: specificity of location, results of losing, use of rules.
   Justifiable analogy: The football game was like a war; the coaches acted like generals, dictating orders and
       doing everything they could think of to win.
   Unjustifiable analogy: The football game was a war; I thought we were all going to be killed.
A family and a group of employees:
   Similarities include: units of more than one, time spent together, established hierarchy.
   Differences include: types of relationships, motivation for cooperation, types of punishment.
   Justifiable analogy: We have such a supportive, close knit work group, I could ask a favor of them as easily
       as my family.
   Unjustifiable analogy: My office mate is like a sister; I knew she wouldn't mind if borrowed her sweater.

"Ethnic Cleansing" in the Balkans and racial discrimination in the US:

    Similarities include: conflict between races, innocent victims.

    Differences include: minority relationships, government stances, position on violence.

    Justifiable analogy: "Ethnic cleansing" in the Balkans, being a highly emotional and volatile issue like our own racial conflict in the United States, has resulted in many victims.

    Unjustifiable analogy: The "Ethnic cleansing" in the Balkans, being a racial conflict similar to that in the United States, will necessarily have similar solutions.

The national debt and one's personal checking account:

    Similarities include: both deal with money, handled by banks, accounts tallied.

    Differences include: proportion of negative cash flow, penalties for overdraft, person(s) accountable.

    Justifiable analogy: The national debt is not unlike my personal checking account; both suffer penalties when there is an "overdraft," only theirs is larger.

    Unjustifiable analogy: The government has full intent to pay off the national debt just as I intend to cover my over charges, so why can't I keep charging like the government does?

Exercise 14. There are some similarities between giving blood and voting; both are moderately inconvenient but not major commitments of time and effort. Both are connected to a sense of civic duty. However, there are also some differences that might make *Wood's* analogy questionable. Voting for candidates serves the individual voter and is not a contribution in the sense of giving blood, therefore less deserving of a reward. And, the tradition of giving juice and cookies to blood donors springs to some degree from a physical need to replenish fluids and elevate blood sugar, needs that are not relevant to voting.

Exercise 15.

"I'm surprised . . . " (*reductio ad absurdum*)

"Anyone who drives . . ." (*ad hominem*)

"You said you could prove . . ." (semantic fallacy)

"It always rains . . ." (hasty generalization)

"Well, either you support . . ." (false dichotomy)

"The jury system should . . ." (confusing sequence with cause)

Exercise 16. I. Inductive reasoning—The speaker could be guilty of making a hasty generalization. It can be argued that five examples do not warrant a generalization regarding all people being dangerous when they are under the influence of marijuana; II. Reasoning by analogy—Some experts argue marijuana is psychologically addictive. Alcohol and cigarettes are physically addictive. If the speaker is using the term addictive to mean physical addiction to cigarettes and alcohol, but psychological addiction to marijuana, a semantic fallacy is being committed; III. Causal reasoning—If this claim had not been qualified ("often causes") this would be a classic post hoc ergo propter hoc fallacy. The fact that some people use harder drugs after they have used marijuana does not warrant a causal relationship; IV. Deductive reasoning—Deductive fallacies are related to form. There is no problem with the form of this argument, but the premises themselves can still be questioned. In this case one would have to ask: How many brain cells must be lost before intelligence is affected?, How many brain cells are lost when marijuana is used?, Do brain cells rejuvenate themselves?

Class Activities

Viewing persuasive speeches

This exercise parallels the viewing informative speeches exercise in the previous section. Once again, students should be divided into four groups. Each group is assigned an area to critique. After viewing a persuasive speech on tape, each group should discuss their assigned area and present their finding to the class. In the persuasive speech, unlike in the informative speech, students should ask the following questions: Did the speaker make a clear link between the evidence presented and his or her claim? What forms of reasoning could you identify? Did the reasoning appear sound? Were appeals made to audience needs and values? Were these appeals effective and appropriate? Did you perceive the speaker as credible? What did the speaker do to establish/diminish credibility? (See also section D-3 of this instructor's manual, on chapter **11**.)

Editorials

Clip several editorials from recent opinion/editorial pages. Have students form small groups and give each group an editorial. Working in their group, students should determine the thesis statement or major claim made in the editorial, the evidence used to support the claim, and the types of reasoning employed in the argument. Students should also identify potential fallacies. Each group should then present its findings to the rest of the class.

Fallacy mini-report

Assign each student a fallacy of reasoning or language. You may want to have sources available in your office for students to research their fallacy or direct them toward the types of books in the library which would define and describe fallacies. Each student will give a report on her or his fallacy which meets the criteria below. This exercise familiarizes students with fallacies so that they may determine the soundness of persuasive appeals and avoid making fallacious arguments in their own appeals. This assignment also gives students another opportunity to speak in front of the class and exercise their public speaking skills. You may also want to require that students bring a handout with the information pertaining to their fallacy for each member of the class.

Fallacy Mini-Report Requirements

1. Your presentation to the class must include:
   —A definition of the fallacy
   —Two examples of the fallacy
   —An explanation of the definition and/or examples in your own words (in other words, do not just read a definition and examples as you wrote them down out of a text; *explain* the fallacy to us).
2. You must cite the source for any information you take directly from a text.
3. If there is any interesting history associated with your fallacy you may want to present it if it helps us understand the fallacy's origin and meaning.
4. Your presentation should be extemporaneous.

Rhetorical analysis project

Adapt the rhetorical analysis essay examination (end of Part IV in this instructor's manual) into a brief written assignment, a major term paper assignment, or a take-home examination.

Supporting a claim

Have students prepare and deliver the "Supporting a Claim" speaking exercise described in Part II (Basic Materials) of this manual. Discuss the strengths and weakness of each student's claim and use of supporting material.

Locating illustrative materials

Have students bring in examples of editorials and letters to the editor, and identify reasoning patterns, fallacies, and supporting materials. Have students bring in examples of advertisements and radio and television commercials that illustrate various motivational appeals to needs, emotions, and values. Have them identify those that fall into the categories of excessive and inappropriate uses discussed in chapter **3**. Have students bring in examples of particularly effective or ineffective style to illustrate concepts from chapter **17**.

Additional Resources

Allen, M., Berkowitz, S., Hunt, S., Louden, A. (1999). A meta-analyses of the impact of forensics and communication education on critical thinking. *Communication Education*, 48(1), 18.

Baesler, E.J. (1997). Persuasive effects of story and statistical evidence. *Argumentation and Advocacy*, 33(4), 170–176.

Cirksena, K. (1996). Sources of "access" and "competence" in women's political persuading, 1964–1984. *Communication Quarterly*, 44(2), 227–246.

Dittus, J.K. (1992). Grade begging as an exercise in argumentation. *Speech Communication Teacher*, (2), 5.

Doloff, S.T. (1997). Caveat audiens (let the audience beware). *The Humanist*, 57(1), 4–6.

Kazoleas, D.C. (1993). A comparison of the persuasive effectiveness of qualitative versus quantitative evidence: A test of explanatory hypothesis. *Communication Quarterly*, 41, 40–50.

MacDonald, M.A. (1992). The key to Persuasion. In Stephen E. Lucas (Ed.), *Selections from the Speech Communication Teacher, 1986-1991.* (p. 67). New York: McGraw-Hill.

O'Keefe, D.J. (1997). Standpoint explicitness ad persuasive effect: A meta analytic review of the effects of varying conclusion articulation in persuasive messages, *Argumentation and Advocacy*, 34(1), 1–12.

Reinard, J.C. (1998). The empirical study of the persuasive effects of evidence: The status after fifty years of research. *Human Communication Research*, 15, 3–59.

Sparks, J.R., Areni, C.S., & Cox, K.C. (1998). An investigation of the effects of language style and communication modality on persuasion. *Communication Monographs*, 65(2), 108–126.

3. Chapter 17: Language and Style

Chapter Exercises

Exercise 1.
After you take off the air filter you can then look for the problem.

We will have performance appraisals for all clerical and administrative personnel twice a year. These are designed to do two things. The first is to evaluate employee competence and the second is to clarify objectives for the next appraisal period.

Exercise 2.
Karen is unique when it comes to making everyone feel good. She's the most respected member of our sales staff.

In fact, being surrounded by smokers caused us considerable irritation.

I feel that we also face a crisis of morale. We need to talk seriously about this problem that has hurt our progress.

Exercise 3. There are a number of possible responses for this exercise. Some examples include:
A wintry, wet day (alliteration); The day was as wet as a polar bear's sweatband (simile).

A policy that is not purposeful, but powerless (antithesis); A square-peg policy in a round world (metaphor).

Performing this procedure is like carving a snowflake (simile/hyperbole).

A leader who can stop a sitcom laugh track with his frown (hyperbole); A leader who believes, not in smiles and handshakes, but in frosty, distant stares (antithesis).

It was a big crowd. A very big crowd. How big of a crowd was it? Big! (repetitive language); The crowd was Goliath: huge (personification).

Exercise 4. Eschewing cliché is sometimes an almost insurmountable task, but if students can accept the challenge to go beyond habitual reliance on the well-worn phrase this can be a fun exercise. For instance, for Like comparing apples and oranges, a "high-tech" type might suggest "like comparing analog and digital," someone from another perspective might suggest, "like measuring weight with a ruler" . . . and so on.

Exercise 5. The Rodriguez speech was replete with imagery. Among a few that might be identified in response to this question are: the green eyes of the great-grandmother, which compared to the green hills of Ohio and the notion of springtime and contrasted to her clawlike hands and her restriction to a wheelchair; The indescribable noise of a space shuttle taking off contrasted to the deep stillness of space; the authors from different corners of Border's Books coming out to play together at night and returning to their designated areas each morning, the middle-aged author going through his mother's dishes and papers and photographs in her empty apartment, the aged mother talking about her feelings of running as a young girl. Rodriguez holding young men who were dying of AIDS, Rodriguez in his college dorm room writing a last minute paper as his roommate snored.

Exercise 6. For group A, the appeal would center on the need for strategic planning to help the organization operate more smoothly. It would be effective to use terms like "take some of the pressure off," "set priorities so that we are not living in a constant state of crisis," "give us a chance to step back, relax in an unpressured setting and talk about our goals." For group B, the appeal would be to efficiency. Effective language in support of the retreat might emphasize the need to "clarify policies," "tighten up procedures," and "streamlining communication." For group C, the appeal would be to a sense of community. The language in support of the retreat would best use phrases such as "build rapport," "strengthen our bonds," "remind ourselves of our common mission and core values."

Class Activities

Speech analysis

Make copies of the Mosely-Braun exchange, "Excerpts from Debate on Senate Amendment 610" in Sample Speeches under Book Resources on the *Speaker's Hanbook* Web site, and have your students respond to the following questions either in writing or in class discussion.

    a. Why does the symbol of the confederate flag seem to represent for each participant in the debate?

    b. Beyond the flag itself, what is symbolized by the action of providing an imprimateur from the national government?

    c. Can anyone determine what the "true meaning" of a symbol is? If so, who gets to decide? If not, how can groups negotiate meanings when there is disagreement?

    d. Do the participants in this debate have different assumptions about the nature of symbols? Identify specific statements that suggest what theory of language/symbolic behavior they hold.

    e. Characterize the different language styles of each participant in this debate as they argue about the issue. Also, note the change in Mosely-Braun's style from her first statement to her second. What changed? Why? What was the impact of each stylistic approach?

Oral and written style

Ask each student to write a paragraph on a familiar topic. After these are turned in, have each student tape record a brief oral statement on the same topic. Then have groups compare the two samples and identify the differences between oral and written style using concepts from **17a**. As an individual homework assignment each student can be asked to transcribe one paragraph from her or his videotaped speech and to analyze the style. Then have the student rewrite the paragraph twice. In the first version, it should be rewritten as if it were to be a paragraph in a paper. In the second version, have the student rewrite the paragraph as it might have been presented orally. In this case it is important to retain the elements of oral style, but to refine the expression for clarity and impact. Have the students read all three versions aloud and discuss the contrasts.

Stylistic devices

Assign each student a stylistic device. The students are required to find a newspaper article, a poem, or an excerpt from a short story, play, or speech which illustrates their assigned device. Each student should read his or her example to the class, then the class can determine what stylistic device was illustrated.

Analyzing a speech

Have students analyze the text of Martin Luther King's "I have a dream speech." Students should focus their analysis on how King uses stylistic devices to enhance the impact of his message.

Analyzing a tribute speech

Have students analyze the text of the speech Princess Diana's brother delivered at her funeral. Students should focus their analysis on how he utilized stylistic devices to enhance the impact of his tribute.

Testing your knowledge of stylistic devices

Have students examine the following quotes to determine which stylistic device is illustrated.

  a. "The mother of all wars." —Saddam Hussein
  b. "Television—a medium. So called because it is neither rare nor well done." —Ernie Kovacs
  c. "Ours is a nation that has shed the blood of war and cried the tears of depression." —George Bush.
  d. "Power, Parity, Personal Responsibility, and Progress . . ." —William H. Harris
  e. ". . . reducing the deficit and at the same time increasing government spending. Well let me tell you, that is like trying to lose weight on a diet of french fries and Big Macs." —J. Peter Grace
  f. "Three things in human life are important. The first is to be kind, the second is to be kind, and the third is to be kind." —Henry James
  g. "When you get to the end of your rope, tie a knot and hang on." —Franklin D. Roosevelt
  h. "The meeting of two personalities is like the contact of two chemical substances: if there is any reaction, both are transformed." —Carl Jung

Adding excitement to your language

This activity is a fun way to get your students to use language creatively. For each of the following "common" words substitute a more uncommon word or phrase—something that is more concrete, animated, or intense.

  Hungry, Tired, Wrong, Sad, Money, Nervous, Decrease, Polite, Fat, Spoiled, Cheap, etc.

Adding Excitement to Your Language

Substitute each of the following phrases with similes or metaphors.

1. Picking a topic was difficult.

2. The man is good-looking.

3. Drugs are addictive.

Rewrite the following sentences using vivid language—paint a picture in the mind of the listener.

1. He is a great piano player.

2. Five new businesses can be seen downtown.

3. We watched the moon come up.

4. She is smart.

5. I was nervous giving my speech.

Additional Resources

Buttney, R. (1997). Reported speech on talking race on campus. *Human Communication Research, 23(4)*, 477–507.

Crawford, M. (1995). *Talking difference. On gender and language.* London: Sage ltd.

Grob, L. M., Meyers, R. A., & Schuh, R. (1997). Powerful/powerless language use in group interactions: Sex differences or similarities? *Communication Quarterly, 41*, 129–144.

Haleta, L.L. (1996). Student perceptions of teachers use of language: The effects of powerful and powerless language on impression formation and uncertainty. *Communication Education, 45*, 16–28.

Hochel, S. (1992). Language awareness and assessment. In Stephen E. Lucas (Ed.), *Selections from the Speech Communication Teacher, 1986-1991.* (p. 39). New York: McGraw-Hill.

Maggio, R. (1991). *The bias free word finder: A dictionary of non-discriminatory language.* Boston: Beacon.

Moon, D.G. (1998). Communication of classism. In M. L. Hecht (ed.), *Communicating Prejudice* (pp. 122–135). Thousand Oaks, CA: Sage.

Sparks, J. R., Areni, C. S., & Cox, K. C. (1998). An investigation of the effects of language style and communication modality on persuasion. *Communication Monographs, 65(2)*, 108–126.

Thimm, C., Rademacher, U., & Kruse, L. (1998). Age stereotypes and patronizing messages: Features of age-adapted speech in technical instructions to the elderly. *Journal of Applied Communication Research, 26(1)*, 282–304.

Weatherall, A. (1998).Women and men in language: An analysis of semi-naturalistic person descriptions. *Human Communication Research, 25*, 276–293.

4. Chapter 18: Attention and Interest

Chapter Exercises

Exercise 1. This exercise is designed to get students thinking about styles of humor. The discussion should reveal our different preferences and the fact that nearly everyone has a funny side.

Exercise 2. Dawson uses humor when he comments, "I may have bumped into some of you on campus—sorry about that." This double meaning of bumping into someone startles and then delights the audience as they realize he is able to take a light touch about the awkward moments that go with being a blind person. He also paints a very humorous image by playing with the cliché of leading a horse to water. First the audience visualizes a horse taking a tiny sip of water, gargling and spitting it out, then another bolder house putting its snout right down in the pool. This technique of extending a metaphor is a nice form of humor for speakers to consider. Dawson also showed humor by choosing to illustrate predictability by mentioning the Monday fish burgers in the De Anza campus cafeteria instead of selecting some weightier example.

Exercise 3.
"A good accountant . . ." The Vital
"You've all heard the phrase . . ." Familiarity
"Our own accounting department . . ." Novelty
"I was trembling when I . . ." Suspense

Exercise 4. Even a short statement can incorporate several attention factors: Whether it's the prestige or really a practical matter (conflict) people have to have alternatives to gas powered vehicles. (The Vital).

Exercise 5. The *McNeil* speech uses Proximity, referring to current events (deforestation and the media coverage of it), injects a healthy dose of The Vital and proceeds to strip away the veneer cloaking the effects of deforestation. At the same time, the speech moves toward a narrative quality. The story becomes: what happens, what are the results, how do they affect me, and what can I do about it? The *Erian* speech used reality in reference to the actual case of Arnell Scott. He used familiarity with reference to familiar food labels. The vital self interest of the audience was engaged with his dramatic warnings about health concerns related to sugar consumption. He uses proximity with phrases like "the average person in this room" and "how much soda do you drink?"

Exercise 6. Brasher's speech is an excellent example of how story telling can capture the interest of an audience. In telling of her experience as a single parent returning to college, she makes all the points that could have been part of an expository speech, but in a highly engaging manner.

Classroom Activities

Critiquing attention and interest factors in political speeches
Show your students part or all of the President's State of the Union Address. Have them identify the way he uses supporting material "that are concrete and close to home" **(18)**. Throughout his speech, he makes references to those individuals whose stories have touched him. In fact, he often asks these individuals to stand and be recognized for their bravery/courage/compassion/ etc. Your students might also find it useful to discuss the ways in which the President tries to adapt his speech to meet all of the needs of the people of the United States.

Watching student speeches

Have students incorporate at least four attention factors into their speeches. After the each round of speeches, ask the class to critique their level of attention and interest. What did the speaker effectively do to keep their interest, what could the speaker have said that would have been even more effective?

Additional Resources

Frances, C. (1996). How to stop boring your audience to death: Databases, anecdotes, and humor. *Vital Speeches, 62(9),* 283–286.

5. Chapter 19: Credibility

Chapter Exercises

Exercise 1. After your students have completed their inventory, you might ask them (if their egos can stand it) to check with friends to get their impression.

Exercise 2. After naming three areas of low credibility, have students focus on specific dimensions and discuss ways they can improve.

Exercise 3. Remember, credibility reflects a perception. Some students have noted that Ronald Reagan tends to be perceived as high on dynamism. How did George Bush the elder overcome the so-called "wimp factor?" The Lewinsky scandal caused many to question Bill Clinton's credibility. George W. Bush's credibility in the wake of the 9/11 terrorist attacks was high, but the perception of his trustworthiness suffered following controversy over the validity of intelligence estimates leading to the invasion of Iraq. Students might focus their discussion on which dimensions Clinton or Bush had high credibility and which areas he had to work very hard to (re)establish. In general, the discussions should center on the different perceptions students have and their rationale for having such views.

Exercise 4. Al Gore is a good example of a public figure whose image suffered due to a perceived lack of dynamism. On the other hand, the Rev. Jesse Jackson is often perceived as being a very dynamic individual. Geraldo Rivera is dynamic but some might question his competence and, even more, his trustworthiness. Try to find local examples of each of these categories: your college president, mayor, etc.

Exercise 5. Carly Fiorina was well known to her audience as perhaps the highest ranking woman CEO in the country and as an expert on Information Technology and business strategy. She had no need to explicitly advance her credentials. She did, however, bolster that image by listing some of the successes of HP and its growth to a company with more than $21 million in annual sales. She establishes her good will and concern for others by expressly thanking the SBA administrators and congratulating the attendees at the breakfast. The simple act of wishing participants a safe trip home adds a warm and human touch in acknowledging that the hurricane had placed many people in danger. She furthers her sense of concern by making several references to the shared interests of large corporations and small businesses. She mentions specific ways that HP has shown respect for colleagues in small businesses through initiatives such as the Business Matchmaking program and the Smart Office Initiative. Finally, she establishes the dimension of credibility related to character and integrity by admitting that technology has not succeeded in reaching its potential and that there is room for improvement.

Exercise 6. At several points in the speech *Wong* lets the audience know that he is very worried about their well being and that he wants them to protect their precious hearing. *McNeil* is in the difficult position of advocating changes for the planet and for people worldwide that might involve some sacrifice or discomfort for people like those in her immediate audience, privileged individuals in a consumption-oriented nation. She tries to address this by appealing to their concern for the long term viability of the environment and for the preservation of the world's beauty and diversity.

Exercise 7. By acknowledging that he is committed to paradoxical tasks, *Poulakos* lets the audience know that he recognizes the complexity of communication and will not oversimplify it. He also states that he does not believe that every speech student can become a Kennedy, Cuomo or Jackson, thus adding credibility to his more realistic goal that all students can improve their speaking. Smith acknowledged the many abuses of the Internet. He stated that the impulse toward censorship of racist, anti-semitic hate speech was fully understandable. He expressed his own horror at the abuses and admitted that defense of first amendment principles often requires very difficult choices.

Classroom Activities

Credibility profile
Have each student prepare a detailed credibility profile of one key source that they cite in their persuasive speech. They should research the person's background, expertise, and public image and write their analysis in terms of concepts from chapter **19**.

Speaker credibility profile
Have student prepare a detailed credibility profile of themselves and at least two other classmates. In groups, have the students exchange their profiles, noting the similarities and differences among the various profiles. Asking students to consider why one classmate saw him/her as highly trustworthy, while another saw him/her as lacking trustworthiness, for example, will allow the student to examine the perceptions of his/her audience.

Chapter exercises as topics for discussion
In one large group, or several ad hoc groups, have the students discuss any one of the seven chapter exercises. These exercises usually serve as good starting points for interesting, and sometimes heated, discussion.

Additional Resources

Gerson, M. J. (1998). Words he dare not speak: Clinton's political power suffers from what he cannot say. *US News and World Report, 125*(11), 33.

Kenton, S. B. (1989). Speaker credibility in persuasive business communication: a model which explains gender differences. *Journal of Business Communication, 26,* 143–157.

6. Chapter 20: Motivational Appeals

Class Exercises

Exercise 1. a. Esteem; b. Security; c. Self-actualization; d. Survival; e. Belonging.

Exercise 2. *Senator Helms* appealed to the value of respect for elders and the value of tradition. He used explicit emotional appeals of pity for the well meaning elderly members of the Daughters of the Confederacy. He also used fear appeals in a quite explicit threat that it would be a "very, very bad mistake" to vote against his amendment because there would be "hard feelings" toward Mosely-Braun. *Senator Mosely-Braun* included appeals to the value of patriotism with her many mentions of the American flag and the struggles it represents, to the value of justice with her references to the history of African Americans who were denied their human rights, to the value of fair play and civility in describing how she had attempted to show restraint and follow Senate rules in her response to the issue under debate. She invokes many emotions such as outrage over the institution of slavery, regret for the deaths in the Civil War and civil rights movement. She used very strong language such as "slipping back into the snake pit of racial hatred." Implicitly, then, she too may have been making a more subtle threat and an appeal to the emotion of fear should racial disharmony turn to violence as it has in the past. *Senator Heflin* appealed very effectively to two contradictory values, the value of tradition that he felt as a Southerner and which was reflected in his loyalty to his ancestors, and the value of progress and change, which was reflected in the need to move forward and try to heal longstanding pain. *Senator Moynihan* appealed to the value of duty, reminding his colleagues of the oath they took to protect the Constitution from all threats, even those from within. *Senator Campbell* appealed to the value of unity among diverse groups. His direct mention of a swastika as a symbol of divisiveness and hate was a strong emotional appeal to fear. *Senator Boxer* appealed to the value of pride, in congratulating her colleagues for the courage they showed and also to the value of freedom when she linked the many different groups who are striving to recover from their historical oppression.

Exercise 3. *Dawson* very explicitly appeals to Maslow's need for self-actualization, the highest level of need. The speech includes appeals to the value of hard work and value of education. *Rodriguez* appeals to the emotions of fear as he dramatically points out the unknown pain and tragedy that life will bring. He also draws out feelings of hope and excitement in reference to some of the joyful experiences that lie ahead. He evokes compassion for the students who died before graduating and those who loved them, and for the young men who died of AIDS, but also for the people who live to old age and grieve for their younger selves. He appeals to the value of family life and friendship. Curiously, he does not directly speak of the value of education, though he is a highly literary person and the day is a celebration of learning, but rather directs the graduates' attention to their "lives as a whole."

Exercise 4. Obviously, this is a matter of individual choice. For the speaker, determining the core values of your audience would be extremely beneficial. Have students discuss which values they think are the most and least salient in the value system of the US today.

Exercise 5.
  a. Following the dress-for-success formula can lead to a more exciting life and may elicit admiration from others.
  b. Having an electronic alarm system will protect your family from intruders and convince your neighbors that you are wealthy and successful enough to have a house full of valuables.

c. Meditation, wisdom, happiness go hand-in-hand.

d. When you stop smoking marijuana, you'll feel better and regain your self-respect.

e. Using X shampoo will win you friends, and if you're not careful you may fall in love.

Exercise 6. This is another exercise that can prompt highly individualized responses.

Exercise 7. Have students share the results of their *InfoTrac* searches and discuss the examples of core values that they found. Note especially the potential conflicts between different values.

Class Activities

Motivational appeals in advertising

After breaking the class into small groups of four or five students, give each group an advertisement which incorporates needs and values in order to motivate consumers to action. Each group should discuss its assigned advertisement's visual images as well as written text. The groups should look for implicit as well as explicit motivational appeals. The following questions should be discussed by each group:

a. What is the purpose or goal of the advertisement?

b. Who is the target audience for this advertisement?

c. What values are appealed to in the advertisement? Provide examples and explain how these values are used as motivator.

d. What needs are appealed to in the advertisement? Provide examples and explain how these needs are used as motivators.

e. Is there a balance of reasoning and motivational appeals in this advertisement?

f. Would you consider this advertisement an ethical use of motivational appeals? Why or why not?

g. Considering the target audience, is the advertisement effective?

After each group has worked with its individual advertisement, it should present its advertisement and the results of its discussion to the entire class. Each group member should present the answer to at least one question the group discussed. If time allows, you may ask each group to develop an attention getter, transitions, and a clincher for its presentation.

Examining motivational appeals in editorials

Clip several editorials from recent opinion/editorial pages. Have students form small groups and give each group an editorial. Working in their group, students should determine the thesis statement or major claim made in the editorial, the evidence used to support the claim, and the types of motivational appeals employed in the argument. Each group should then present its findings to the rest of the class.

Unethical use of appeals

Show students examples of infomercials that contain questionable use(s) of emotional appeals. Have students evaluate the use of emotional appeal according to the principles suggested in this chapter and **3e.3** of the *Handbook*.

Additional Resources

Stutman, R. K., & Newell, S. E. (1984). Beliefs versus values: Silent beliefs in designing a persuasive message. *Western Journal of Speech Communication* 48(4), 364.

7. Chapter 21: Informative Strategies

Chapter Exercises

Exercise 1. The object of this exercise is not merely to count the number of analogies and metaphors but to discuss how they help clarify and make the material more interesting. The phrase, "Do not engulf listeners with a tidal wave of facts or bury them under an avalanche of data" uses metaphors to create a vivid image of information overload. The authors also use analogies comparing jigsaw puzzles and a road map to the principle of organizing information.

Exercise 2. This activity is designed to tax your students' creativity and provide some fun.

A motorcycle club about nutrition: You could relate the inner workings of a motorcycle engine to the human body. Although there are *obvious* differences between the two, the members in the motorcycle club could relate to the importance of taking care of their motorcycle engine to taking care of their bodies. Just like bikes need care to run properly, so does the human body.

Elementary school students about endangered species: Because elementary students may not be familiar with the concept of endangered species, it will be important to link it to something they can relate to. Asking the students to imagine how they would feel if people could no longer have fish, cats, or dogs as pets; imagine if they went to the zoo and there were no animals in the compounds. For even younger children, relating endangered animals to the depletion of resources they commonly use (food, toys, bath products, etc.) will, in a very simple way, help them grasp the meaning of "endangered."

Exercise 3. Among the clear explanation techniques *Harikul* used are: the informative strategy of linking the familiar to the unfamiliar when she compared the eye chip to cochlear implants and also to Geordie La Forge's "magical" glasses that gave him vision. She used multiple channels and modes by supplementing her verbal explanation with gestures and visual aids. She used the analogy of the bridge to explain how the optical nerve works. *McDermott* made extensive use of examples. He utilized multiple modes and channels by relying on a visual aid and specific gestures to reinforce his verbal explanations. McDermott moved from the simple to the complex by beginning with a "stripped down" hypothetical example of an election with only 100 electoral votes, then transferred the principle to the complexities of an actual presidential election. He also used repetition of phrases like "winner takes all" and "all a candidate has to do."

Class Activities

There are no specific activities for this chapter.

Additional Resources

See Part V, Resource Integration Guide.

8. Chapter 22: Persuasive Strategies

Chapter Exercises

Exercise 1. The cost of maintaining the International Space Station will be astronomical (fact—assuming reasonable agreement on what constitutes an astronomical cost). Music on MTV is simplistic and tasteless (value). Cats make better pets than dogs (value). Children should learn a foreign language before fifth grade (policy).

Exercise 2. *Atheism:* Father Duffy left the priesthood and became an atheist (fact). Being an agnostic seems to make more sense than being an atheist (value). Father Duffy should not be allowed to continue teaching catechism (policy).
Nutrition: Eating food high in fat will increase the risk of heart disease (fact). Tofu burgers taste wonderful (value). Fast food establishments should be forced to label the nutritional value of their food on each package (policy).
Women in the military The percentage of women in the military has grown in the last 15 years (fact). The new uniforms for women look lousy (value). The military should implement a quota system that requires at least 10% women in the officer's program (policy).

Exercise 3. 1) Is the need inherent in the very structure of the present system? 2) Will the proposed solution meet the need presented? 3) Is there a compelling need for change?

Exercise 4. *McNeil:* As stated in the lead-in, she had good reason to assume that she was speaking to a generally positive but rather uninformed audience. At the end of a semester class she had observed their responses to other environmentally oriented topics. She chose to rely heavily on evidence and reasoning to explicate the seriousness of the problem, but she also included healthy doses of motivational appeals to arouse her listeners' anger, sympathy, fear, and shame. If she had been speaking to an unfavorable audience she would have needed to build her own credibility even more and she would have needed more support of her analysis that US policy has actively contributed to the exploitation of the rainforests. With a neutral audience, she probably would have used even more examples of the horrors of deforestation and tried to emphasize a sense of urgency she captured in the phrase "even as we speak." Neutral audiences with many important topics to decide about would have to be convinced that this one requires attention now and cannot be left on the back burner for even a day.

Exercise 5. Smith addresses the reasons that some people support censorship in paragraphs 4–6, and 11–13. On a topic this controversial, with a great deal of media attention focused on dangers of the Internet, it seems very wise for Smith to summarize and acknowledge the motivation behind efforts for censorship as a necessary step in building his own anti-censorship argument.

Exercise 6. These should be modeled after the examples in **22f**.

Class Activities

The clash
This exercise gives students an opportunity to argue a policy proposition (In the past students have chosen to debate everything from "People who subscribe to tabloids should be banished to a desert island" to "Prostitution

should be legalized.") You may want students to come to class with a debatable proposition in mind to save time in the topic selection phase of this exercise. Here are the instructions that can be distributed to class members.

Step 1: Selecting a topic

The topic must be phrased as a debatable policy. The class will narrow the possibilities and vote on the final choice. The most important thing is that an approximately equal number of people be for and against the policy proposal. The "clash" won't be much of a "clash" if everyone already agrees. It is okay to have a couple of neutral individuals, but you are encouraged to go with the side you are leaning toward.

Step 2: Procedures for "clash"

Move your desks so supporters of the policy are on one side of the room and those opposing the policy are on the other side of the room. Neutral individuals can move to the front of the room. The moderator (your instructor) will count the number of individuals on either side as well as the number of neutral individuals.

Five minutes will be given for each group to discuss the reasons for their position. The group advocating the policy should select someone to speak first. This spokesperson will begin the clash with a brief explanation of why the group supports the policy. After the initial statement, the "clash" begins.

Members of the opposing side must raise their hand if they have a response or counter argument. You will be recognized by the moderator. If several people raise their hands in response, the moderator will select one individual to speak. The clash will continue back and forth in this manner.

Every individual on a side must speak! The moderator will keep track of who has spoken. Teams can whisper among themselves quietly while the clash is going on, but this is a team effort; no single individual should dominate or tell others what to say.

If you change your position during the exercise, you are encouraged to get up and move to the other side. Neutral individuals should join a team whenever you find yourself leaning either way. Anyone who is on a team, but finds themselves feeling neutral may also move.

The "clash" ends when either team gives, arguments are exhausted, consensus is reached, or the moderator calls the "clash" complete.

The moderator will ask if anyone on either side has changed his or her mind or if any neutral individuals were swayed to a side (whether or not they physically moved). The "clash winner" is the side persuading change in the most people. If no one switches position, or if an equal number of neutral individuals join the opposing sides, the "clash" is tied.

Step 3: Discussion

After the clash is completed, discuss the claims made by each side, the evidence which was used to support those claims, the types of reasoning employed, any fallacies which were noticed, and the motivational appeals employed. Individuals who moved during the course of the clash should discuss what arguments compelled them to move.

Audience analysis project

This project asks students to analyze their listeners' possible reactions to their propositions. Have students complete the audience analysis project that is described in Part II (Basic Materials) of this Instructor's Manual. Once the surveys and analyses have been completed, have students identify which type of audience they will be speaking to (favorable, neutral, hostile), and discuss the ways they plan to adapt their speech to their intended audience's attitude toward their topics.

Advertisement speaking exercise
Have students deliver the "advertising speaking" exercise contained in the Basic Materials section of this manual. This exercise asks students to use Monroe's Motivated Sequence to organize a persuasive speech in which they are trying to sell some idea or product. After each speech, have the students critique each speaker's ability to use this organizational pattern.

Additional Resources

See Part V, Resource Integration Guide.

15. Chapter 23: Adapting to Speaking Contexts

Chapter Exercises

Exercise 1. Pep rallies are often conducted in the public sphere by an existing community and are informal in demeanor. By their very nature, pep rallies are dialogic, more open to rules of speaking. An opening statement in a courtroom, however, is usually private, more formal and monologic—with highly prescribed rules of speaking for a one-time assembly, etc.

Exercise 2. Have students think of contexts not mentioned in chapter **23**. Ask them to brainstorm the dimensions along which those speaking contexts may vary.

Exercise 3. Have students write their responses out, or tape them and submit the tape to you. There are a variety of ways students could complete this exercise. For example, one could develop a PSR that recounted a time where he/she demonstrated his/her Adaptability [Specific Personal Attribute] by saving the day for a group doing a class project when he/she stepped in to take the place of a student who dropped the class; and then develop a PSR that tells of a time where his/her Facility with computers [Specific Work Skill] resulted in a success of some sort; and then develop a PSR that tells of the good things that happened after he/she discovered and implemented ways to Lower costs [Accomplishment] in some project or area.

Exercise 4. Established and informal groups can rely on implicit understandings of norms and rules. However, explicit rules and norms are often needed in more formal settings and when new members or visitors are present. Have students discuss the implicit and explicit norms and rules of groups in which they participate.

Exercise 5. Verbal and nonverbal hecklers can be very distracting to any speaker. Speakers should always respond to interruptions firmly and calmly. For an extensive discussion specific techniques for handling various distractions see sections **29c** and **30c**.

Class Activities

Tribute speeches
Have students prepare and deliver a tribute speech. See Part II (Basic Materials) of this manual for a description of the tribute speaking exercise.

Special occasion speeches and film
For a fun alternative to the previous exercise, bring in several clips from films where special occasion speeches are delivered. Have students use the guidelines in this chapter to critique the speeches.

Additional Resources

Kahney, L. (1996). Model speeches and toasts. *PC/Computing, 9*(12), 272.

F. Teaching Chapters 24–30: Presentation

1. Chapter 24: Modes of Delivery

Chapter Exercises

Exercise 1. Each of the speeches blended at least one other mode with the primary mode of delivery. *Dawson* —This was clearly a memorized speech. Dawson had carefully planned the speech and chosen most of the words to use. However, notice that there are still some phrases that were generated in the moment in a more extemporaneous mode. The word choice in these places may be les than perfect, but it sounds conversational and natural *Mineta*—This was probably written as a manuscript speech, then read over several times by the author so that the actual delivery was a combination of memorized and extemporaneous. This blend works for experienced speakers who have a high comfort level with the content of their ideas and want to craft a few phrases for special impact. It is a difficult blend for beginning speakers. (The comments on his coughing, were of course, impromptu.) *Fiorina*—This was a manuscript speech that was delivered in a very conversational tone. If the speech had been presented to a live audience as originally planned, it is likely that she would have used a combination of memorized delivery and reading. Therefore, she had no doubt read it over and practiced it to the point where it was partially memorized. When circumstances forced Fiorina to present the speech via teleconferencing, she transferred her manuscript to a teleprompter, but was so familiar with the ideas that she did not have to concentrate on the script word by word. She was able to maintain a natural and conversational delivery that approximated extemporaneous speaking. *Wood*—This was an impromptu speech. As a result she drew heavily on the resource of conversation and had an appealing informal style of speaking.

Class Activities

Identify and discuss the mode of delivery
Ask students to discuss the advantages and disadvantages of each mode of delivery. In addition, students should be able to provide several "real life" examples when each mode would be most effective.

Gather a variety of political and/or student speeches that represent each mode of delivery
Show the clips to students and ask them to discuss the impact of each mode. Examples to consider: Earl Spencer's tribute to Princess Diana (manuscript); Elizabeth Dole, 2000 Republican Convention (extemporaneous); President George W. Bush, State of the Union Address (teleprompter), etc.

Additional Resources

Bakshian, A. (1997). Applause, applause. Anyone can win over a tough audience, says hailed speech writer. Just ask Colin Powell. *The Economist, 345*(8039), p. S2.

Branham, R. J., & Pearce, W. B. (1996). The conversational frame in public address. *Communication Quarterly, 44*(4), 423–440.

Edwards, O. (1996). The plod thickens (teleprompters and speaking). *Forbes, 158*(5), S108.

Hinton, J. S. & Kramer, M. W. (1998). The impact of self directed videotape feedback on students' self-reported levels of communication competence and apprehension. *Communication Education, 47*(2), 151–160.

Lewis, B. J. (1998). Before you stand up to speak. *Journal of Management in Engineering, 14*(3), 9–12.

Slade-White, J. (1997). Candidate speaking t.v. spots: When they're good . . . they're very, very good. *Campaigns and Elections, 18*(6), 35–38.

2. Chapter 25: Practice Sessions

Chapter Exercises

There are no exercises in this chapter.

Class Activities

"Practice Makes Perfect"
This assignment, developed by Ayres, D. and Ayres, J. (1999), "helps students develop their practice habit as they prepare for their public speaking assignments" (p. 14). Tell students that they are required to provide proof they practiced their speeches by providing you with an audio or video tape of their speech. These tapes should be collected several days prior to the date of their presentation. A variation of this assignment is to also have the students practice their speeches in small groups. Requiring proof motivates students to plan their speeches well in advance of their due dates.

For a complete description of this assignment, see: Ayres, J. & Ayres, D. (1999). Practice makes perfect. *Speech Communication Teacher,* 13(2), 14–15.

Additional Resources

Ayres, J. (1997). Reducing public speaking apprehension through speech preparation. *Speech Communication Teacher,* 11, 6–7.

Ayres, J. & Ayres, D. (1999). Practice makes perfect. *Speech Communication Teacher,* 13(2), 14–15.

Crandall, H. (1999). Practicing impromptu speeches. *Speech Communication Teacher,* 13(2), 3–4.

3. Chapter 26: Vocal Delivery

Chapter Exercises

Exercise 1. *Luebbering*—Anna starts out with a statement in her native language, which gives her audience a moment to adjust to her physical and vocal presence before they need to begin to focus on her words. She speaks rather rapidly and some of her words may be clipped off, but generally she seems to pronounce words clearly. Luebbering seems to successfully work past any problems that could have been linked to her slight accent by her very strong nonverbal communication. Everything about her demeanor conveys a strong will to connect with her audience. She reaches out with her facial expression, her eye contact, her animated movement and gestures and the high energy level in her voice.

Exercise 2. *Harikul* has a very pleasant and expressive voice. Her rate is quite rapid but she pauses for emphasis. She has a great deal of inflection which is used to emphasize points, but generally her vocal delivery is quite natural and conversational. *Fiorina*—The speech was delivered with clear and expressive vocal qualities. Fiorina varies her pitch and inflection to show warmth and sincerity. Perhaps most striking is the control she shows in the pacing of her speech. There is a great tendency for many speakers to rush through a speech and to swallow the ends of sentences, but Fiorina resists that tendency. Her professionalism is projected with a very measured rate. She articulates each word and pauses between sentences, yet maintains a natural and conversational flow. This is a difficult task in any situation and particularly for a speech that is not in the presence of the audience. She had to gauge the tempo and rate, allowing for response, without being able to see and hear the audience reaction. *McDermott* is fortunate to have a very pleasant natural vocal quality. He makes the most of this by introducing a great deal of inflection in his speech. He articulates clearly and has excellent diction, yet does not speak in an artificial or overly precise manner. He emphasizes key words that are essential to the main points he is making. He varies his rate considerably, speaking quite rapidly at some points, yet slowing down for emphasis at others.

Class Activities

Vocal variety exercise
This is a lively game designed to get students to make full use of their vocal expressiveness. Facial and bodily expression almost always enter into the picture as well. Each student draws a slip of paper and is to read twice the sentence written on it. The first time it is to be read with no expression whatsoever. The second time it is to be read as expressively as possible. The "prize" goes to the student with the greatest contrast between the two readings. Besides the hilarity that usually ensues, several points about delivery come out in discussing the experience. One is that it is actually difficult to speak with no expression. Your voice just "wants" to emphasize certain words. Another point is that people who think they are really hamming it up do not sound as ridiculous as they feel. The conscious competence of using vocal emphasis just seems odd because it is new. Another point that comes out is the importance of pausing. Most of the phrases go by too quickly for really effective emphasis to occur. Here are a few of our phrases. Add some of your own tailored to local events or your class' personal history.

Wait a minute. Let me get this straight. You're telling me I have to give a speech tomorrow?

Today started out to be so perfect and then I ran into you.

She's such a cute little baby with those curls. She'll be a real doll when she grows up. What's her name? Fred? Oops.

How about those 49ers? Was that a fantastic game Sunday or what?

I can't wait to get out of these filthy, disgusting clothes and slip into a nice warm fragrant bubble bath.

If I ever catch you flirting with my honey again, you'll wish you'd never been born.

This is much too complicated for little old me to understand. I'm just totally lost. Can you help me?

You expect me to lend you money? After last time? Give me a break.

This trial is a mockery, a sham, a travesty. It's a mockery of a travesty and two shams of a mockery.

Can you ever forgive me? I'll do anything to make it up to you. Just please stop looking at me that way.

What a breeze this speech class is. I can knock those outlines off in ten minutes.

Oh, what a beautiful morning. Oh, what a beautiful day. I've got a wonderful feeling everything's going my way.

Additional Resources

Dale, P., & Pons, L. (1993). *English pronunciation for international students.* Englewood Cliffs, NJ: Prentice Hall.

Dauer, R. M. (1994). *Accurate English: A complete course in pronunciation.* Englewood Cliffs, NJ: Prentice-Hall Regents.

Gitterman, M. R. (1996). Improving the pronunciation of English as a second language (ESL) students. *Speech Communication Teacher*, 10(4), 5–6.

Hahner, J. C., Sokoloff, M. A., & Salishch, S. L. (1993) *Speaking clearly: Improving voice and diction* (4th ed.). New York: McGraw Hill.

Modisett, N. F., & Luter, J. G. (1988). *The basics of voice and articulation* (3rd. ed.). Minneapolis: Burgess.

Porter, P. A., Grant, M., & Draper, M. (1985*). Communicating effectively in English: Oral communication for non-native speakers.* Belmont: Wadsworth.

Prator, C. H., Jr., & Robinett, B. W. (1985). *Manual of American English Pronunciation* (4th ed.). New York: Holt.

Wells, L. K. (1989). *The articulate voice.* Scottsdale: Gorsuch Scarisbrick.

4. Chapter 27: Physical Delivery

Chapter Exercises

Exercise 1. *Brasher* has a very poised manner and makes good use of gestures and movement to emphasize her ideas. Probably most effective is her expressive face and the way she uses facial expression to reinforce the feelings she wants to convey. *Erian*—Most observers would agree that Erian is an energetic, animated, intense speaker with considerable variety in vocal and physical expression. Of course, judgments of effectiveness are subjective. Some may be critical of the overly structured gestures and planned movement or of the memorized sound of his speech which could be conceived as distracting from his message or even as too dramatic to appear sincere and natural. *Harikul* is professionally dressed, has excellent posture and is very poised. She has pleasant facial expressions that forecast the emotional content of her speech. She smiled several times as appropriate to the content. She used gestures to emphasize her points and to illustrate the processes she was describing.

Class Activities

Charades
This exercise asks students to convey emotions non-verbally. Prepare a set of slips of paper on which you have written emotions such as happiness, sadness, fear, anger, hate, love, nervousness, sympathy. Each student draws a slip and attempts to convey that emotion to the class through the *tone of voice* he or she uses while slowly counting from one to ten. Ideally, the player should be visually separated from the class (speaking from behind a curtain, a makeshift partition, or turned away from the audience) so there is no chance to interpret other nonverbal cues such as facial expression or gestures. Ask the class to check off on lists you have given them the emotion they think the player is trying to express. Students should keep track of correct and incorrect guesses and make a final tally at the end of the exercise.

After going through all or part of the list, repeat the exercise, but this time do not allow the players to speak at all. They must use nothing other than facial expressions to convey the emotions. Afterward, have the participants discuss their feelings (using words this time) about the ease or difficulties of sending messages without words. Also explore why some individuals are more adept at picking up nonverbal messages. You might make this exercise a bit more competitive by dividing the class into two teams. Each team would select participants to convey the emotions. [Based on J. R. Davitz and L. J. Davitz, "The Communication of Feelings by Content-Free Speech," *Journal of Communication*, no. 9, 1959, pp. 6–13.]

Observation of nonverbal behavior
Select several students (or ask for volunteers) to participate in a discussion. Have the participants leave the classroom for a few minutes so that they can select a controversial issue to discuss, one on which no two of the speakers hold a similar position. While the participants are outside, reveal the real purpose of the exercise to the class: the observation of nonverbal behavior. Specifically, ask the class to observe the facial expressions, eye contact, gestures, vocal variety that are so important in public presentation and to notice how these come into play in an animated conversation. So that the participants will be as natural as possible, it is important that they remain unaware that the class is observing their delivery skills. You may want to ask certain students to watch for certain things or you may have a few people observe each participant. A checklist of vocal and physical delivery skills might focus their observations.

Bring the discussion group back, have them sit in a circle in the center of the room and discuss the controversial topic for ten to fifteen minutes. Conclude the discussion whether they have reached agreement or not. Ask the observers to comment on the physical and vocal delivery skills of the participants. Emphasize that the comments should be constructive and should not be embarrassing to any student with poor delivery skills. Ideally, this exercise should be videotaped so the participants can see themselves and you can make appropriate comments.

Eye contact exercise

Have every audience member raise his or her hand at the beginning of a speech. The speaker's goal is to get all hands lowered. When the speaker engages an audience member in direct eye contact, that person should silently count off three seconds and then lower the hand. The exercise provides immediate reinforcement for students who need to improve eye contact. Seeing that last hand go down is like blowing out the last candle on a birthday cake. Obviously, this exercise is best used with an ungraded short speech or an impromptu speech rather than a major graded assignment, since a circus atmosphere sometimes ensues.

Emphasizing & identifying poor delivery

This classic activity illustrates how poor delivery skills can impact a speech. Volunteer students are asked to give a brief impromptu speech that incorporates one of the following ineffective delivery styles:

> Ineffective Delivery Style: Speak quickly and loudly
> Ineffective Delivery Style: Avoid eye contact
> Ineffective Delivery Style: Speak in a monotone voice
> Ineffective Delivery Style: Pace back and forth in front of the audience
> Ineffective Delivery Style: Use excessive and/or exaggerated gestures
> Ineffective Delivery Style: Fidget with your clothing, note cards, or the lectern

Afterwards, discuss the impact the ineffective delivery style had on the impromptu speech.

Delivery coach activity

Each student is designated as delivery coach for another. This can be reciprocal in pairs if there is an even number of students. It is perhaps more effective, however, to have a student serve as coach for one person and be coached by another. If you are using a support group format, this is easily done in a round robin fashion: Bob is coach for Carol, Carol for Ted, Ted for Alice, and Alice for Bob.

Coach and "coachee" must meet and discuss delivery goals. Based on introductory exercises they should identify areas for improvement and prioritize them starting with areas that create actual distractions, and moving to areas where improvement would add impact to the speech. They are to set at least one but no more than three short term goals for the upcoming speech. There should be no more than one in each of the following categories: vocal delivery, physical delivery, and overall speaker image. Both should agree on the importance of the goal.

Next have them develop a clear and simple signaling system to remind the speaker of these goals. Bring note cards and colored markers to class and let their creativity take over. Many will devise cards like:

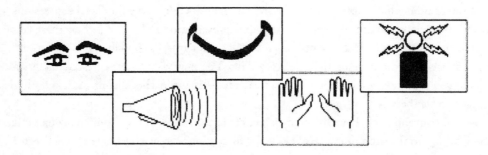

Others will develop simple reinforcers like:

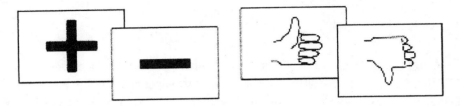

Still others will create private and mysterious signals not unlike third base coaches. Let them have fun with the coaching analogy.

During the speech the coachees are to be consciously competent of the one, two, or three delivery goals *only*. All the rest of their attention is to be directed toward content and audience response. Coaches are to signal encouragement and reminders. After each speech they are to meet, perhaps watch the videotape together, and discuss the status of the goals. If a skill has moved into the domain of unconscious competence, the students may move on to a new goal in that area. For instance, if confidence was the goal for the overall category and the student now feels and appears confident, the new goal may be a higher energy level. If the distracting mannerism of sleeve pushing has been eliminated, the new goal for physical delivery may be to gesture a few times during the speech. If a goal has not been met, coach and coachee should continue to focus on that area in the next speech.

You may have students write a short paper about this coaching experience at the end of the course. Some teachers have each student list his or her short term delivery goals on the critique form for each speech so the teacher can be sure to give feedback in this area.

Additional Resources

Manusov, V. (1991). Perceiving nonverbal messages: Effects of immediacy and encoded intent on receiver judgments. *Western Journal of Speech Communication, 55*, 235–253.

Mills, D. D. (1992). Tag team championship: Improving delivery skills. In Stephen E. Lucas (Ed.), *Selections from the Speech Communication Teacher, 1986-1991.* (pp. 23–24). New York: McGraw-Hill.

Roach, T.J., & Goodnight, L.J. (1998). Eye contact shooting gallery. *Speech Communication Teacher, 13*(1), 7–8.

Rollman, S. A. (1992). Classroom exercises for teaching nonverbal communication. In Stephen E. Lucas (Ed.), *Selections from the Speech Communication Teacher, 1986-1991.* (pp. 49–50). New York: McGraw-Hill.

Streek, J. (1993). Gesture as communication I: Its coordination with gaze and speech. *Communication Monographs, 60*, 275–299.

Sullivan, G. F. (1997). Improving delivery skills: The practice impromptu. *Speech Communication Teacher, 1,* 2.

5. Chapter 28: Presentation Aids

Chapter Exercises

Exercise 1. *Carpool lanes:* Charts and graphs would complement a speech on carpool lanes. A line graph could chart the relationship between increasing numbers of cars traveling on a city's freeways and increasing levels of air pollution. A bar graph comparing the number of cars traveling on a major freeway during commute hours before and after a city designating a carpool lane could be displayed to illustrate a decrease in traffic congestion due to carpool lanes. A pie chart could reflect the results of a poll which found a high percentage of commuters say they would carpool with their coworkers if the city designated carpool lanes.

Exercise 2. *Harikul* uses two large, colorful charts, one of the eye and one of the eye chip. Both seem to contain the key elements without unnecessary detail and are easy to see. She keeps them covered when not in use and points to the part of the process she is describing without blocking the presentation aid or losing contact with the audience. *Erian* had four charts, one that listed the good and bad kinds of sugar and three that showed blown up labels with ingredients of popular foods and beverages. These were all large enough to read and were clear. He kept them covered when they were not in use and pointed to the elements of each chart as he spoke.

Class Activities

Critiquing presentation aids

This exercise requires that you have sample presentation aids that have been collected from previous students (Note: We recommend that you have students sign a permission form whenever they donate their work. This form should include the student's name, address, phone number, and the item[s] which they are granting you permission to use.) Have students form groups of four or five people. Give each group an aid to critique. Using the guidelines in the text, ask the groups to discuss those aspects of their aid which are effective and ineffective. Groups should then present their aid to the class with their assessment. Features of discrete and continuous aids will most likely be part of the discussion. This is also a good time to clarify the types of information for which pie charts, line graphs, and bar graphs are appropriate.

Viewing sample speeches

Have students view an informative or persuasive speech and critique the speaker's use of presentation aids.

Have students orally discuss their responses to chapter exercise 1 above

Compare and contrast each student's response.

Additional Resources

Bohn, E., & Jabusch, D. (1982). The effect of four methods of instruction on the use of visual aids in speeches. *Western Journal of Speech Communication, 46,* 253-265.

Gutgold, N. (1998). Pointing groups to power-point. *Speech Communication Teacher, 13*(1), 5-6.

Tufte, Edward R. (2001). *The visual display of qualitative information* (2nd ed). Graphics Press, Cheshire, Connecticut.

Zelazny, G. (1991). *Irwin professional says it with charts: The executive's guide to successful presentations in the 1990's,* (2nd ed). Burr Ridge, Illinois.

6. Chapter 29: Adapting to the Speech Situation

Chapter Exercises

There are no exercises in this chapter.

Class Activities

Overcoming speech distractions

Create realistic situations/scenarios students may encounter while delivering their speeches. Examples of distractions might include: (1) several of the students in your speech class fall asleep during your presentation; (2) several students walk in late while you are speaking, causing a noisy disruption; (3) the maintenance crew is knocking down the building outside of the classroom, making it nearly impossible for anyone to hear you; (4) the light in the overhead projector you had planned on using burns out just after you turn it on; (5) you had planned to conduct an audience activity that involved the audience moving their chairs into a circle. Unfortunately, the classroom you've been assigned to is a large lecture room with chairs bolted to the ground; (6) several students engage in small-talk throughout your presentation, etc.

As a large group discussion or in small groups, have students brainstorm solutions or remedies for adapting to the speech situations you presented them with.

Additional Resources

Bakshian, A. (1997). Applause, applause. Anyone can win over a tough audience, says hailed speech writer. Just ask Colin Powell. *The Economist*, 345, pS2.

Branham, R. J., & Pearce, W. B. (1996). The conversational frame in public address. *Communication Quarterly*, 44(4), 423–440.

Slade-White, J. (1997). Candidate speaking t.v. spots: When they're good . . . they're very, very good. *Campaigns and Elections*, 18(6), 35–38.

Lewis, B. J. (1998). Before you stand up to speak. *Journal of Management in Engineering*, 14(3), 9–12.

Manusov, V. (1991). Perceiving nonverbal messages: Effects of immediacy and encoded intent on receiver judgments. *Western Journal of Speech Communication*, 55, 235–253.

7. Chapter 30: Answering Questions

Chapter Exercises

There are no exercises in this chapter.

Class Activities

Answering questions effectively
Have each student stand in front of the class and discuss some topic of interest to him/her. After about a minute, have the audience ask the speaker both interpretive and factual questions about his/her speech. Following the guidelines in the text, the speaker should answer the questions. For an added challenge, ask a couple of your students to take on the role of a hostile audience member. This activity provides a fun, non-threatening atmosphere for students to practice answering questions prior to their formal speeches.

Asking effective questions
Have students watch a sample informative or persuasive speech. Ask the students to write down 2–3 questions they might ask the speaker if they had the opportunity. Discuss the type of questions the students pose, emphasizing the difference between a question and a comment.

Political press conferences
Show a brief presidential press conference where reporters are allowed to ask the president questions. Discuss the effectiveness of the questions and the answers that are reported. Students find this timely activity interesting in that they often find that the speaker does not often answer questions completely.

Additional Resources

International City-Country Management Association. (1998). How do I deal with hostile questions? *Public Management*, 80(4), 27–29.

Part IV
Sample Test Questions

Correct answers are marked with an asterisk. The places in the *Handbook* where the information was presented are shown in brackets.

Chapter 1: Understanding Speaking

True/False Questions

T   F*   1. It is generally correct to say effective public speakers are born, not made.   [1e]

T   F*   2. If you are not a "born" public speaker, you will find it difficult to achieve an adequate degree of competence.   [1e]

T*   F   3. Like many other skills, public speaking should become easier with experience.   [1e]

T   F*   4. Effective public speakers, from the very beginning, generally find public speaking to be an easy task.   [1e]

T   F*   5. Conscious competence is the highest skill level that a speaker can reach.   [1d]

T   F*   6. Speakers give speeches to audiences, therefore meaning is transmitted from a speaker to an audience.   [1b.1&.2]

T*   F   7. Approach public speaking by drawing on your conversation skills, writing skills, and performance skills.   [1c.1–.3]

T   F*   8. The sender controls the true meanings of a speaker's statement.   [1b.2]

T*   F   9. Once the speech context changes, the meaning of the speaker's words change.   [1b.2]

T   F*   10. A speaker who is spontaneous and responsive during everyday conversations and also in his speech is drawing on his performance skills.   [1c.1]

Multiple Choice Questions

11.   The three familiar communicative resources public speakers should draw on are:
    A. Writing, speaking, and performing skills
    B. Acting, singing, and conversational skills
    *C. Conversation, writing, performing skills
    D. None of the above resources will help a speaker who is ill prepared for her speech.   [1c]

12.   Which of the following is not one of the steps in the skill learning process?
    A. Conscious competence
    B. Unconscious incompetence
    *C. Incompetent competence

D. Conscious incompetence

E. Unconscious competence [1d]

13. A person in the _____ stage has made the realization that she or he is doing something ineptly and that there is room for improvement.
    A. Conscious competence
    B. Unconscious incompetence
    *C. Conscious incompetence
    D. Unconscious competence [1d]

14. Without realizing it, Jane twirls her hair every time she delivers a speech. Jane is in which of the four stages?
    *A. Unconscious incompetence
    B. Conscious incompetence
    C. Conscious competence
    D. Unconscious competence [1d]

15. After watching the videotape of his second speech, Tim is aware of his abundant use of "ums" and "ahs." He then makes the commitment to eliminate non-fluencies from his speaking. From then on, he is able to cut down on non-fluencies when he speaks. He is operating at the _____ level of skill mastery.
    A. Unconscious incompetence
    B. Conscious incompetence
    *C. Conscious competence
    D. Unconscious competence [1d]

Essay and Short Answer Questions

16. Discuss at least one way that public speaking is like acting, writing and conversing. Then discuss at least one way that public speaking is different from each of these other forms of communication. [1c]

17. Identify a skill that you have mastered and describe how you progressed through the four stages of skill learning. [1d]

18. What do the authors of your textbook mean when they write, "think about communication as the joint creation of meaning"? [1a, b.1&.2]

19. Discuss two misconceptions that often affect speakers. [1e]

20. Assess the resources you have to draw upon as a public speaker by discussing your strengths and weaknesses as a conversationalist, writer, and performer. Which of these three resources promises to be the most transferable to your public speaking success? [1c]

Chapter 2: Listening

True/False Questions

T*   F   1. A message does not really exist until it is received and shaped by a listener. [2a]

T*   F   2. It is important to take time to prepare before a situation that requires skilled listening.   [2a]

T   F*   3. Effective listeners know when to uncritically accept ideas and information they encounter.   [2c]

T*   F   4. Holistic listening involves listening with our ears, eyes, and hearts.   [2f.2]

T*   F   5. Listeners share the ethical responsibility for meanings that come out of speeches.   [2g.3]

T   F*   6. According to the 90/10 principle, all people's weaknesses are the opposite of their strengths.   [2d.6]

T*   F   7. "Salim, I really enjoyed your high energy level, except that by the end of the speech I was almost exhausted. Is it possible to keep that momentum, but to tone it down just a little?" This response is an example of feedback based on the 90/10 principle.   [2d.6]

Multiple Choice Questions

8.   If you were going to give a person all of these comments, which would most appropriately give first?
   A. You mispronounced the word "athlete."
   *B. Your main points were very clear.
   C. I was distracted a few times by your pacing.
   D. The colors on your visual aid really caught my eye.
   E. Next time, use even more personal examples.   [2d]

9.   When giving feedback, which of the following is *not* suggested by your text?
   A. Give positive suggestions first.
   B. Give suggestions not orders.
   C. Be realistic about the amount of feedback a speaker can receive.
   D. Prioritize feedback, focusing on giving the most important feedback first.
   *E. Make feedback general rather than specific.   [2d]

10.   The body of your speech should generally comprise _____ of your speech.
   A. 50 %
   B. 25%
   C. 30%
   *D. 75%   [2d]

11.   When listening as a consultant to a speaker, use the following principles of constructive feedback *except*:
   A. Be vague to avoid hurting the speaker's feelings.
   B. Start with the negative.
   C. Give suggestions, not orders.
   D. Make important comments first.
   *E. Both "A" and "B" should be avoided.   [2d]

12.   All of the following are listening pitfalls *except*:
   A. Daydreaming, doodling, disengaging.
   B. Allowing yourself to be distracted by superficial qualities of the speaker.
   C. Failing to monitor your nonverbal behaviors as a listener.

*D. All of the above are listening pitfalls and should be avoided. [2g]

13. Which of the following is the most effective example of constructive criticism?
    A. Your speech was great!
    B. I couldn't really hear you in the back.
    *C. Your thesis was clearly stated and well supported with evidence.
    D. Your introduction was too long and disorganized. [2d]

Essay and Short Answer Questions

14. Revise the following statements so they better adhere to the principles of constructive feedback:
    You sound boring when you speak.
    I can't understand you.
    Your speech was good. [2d]

15. Of the six listening pitfalls mentioned in chapter **2**, which two do you find yourself engaging in most? How can you avoid these pitfalls? [2g]

16. How can a listener be both curious and critical? [2c]

17. Describe the relationship between effective speaking and listening. [2a]

18. What do your authors mean when they say you should prepare to listen? [2b]

19. Briefly describe two ways you might listen to optimize your learning when gathering information for your speech. [2e]

20. What do your authors mean when they suggest using the "90/10" principle? [2d]

21. What three guidelines should listeners adhere to when giving feedback to a speaker? [2d]

Chapter 3: Speaking Ethics

True/False Questions

T* F 1. Every action has an ethical dimension. [3a.1]

T* F 2. Ethical decisions are rarely clear cut. [3a.2]

T* F 3. Ethical decisions vary with context. [3a.3]

T F* 4. Ethical questions are concerned with what works in a speech. [3]

T* F 5. Appeals to your listeners' feelings are legitimate ways to support and emphasize your points. [3e.2]

T* F 6. Speakers who use the bandwagon technique discourage independent thinking. [3e.3]

T   F*   7. Speakers who build identification with their audience so they will be receptive to their ideas are
            using the card-stacking technique.   [3e.3]

Multiple Choice Questions

8. Speakers can respect the integrity of ideas by not
    A. Plagiarizing
    B. Lying
    C. Oversimplifying
    *D. Doing any of the above   [3d]

9. Lying includes
    A. Making statements that are completely counterfactual
    B. Playing word games to create false impressions
    C. Leaving out part of the whole truth
    *D. All of the above   [3d.2]

10. All of the following may be considered propaganda devices except for:
    A. Just plain folks
    B. Card stacking
    C. Transference
    *D. False Analogy
    E. Testimonials   [3e.3]

11. When a speaker tries to gloss over his position by calling his opponent a "sexist," he is using which
    propaganda device?
    A. Just plain folks
    B. Card stacking
    C. Transference
    *D. Name-calling
    E. Testimonials   [3e.3]

12. When a speaker tries to discourage independent thinking by making statements like "everyone is
    investing in this product," he/she is using which propaganda device?
    *A. Bandwagon
    B. Card stacking
    C. Transference
    D. False Analogy
    E. Testimonials   [3e.3]

Essay and Short Answer Questions

13. Describe what conditions make a reliance on appeals to needs, emotions, or values suspect.   [3e.2]

14. Explain the following statement "every time you speak you exercise power and take on some
    responsibility for the consequences of what you do or do not say."   [3a]

15. Define and provide examples of three propaganda devices ethical speakers should avoid. [3e.3]

16. Provide two ways a speaker can avoid plagiarizing the ideas and words of another. [3d.1]

17. What is plagiarism? Are there degrees/types of plagiarism that are worse than other types of plagiarism? Why or why not? [3d.1]

18. What can a listener reasonably expect from an ethical public speaker? [3]

19. Evaluate the use of the following emotional appeals according to the principles suggested in chapter 3:
We need to increase defense spending by 40 billion dollars if we are to protect ourselves against outside aggression.
You are either with us or against us! [3e]

20. Suppose your opponent or adversary makes extensive and effective use of propaganda techniques. Are you then justified in countering with similar strategies? In a well developed paragraph, explain your response. [3e]

21. According to your authors, "ethical decisions often involve weighing complex factors and competing goals." Select and discuss with an original example one of the balances speakers should consider. [3e.1&.2]

Chapter 4: Overcoming Fear of Speaking

True/False Questions

T* F 1. All speakers experience some fear of speaking. [4a]

T* F 2. Visualizing success is a method that can relieve some of the anxiety related to public speaking. [4d.1]

T* F 3. Relaxation techniques have been shown to reduce speaker apprehension. [4c]

T F* 4. Build your confidence by picturing yourself delivering an absolutely flawless speech. [4d.1]

T F* 5. If you are an extremely nervous speaker, having several glasses of wine before your speech will relax you and make you a more effective speaker. [4c]

T* F 6. Unproductive internal statements are habitual and will not change easily. [4d.2]

T* F 7. Visualizing the successful delivery of your speech will positively influence your presentation. [4d.1]

T* F 8. Speakers can handle symptoms of nervousness by learning relaxation techniques. [4c]

Multiple Choice Questions

9.   If you have a high degree of speaker apprehension you should try all of the following *except*
    A. Use tension release techniques
    B. Accept fear as normal
    *C. Imagine yourself giving a perfect speech
    D. Use positive self-suggestions
    E. All of the above are good ways to reduce anxiety   [4]

Essay and Short Answer Questions

10.   Discuss the rationale for and give examples of how the use of positive self-suggestions can help to reduce speaker apprehension.   [4d]

11.   List negative statements that relate to a public speaking situation and replace them with positive ones.   [4d.2]

12.   Discuss several ways a speaker can cope with the physical effects of fear.   [4c]

13.   Describe and explain the technique called "cognitive restructuring"?   [4d.2]

14.   Describe your greatest fear of public speaking. In what way(s) will you over come that fear?   [4]

Chapter 5: Planning

True/False Questions

T*   F   1. Practicing in front of colleagues or friends is a good way to receive feedback.   [5c]

T   F*   2. Contemplation is the first step in the creative process.   [5a]

T*   F   3. The four phases of creativity are: preparation, incubation, illumination, and refinement.   [5a]

Multiple Choice Questions

4.   In planning and practicing his persuasive speech on environmental preservation, Paul comes to a revelation of how the information could be organized into past, present, and future regarding our role of caring for the earth. He has reached the _____ stage of the creative process.
    A. preparation
    B. incubation
    *C. illumination
    D. refinement
    E. contemplation   [5a]

5.   Which of the following planning pitfalls should you avoid?
    A. Not allowing time for incubation
    B. Not allowing margin for error

    C. Experiencing "Writer's" block

    D. Experiencing "Speaker's" block

    *E. All of the above are pitfalls that should be avoided [5e]

Essay and Short Answer Questions

6. What are the advantages of talking aloud throughout the process of speech preparation? [5c]

7. What are the advantages of using a collaborative approach to speech preparation? [5c]

8. Briefly describe two reasons a speaker should practice her speech aloud. [5c,e]

9. What considerations should a speaker make when creating a timetable for his speech preparation? [5b]

Chapter 6: Topic Selection and Analysis

True/False Questions

T*   F   1. When selecting a speech topic, you should rely on your own experience, expertise, and interests. [6a.1]

T*   F   2. It is generally a good idea to select a topic that is both timely and timeless. [6a.3]

T*   F   3. Limiting the number of ideas in your speech may be necessary to ensure adequate depth of analysis. [6b]

T*   F   4. Your text suggests that it is helpful to make a distinction between your purpose and audience outcomes. [6c]

T   F*   5. A thesis sentence and the speech title are essentially the same thing. [6d,e]

T   F*   6. Thesis statements should be written as questions your audience should answer. [6d.1]

T   F*   7. It is generally a good idea to settle on the first speech topic that occurs to you. [6]

T*   F   8. The average speaker speaks between 100 and 150 words per minute. [6b.1]

T*   F   9. A thesis statement should be stated as a single declarative statement. [6d.1]

T   F*   10. All good speeches have titles. [6e]

Multiple Choice Questions

11. Which of the following is *not* a criterion for selecting a speech topic?
    A. Appropriate to the audience
    *B. Non-controversial
    C. Related to speaker's interests
    D. Timely
    E. Timeless [6a]

12. Which of the following is one of the three general purposes of a speech as classified in your text?
    A. Describe
    B. Transmit
    C. Recognize
    *D. Evoke
    E. Explain   [6c.1]

13. Chong is going to speak formally to the cafeteria staff about getting more vegetarian options in the dining hall on campus. The purpose of his speech will most likely be:
    A. to debate
    B. to inform
    C. to evoke
    *D. to persuade
    E. to educate   [6c.1]

14. The phrase "to inform the audience about the three necessary elements to hosting a successful party" would be considered a:
    A. General purpose
    *B. Specific purpose
    C. Primary audience analysis
    D. Thesis statement   [6c.1]

15. A speech explaining the procedure in passing a law on gun control would most likely be an example of a speech to:
    *A. Inform
    B. Persuade
    C. Evoke
    D. None of the above   [6c.1]

16. Which of the following intentions would be appropriate in a speech to evoke?
    A. Explain
    B. Convince
    C. Influence
    *D. Inspire   [6c.1]

17. Which of the following intentions would be appropriate in a speech to persuade?
    A. Motivate
    B. Convince
    C. Stimulate action
    *D. All of the above   [6c.1]

18. Which of the following intentions would be appropriate in a speech to inform?
    A. Celebrate
    B. Preach
    *C. Define
    D. Entertain   [6c.1]

Essay and Short Answer Questions

19.   Rewrite the following ineffective thesis statement: The need for mandatory drug testing for college athletes.   [6d.1&.2]

20.   Explain what is wrong, if anything, with the following thesis statements:
       What kinds of special effects are used in the film Star Wars, Episode I: The Phantom Menace?
       The United States government should oppose terrorism.
       How much money from the state lottery actually goes to education?   [6d]

21.   Name three things you should consider before selecting your speech topic.   [6a.1–.3]

22.   Explain why the best speech topics are not just timely or just timeless.   [6a.3]

23.   Suppose you were speaking on depression. Phrase a thesis sentence and then state your primary and contributing audience outcomes.   [6c,d]

24.   Select one of the following topics and describe how it could be made into a speech to inform, persuade, and evoke.
       Topics: Skin cancer, Cardio athletic kickboxing, Politics, Vegetarianism, Education, Home schooling
                                                                                            [6c]

25.   Select a catchy title for a speech on the positive outcomes of cosmetic surgery.   [6e]

Chapter 7: Audience Analysis

True/False Questions

T   F*   1. Intelligent inference and empathy are unrealistic methods to use when attempting to gather information on your audience.   [7a]

T*   F   2. If the majority of your audience is in extreme disagreement with your thesis, you might consider them an unfavorable audience.   [7d]

T*   F   3. Audience analysis is the constant awareness of those who are the "co-authors" of your speech.[7]

T   F*   4. The most unreliable source of audience analysis is direct observation.   [7a.1]

T*   F   5. It is possible to infer from your audience's ages certain experiences they have had.   [7a.1]

T   F*   6. Speakers should say what is on their minds and not worry about offending their audience.   [7]

T*   F   7. When planning your speech you should try to consider what is meaningful to you audience.[7c]

Multiple Choice Questions

8.   Generally, the most reliable source of audience analysis is
       A. Administering a questionnaire

     B. Inference and empathy

     C. Selected interviews

     D. A contact person

    *E. Direct observation   [7a]

9.   Monty has completed the audience analysis portion of his speech preparation. Below are several pieces of information he collected. Which of the following is *not* an example of demographic data?

     A. The average age of the audience is 31

    *B. Most audience members are in favor of his topic

     C. Most audience members are African American females

     D. Most of the audience members are middle class college graduates

     E. All of the above are pieces of demographic data   [7b]

10.   Which of the following questions would yield the *least* useful information about your audience?

     A. What does your audience know about your topic?

     B. What is the history of your audience as a group?

    *C. What does the audience think of themselves as a group?

     D. What does the audience think of you?

     E. What will be the program surrounding your speech?   [7e]

11.   A speaker can anticipate her audience's expectations by gathering details specific to the speech situation including asking the following questions:

     A. What do they know about your topic?

     B. What do they think about you?

     C. What is the history of the group?

     D. What is the program surrounding your speech?

    *E. All the above   [7e]

Essay and Short Answer Questions

12.   List four ways that a speaker can gain information about an audience, and give at least one advantage of each.   [7a]

13.   Suppose your instructor has just informed you that you need to prepare a speech to deliver to a group of approximately 40 individuals. Unfortunately, the *only* information you know about this group is that the individuals are avid readers of *Rolling Stone* magazine. Relying on your knowledge of the importance of audience analysis, intelligent inferences and reasonable assumptions, develop an audience profile that summarizes the most relevant demographic and attitudinal data. Finally, what two potential topics might this group be interested in hearing about?   [7b,c,d]

14.   Based on the textbook and class discussions, write a paragraph explaining how audience analysis information will aid you in customizing your informative speech to the specific audience in this class.[7]

15.   Explain the following statement: "To anticipate your audience's expectations, gather details about the specific speech situation."   [7e]

16.   Discuss several advantages and disadvantages (caveats) of analyzing audience demographics.   [7b]

Chapter 8: Research

True/False Questions

T* F 1. Generally, when gathering research for your speech it is best to start with recorded information, and then seek out knowledgeable individuals. [8a.2]

T F* 2. Research your topic so that you progress from the specific to the general. [8a.2]

T* F 3. When researching information on a matrimonial ritual of Spain, Kim should begin with the general cultural themes of the country before directing her research through the specific procedures of the ceremony. [8a.2]

T* F 4. You should use an analysis question based on your thesis statement to direct your research.[8a.4]

T F* 5. Your family and coworkers are rarely valuable sources of information. [8d]

T F* 6. Conducting interview(s) for your speech can substitute for library and electronic research. [8d]

T* F 7. Web-based materials should be scrutinized and subjected to tests of credibility and reliability.[8c]

T* F 8. InfoTrac College Edition is an electronic virtual library that is available 24 hours a day via an Internet connection. [8c]

T* F 9. Your audience's attitude toward you and your topic is a determinant of how brief your in-speech resource citations can be. [8e.2]

Multiple Choice Questions

9. Which of the following steps would probably come first if you were starting out to do research for your speech on freedom of speech?
   A. Develop a lexicon of key words and phrases like "clear and present danger," "a chilling effect," "obscenity"
   B. Make an appointment to interview a judge
   *C. Read some general sources to get background on the topic
   D. Talk to a librarian to see where books of court cases are located
   E. Prepare a reference list [8a,b,c,d]

10. When seeking information from other people, you should consider
    A. Family
    B. Educators
    C. Public officials
    D. Acquaintances
    *E. All of the above [8d.1]

11. During the initial moments of an interview, you should
    A. Ask specific questions about the topic
    B. Ask general questions about the topic

*C. Set a context for the interview

D. Explain your position regarding the topic

E. None of the above [8d.2]

12. The closing phase of an interview allows you to

*A. Summarize your perspective of the interview

B. Ask the expert open-ended questions

C. Hold forth on your opinion of the subject

D. Make encouraging comments such as "mm-hmm," "I see," etc.

E. None of the above [8d.2]

13. All of the following are suggestions when using note cards to record information *except*

A. For each promising source, write the author's last name on a card

*B. Use several note cards for each source

C. Write a few key words of the book's title until you locate the book

D. Indicate the call number

E. Use 4" x 6" cards [8e]

14. Having a research strategy includes:

A. Fitting your research to the time allotted

B. Approaching your topic so that you progress from the general to the specific

C. Develop a lexicon of the terminology peculiar to your topic

*D. All of the above [8a]

15. When evaluating the reliability of a Web site's content, which of the following questions about the site is *not* relevant:

A. Is it up to date?

*B. Is the site navigation logical?

C. What company does it keep?

D. Who is it?

E. What's its slant? [8c]

Essay and Short Answer Questions

16. Jose is delivering an informative speech on the advantages and disadvantages of home schooling, due in three weeks. Although he has retrieved several published sources on this topic, he would also like to talk to "human resources" to supplement his research. He has asked you to provide him with some suggestions on who he should contact and how he should conduct an interview. In a well developed paragraph, identify and discuss several human resources Jose could contact and how he should conduct the interviews with each subject. [8d.1&.2]

17. Discuss several of the advantages and disadvantages of conducting research on the Internet. [8c]

Chapter 9: Transforming Ideas into Speech Points

True/False Questions

T F* 1. Breaking a speech topic down into its component parts is the process known as synthesis.[ORG INTRO]

T* F 2. At the early stage of speech preparation a topic outline is more appropriate than a full sentence outline. [9b]

T F* 3. Ideally, a speech should have between two and seven main points. [9e]

T* F 4. The concept "Junior High School" bears a coordinate relationship to "Elementary School" and a subordinate relation to "Education." [9f]

T F* 5. Ideas of equal importance are called subordinate points. [9f]

T F* 6. Points of lesser significance that support or explain other ideas are called coordinate points. [9f]

T* F 7. Concept mapping is a visual method of taking your ideas and showing how they relate to each other. [9b.2]

Multiple Choice Questions

8. Which of the following is a form of concept mapping?
 A. Marshaling
 B. Manipulating moveable components
 *C. Clustering
 D. A rudimentary verbal outline
 E. All of the above [9b]

9. Suppose that your thesis sentence is "government regulation such as devaluation, tariffs and subsidies will not solve the US trade deficit, so we need to address this serious problem through increasing the productivity of our industries." Which of the following statements would *not* be an appropriate main point?
 A. The trade deficit is a serious problem in the US.
 *B. Japanese and German industries have much better quality control methods than we do.
 C. Current governmental solutions are not effective in reducing the trade deficit.
 D. Certain changes in our management and production practices would increase productivity enough to reduce the deficit.
 E. None of the above. Any of these statements could be used as a main point. [9c]

10. Suppose that a speech had these three main points:
 I. Good nutrition will help you resist disease.
 II. Good nutrition will help you in all your physical activities.
 III. Good nutrition will improve your sports performance.

Which criterion for the selection of main points is most clearly violated?

A. Have an appropriate number of main points

B. Phrase main points clearly

*C. Select main points that are mutually exclusive

D. State main points as declarative sentences

E. All main points should relate to the topic   [9d,e,f]

Essay and Short Answer Questions

11.   Describe what the process of organizing entails.   [9]

12.   Rewrite the main points and/or thesis statement so that the following main points correspond to the thesis statement.
      Thesis: Body piercing is a form of art and a way for one to express individualism.
      I.   Body piercing is a personal choice
      II. Body piercing does not leave permanent damage to a person's body.   [9c]

13.   What does it mean to "select main points that are mutually exclusive"?   [9d]

14.   Are the following main points mutually exclusive? Explain.   [9d]
      I.   Parents should be responsible for their children's criminal behavior.
      II.   Children under the age of 18 should not be held accountable for their criminal actions.
      III. There are too many children committing crimes.

15.   Suppose you are designing a workshop on delivering effective speeches. What two pieces of advice would you give participants on transforming their general topics and ideas into effective speech points?   [9a–f]

16.   What types of organizational tools can you use to identify potential main points?   [9b]

17.   Defend the statement, "have at least two, but not more than five, main points in the average speech." [9e]

Chapter 10: Arranging Points

True/False Questions

T   F*   1. There is basically one universal way to organize a speech.   [10]

*T   F   2. According to the text, the most frequently used speech organizational pattern is the topical pattern.   [10a.5]

T*   F   3. The Chronological pattern orders ideas in a time sequence.   [10a.1]

T   F*   4. The cause and effect pattern examines the symptoms of a problem and then suggests a remedy.   [10a.4]

T*   F   5. Sometimes topical patterns may combine aspects of other organizational patterns.   [10a.5]

T   F*   6. Subpoints should echo the organizational pattern of the main points.   [10b]

T*   F   7. When two or more organizational patterns seem to fit your topic equally well, try to understand your audience's frame of reference to determine to which sequence they will most relate.   [10a.5]

Multiple Choice Questions

8.   Suppose the main points in a speech on vitamin C are:
   I.   Americans are not getting enough vitamin C.
   II.   Americans should consume more citrus fruits and vegetables to maintain vitamin C balance.

   What is the arrangement of the speech?
   A. Chronological pattern
   *B. Problem-solution pattern
   C. Spatial pattern
   D. Topical pattern
   E. Cause-effect pattern   [10a.4]

9.   Geographical topics seem often to lend themselves to a
   A. Chronological pattern
   B. Problem-solution pattern
   *C. Spatial pattern
   D. Topical pattern
   E. Cause-effect pattern   [10a.2]

10.   Historical developments frequently lend themselves to a
   *A. Chronological pattern
   B. Problem-solution pattern
   C. Spatial pattern
   D. Topical pattern
   E. Cause-effect pattern   [10a.1]

11.   Suppose the main points in a speech on event planning are:
   I.   Providing a variety of food is an important element to a successful event.
   II.   Providing entertainment is also an important element to a successful event.

   What is the arrangement of the speech?
   A. Chronological pattern
   B. Problem-solution pattern
   C. Spatial pattern
   *D. Topical pattern
   E. Cause-effect pattern   [10a.5]

Essay and Short Answer Questions

12.   Suppose that you are speaking about health. Show in a rough outline three different organizational patterns you could use. Label each.   [10]

13.   Discuss the benefits and limitations of each organizational pattern discussed in your text.   [10a]

14. Describe two speech topics that would benefit from a spatial organizational pattern.   [10a.2]

15. Describe three factors you should consider before selecting an organizational pattern.   [10]

Chapter 11: Outlining

True/False Questions

*T   F   1. Full sentences must have both a subject and a predicate in order to provide a criterion against which to test the relevance of subordinate points.   [11b]

T   F*   2. Each symbol on an outline should designate at least two different ideas.   [11a.4]

T*   F   3. Outline development can help you avoid overestimating or underestimating your preparedness.   [11]

T*   F   4. Following the rules of conventional outline format will help you to visualize the relationships among the ideas of your speech.   [11a]

T   F*   5. The main points of the outline should not forecast the subpoints that will be developed.   [11c]

Multiple Choice Questions

6. Which of the following is *not* recommended in preparing an outline?
    A. Show relationships through indenting
    B. Use consistent symbols
    *C. State points as questions the speech must answer
    D. Have at least two points at each level of subordination
    E. Have only one point for each symbol   [11a]

7. A full-sentence outline is useful primarily because
    A. It can also be used for speech notes
    B. It helps you write out the speech word for word
    C. You can plan how to do your research by following the outline
    *D. It helps you develop your speech logically and coherently
    E. All of the above   [11b]

8. The speech outline is essentially the same thing as
    A. your research notes
    B. your preliminary organizational scheme
    C. your speech notes
    D. all of the above
    *E. none of the above   [11]

9. Which would be the most effective phrasing of main points in an outline?
    A.   I. I will explain the problem of drugs.
           II. I will tell what's wrong with our current approach.
           III. I will offer a better solution.

B.　I. Is there a drug problem?

　　II. What has been tried?

　　III. What shall we do about it?

*C　I. Our country has a serious drug problem.

　　II. Our country's efforts to solve the drug problem have failed to get at the causes.

　　III. Our country needs a more comprehensive and fully funded program to deal with drugs.

D.　I. Drug use is on the rise.

　　II. When we have tried governmental programs in the past they have been too oriented toward the small time drug dealers.

　　III. New legislation and better education: these are the ways to stop drug usage once and for all.

E.　I. The scope of the drug problem

　　II. The causes of the drug problem

　　III. The solution to the drug problem　　　　　　　　　　　　　　　　[11b,c]

10.　Your outline so far reflects the following format:

　　I.

　　　A.

　　　　1.

　　　　　a.

What comes next?

　A. II.

　B. B.

　C. 2.

*D. b.

　E. None of the above　　　　　　　　　　　　　　　　　　　　　　[11a.3]

Essay and Short Answer Questions

11.　Write a brief paragraph explaining what is wrong with the following outline of one point of a speech. Include at least three separate reasons.

　　I. Things citizens are concerned about in our city

　　　A. Crime is a concern

　　　　1. Gangs

　　　B. Traffic is a concern

　　　　1. During commuter time

　　　　2. Lack of parking

　　　C. Pollution is a concern

　　　　a. from buses

　　　　b. from cars　　　　　　　　　　　　　　　　　　　　　　[11a–d]

12.　The thesis statement, _____, and at least the first level of subordination should be phrased as declarative statements.　　　　　　　　　　　　　　　　　　[11b]

13.　Each symbol in an outline should designate _____ point(s).　　　　[11a.4]

14.　Describe some of the differences between a topical outline and a formal, conventional outline.　　[11b]

15. Why is it important to "phrase main points and subpoints in clear, effective, and parallel language?"[11d]

16. Provide an example of clear, effective and parallel main points for the following thesis statement: "Physical and verbal abuse are two of the many types of child abuse." [11d]

17. The following main points are worded incorrectly. Rephrase them for coherency. [11b]
    What are the causes of crime?
    History of the feminist movement in the US.
    Buying a house will have tax advantages. You will also build equity. Ownership is fun and fosters pride.

18. What does it mean to "phrase main points and subpoints in clear, effective, and parallel language?" Provide an example. [11d]

Chapter 12: Transitions

True/False Questions

T* F   1. Transitions are more important in speaking than in writing. [12]

T   F* 2. "So", "since," "thus" are examples of chronological transition words. [12a]

T* F   3. Transitions can be internal summaries or internal previews that link main points. [12b]

T* F   4. A speaker should not use the phrase, "In summary," anywhere but in the conclusion. [12b]

T* F   5. A speaker's transitions should illuminate the basic organizational structure of the speech. [12a]

Multiple Choice Questions

6. Transitional words like "but," "though," and "however," show what sort of relationship among the points being linked?
    A. Chronological
    B. Cause-effect
    C. Part to whole
    D. Equality
    *E. Opposition [12a]

7. "In discussing the first problem, America's deteriorating public works system, we shall deal first with our streets and highways, second with our bridges, and third with our water systems." This sentence is an example of a(n):
    A. Internal Summary
    *B. Internal Preview
    C. Introduction
    D. External Summary
    E. None of the above [12b]

Essay and Short Answer Questions

8.   Write a transitional phrase a speaker could use when moving from main point I to main point II.

     I.   The amount of violence on the Jerry Springer talk show has increased over the last 5 years.

Transition: _____

     II. The FCC should ban violence on the Jerry Springer show.   [12b]

9.   Write an internal preview and an internal summary on the following speech on animal cruelty. Write out exactly how you could phrase them.

     I.   Circus animals are often beaten into submission.

          A.   Elephants are guided to their proper destinations with sharp hooks (Owen, 1993)

          B.   Bears are often beaten with steel rods until they dance (Owen, 1993).

          C.   Chimpanzees endure shocks from an electric prod until they ride bikes and turn somersaults on command (Owen, 1993)

Transition: _____

     II. Circus animals' basic needs are not met.

          A.   Most of the animals at a circus are malnourished.

          B.   Many of the animals are dehydrated.   [12b]

10.   Briefly describe why transitions are so important.   [12]

Chapter 13: Introductions

True/False Questions

T   F*   1. Each of the three parts of your introduction should stand out as a clear and separate step.   [13e]

T   F*   2. Introductions, to be effective, often take up to 30% of the entire speech.   [13e]

T   F*   3. In an introduction, begin with "Before I start . . ." if you have something to say before your speech.   [13e]

T*   F   4. An attention getter should be consistent with your personality and the situation.   [13b]

T*   F   5. The Psychological orientation has two parts: establishing a good relationship with the listeners and interesting them in what you have to say.   [13c]

T*   F   6. It is not necessary to tell an audience how important the topic is if the audience is already angry and informed on the subject.   [13c,d]

T*   F   7 In addition to combining parts of the introduction, it is often appropriate to omit steps altogether.   [13e]

T   F*   8. The introduction is so important to the overall success of the speech, speakers should read it to their audiences.   [13f]

Multiple Choice Questions

9.   Which of the following is *not* recommended as part of the psychological orientation phase of an introduction?
      A. Referring to the setting or occasion
      *B. Previewing your main points
      C. Building common ground
      D. Flattering the audience
      E. Using humor   [13c]

10.   Which of the following is *not* a function of the logical orientation phase of an introduction?
      A. Establishing a context for your speech
      B. Orienting the audience to your approach to the topic
      *C. Establishing rapport with the audience
      D. Defining unfamiliar terms
      E. Setting a historical framework   [13d]

11.   Which of the following is *not* an introduction pitfall?
      A. Using familiar phrases like "Unaccustomed as I am to public speaking"
      B. Beginning your speech with an apology for not being as prepared as you'd like
      C. Starting off with a quotation that keeps the audience guessing where the quotation ends and your words begin
      *D. Using a straightforward conversational approach to get the attention of the audience
      E. All of the above are introduction pitfalls   [13f]

12.   The introduction should be _____ percent of your speaking time.
      A. 1-5%
      B. 5-10%
      *C. 10-15%
      D. 15-20%
      E. The amount of time a speaker spends on the introduction depends on the speech topic.   [13e]

13.   Which of the following statements most effectively fulfills the psychological orientation function of an introduction on a speech about the price of gasoline?
      A. Gas prices have continued to rise since the year 2000.
      *B. The rising cost of gasoline affects all of us.
      C. Gasoline: The effects of high prices.
      D. People who buy sport utility vehicles contribute to the high gas prices.   [13c]

Essay and Short Answer Questions

14.   Discuss the two functions of the psychological orientation step of an introduction and give at least three examples of specific techniques a speaker could use in this phase of a speech.   [13c]

15.   What two techniques could a speaker use in the attention getter phase of the speech?   [13b]

16. How would you motivate a group of teenagers to listen further to your speech on the advantages and disadvantages of buying products on the Internet? How about a group of senior citizens? [13c]

17. Describe three introduction pitfalls speakers should avoid. [13f]

18. Why is it so important to establish your credibility in the introduction? [13c.1]

19. What is the "logical orientation"? Why should the introduction of a speech include this step? [13d]

20. Evaluate the following introduction based on the guidelines for an effective introduction described in your text.
Every day thousands of animals are literally placed on what could be called stages and forced to perform for people who receive pleasure from watching this cruelty. I have always loved animals and have likewise enjoyed watching them at zoos, circuses, theme parks and on television. That is, until I found out the real story about what happens to those cute animals. Today I will talk about why animal exploitation should be banned. I will show you why the exploitation of animals is wrong. I will show you that the cruel treatment of these animals needs to be stopped, and that this unethical treatment is a big moneymaker. [13]

21. Evaluate the following introduction based on the guidelines for an effective introduction described in your text.
"The greatest thing in this world is not so much where we are, but in what direction we are moving." (O.W. Holmes). All of us in this room are moving on the right path as we all come to this school not only to fulfill requirements in our majors but also to enhance our knowledge. What can be more important than to learn about the most beneficial part of our body—the nervous system? I am sure most of you must think that this is a boring topic because that is what I thought one year ago. My views changed though when in an animal biology class I learned about the importance of the nervous system in our daily lives. First, I will share with you some of the functions that the nervous system performs in controlling our body. Second, I will share with you the structure and working of the neurons which are the basic units of the nervous system and how these neurons connect to all of our body parts. The nervous system is the main control center of the body and communicates with the body through neurons. [13]

22. Briefly describe how you would go about building a positive relationship on the following topic: A group of women about the need for reducing the dependence on cosmetics to build self esteem. [13c.1&.2]

23. Describe one risk and one benefit of telling a joke as an attention getter. [13b]

24. How would you motivate the following audiences to listen further to your speech? [13c.2]
Dog owners about the increase in dog mauling incidents
A moms group on the benefits of using the Internet to buy groceries
A group of new parents on the importance of having their children immunized
Senior citizens on the benefits of on-line banking

Chapter 14: Conclusions

True/False Questions

T   F*   1. A speaker should always say "thank you" at the end of a speech.   [14c]

T*   F   2. Your conclusion should be carefully planned because audiences are most likely to remember what they hear last.   [14]

T   F*   3. Arguments and information that are not covered in the body of your speech should be introduced in the conclusion.   [14d]

T*   F   4. Providing logical closure means summarizing the main ideas of the speech.   [14a.1]

T   F*   5. It is not necessary to summarize the main ideas of your speech unless your speech is more than 15 minutes long.   [14a.1]

T*   F   6. It is just as important to plan your last sentence as it is your first.   [14c]

T*   F   7. You should avoid ending your speech with an apology.   [14d]

T*   F   8. Part of the psychological wrap-up of a speech can be a direct appeal to your audience.   [14b.2]

T   F*   9. It is not wise to refer back to your attention getter during the conclusion of your speech.   [14c]

Multiple Choice Questions

10. In order of occurrence, the proper conclusion will have
    A. Psychological closure, logical closure, clincher
    B. Psychological closure, motivational appeal, clincher
    C. Logical closure, attention getter, clincher
  *D. Logical closure, psychological closure, clincher
    E. Summary, logical closure, clincher   [14]

11. Which of the following is *not* recommended for use as a clincher?
  *A. A summary of your key ideas
    B. A tie-back to the introduction
    C. A quotation
    D. A proverb
    E. A snatch of poetry   [14c]

12. Which of the following is *not* a conclusion pitfall?
  *A. Using the phrase "in summary" or "in conclusion"
    B. Using a style or mood different from the tenor of the speech
    C. Ending with an apology for taking the audience's time
    D. Introducing a new idea to enlighten the audience
    E. Trailing off so the audience knows you are through   [14d]

Essay and Short Answer Questions

13.   Describe three conclusion pitfalls speakers should avoid.   [14d]

14.   Why is it so important to provide a psychological closure?   [14b]

15.   What is the "logical closure"? Why should the conclusion of a speech include this step?   [14a.1]

16.   Evaluate the following clincher of a conclusion based on the guidelines presented in your text.
       Like a Chinese Proverb says, "A journey of a thousand miles starts with a single step." In order for
       society to get things done right, it must start with one single person. So let that one person be you. Vote
       for the legalization of marijuana for medicinal purposes.   [14c]

17.   Evaluate the following conclusion based on the guidelines presented in your text.
       Today I have proved that cigarettes are addictive and affect both smokers and non-smokers. I have also
       provided what I believe to be a reasonable solution to this problem, to ban smoking in *all* public places. I
       am sure that none of you want to see a loved one lying in a hospital bed with tubes all over his or her
       body. I urge you to write letters to the Governor asking him to sign the bill banning smoking in *all*
       public places. Let's do our part in saving the millions of innocent lives whom are forced to breathe smoke
       filled air. Remember, "we cannot direct the wind. . . But we can adjust the sails."   [14]

18.   Compare and contrast logical and psychological closure as tasks of a speech conclusion. What do the two
       steps have in common? How do they differ?   [14a,b]

19.   Describe how you can let your audience know you have come to the conclusion of your speech, both
       verbally, and nonverbally.   [14c]

20.   Suppose you are trying to persuade a group of citizens that there needs to be bathrooms in the vicinity of
       all city parks. What kind of direct appeal could you make to them during your conclusion?   [14b.2]

Chapter 15: Supporting Materials

True/False Questions

T   F*   1. Hypothetical examples can serve to amplify, clarify, or prove a point.   [15b.2]

T*   F   2. Generally, it is a good idea to make frequent use of examples.   [15b]

T   F*   3. Rather than building your credibility, citing sources during your speech can be distracting and is
               often unnecessary.   [15e]

T   F*   4. Speakers should always use as many statistics as possible.   [15c]

T   F*   5. It is not necessary to evaluate the credibility of the authorities you cite when you use testimony
               as proof.   [15d.1]

T*   F   6. A person does not have to be famous to be an authority.   [15d.1]

T   F*   7. The etymological definition is known as genus-species or dictionary definition.   [15a.2]

Multiple Choice Questions

8.   The validity of statistical evidence can be checked by applying the following tests *except* for
     A. Who collected the data?
     B. Why was the data collected?
     C. When was the data collected?
     *D. How much of the data was used?
     E. How was the data collected?   [15c.1]

9.   Which of the following is *not* a fallacy involving statistics?
     A. The fallacy of the average
     B. The fallacy of the unknown base
     C. The fallacy of the atypical time frame
     D. The fallacy of the arbitrary time frame
     *E. The fallacy of the variance   [15c.2]

10.   General Marlatt of the Joint Chiefs of Staff states that diplomatic solutions have failed in western Africa and that military intervention is necessary. Which criterion of adequate testimony is most likely to be violated?
     A. Does the authority have access to the necessary information?
     B. Is the authority qualified to interpret the data?
     C. Is the person an acknowledged expert on this subject?
     *D. Is the person free of bias and self interest?
     E. All of the above   [15d.2]

11.   Paste is what you get when you mix flour and water. This is an example of what sort of definition?
     *A. Operational definition
     B. Definition by negation
     C. Definition by example
     D. Etymological definition
     E. None of the above   [15a]

12.   Speakers should test the credibility of the authorities they quote by asking the following questions:
     A. Does the authority have access to the necessary information?
     B. Is the authority qualified to interpret data?
     C. Is the person acknowledged as an expert on this subject?
     D. Is the authority figure free of bias and self-interest?
     *E. All of the above should be considered.   [15c]

13.   Definition by _____ is useful for controversial or vague terms where a choice must be made among plausible alternatives.
     *A. authority
     B. example
     C. negation
     D. history   [15a.5]

Essay and Short Answer Questions

14. Select a simple point you might want to develop in a speech. Show how you could support it by a factual example and a hypothetical example. [15b]

15. Suppose a speaker said that each year 20,000 to 40,000 qualified high school graduates were unable to attend college due to financial reasons. What specific questions would you ask to determine the validity of that evidence? [15c.1]

16. Choose one of these terms and define it at least four different ways. Label the four different definitions.
Credibility
Democracy
Leisure time [15a]

17. What additional information would you need before accepting the following statistical evidence?
"Two out of three dentists recommend Colgate toothpaste."
"Laura Bush has a 85% approval rating."
"A high percentage of licensed drivers has driven while under the influence of alcohol." [15c.1–.3]

18. What do the authors of the text mean when they write, "speakers should use a variety of lead-ins for stylistic effectiveness" [15e.2]

19. What is the difference between factual and hypothetical examples? What are the merits and limitations of each? [15b.1&.2]

20. Why do the authors of your text suggest that you "make frequent use of examples"? [15b]

21. What guidelines should a speaker use when incorporating or using statistics in his/her speech? [15c]

22. When and how should a speaker draw on testimony from authorities? [15d]

Matching

23.

A. Logical definition
B. Etymological or historical definition
C. Operational definition
D. Definition by negation
E. Definition from authority
F. Definition by example

1. The American Medical Association classifies angioplasty as a surgical procedure.
2. Angioplasty is a medical procedure used to clear blocked arteries.
3. Remember me talking about that procedure my Uncle Edward had? That's angioplasty.
4. Angioplasty involves inserting a small deflated balloon into the artery and inflating the balloon, thus pressing plaque to the walls of the artery and allowing for the free flow of blood.
5. Although angioplasty is a surgical procedure, it is not the same type of surgery as a heart bypass procedure.

6. Angio is derived from the Greek and refers to blood vessel. Plasty refers to surgery. Therefore, angioplasty can be loosely understood as blood vessel surgery.

*A-2, B-6, C-4, D-5, E-1, F-3   [15a]

Chapter 16: Reasoning

True/False Questions

T   F*   1. A speaker using induction is trying to lead an audience to a conclusion by demonstrating relationships between established premises.   [16b,c]

T   F*   2. When making a deductive argument, if A follows B, then B also follows A.   [16f.8]

T   F*   3. A figurative analogy can often be a more powerful form of reasoning than a literal analogy.   [16e.2]

T   F*   4. My sister is a lousy driver, which leads me to believe that most women are lousy drivers. This is an example of a semantic fallacy.   [16f.6]

T*   F   5. The president of a company was asked whether her decision to implement mandatory drug testing for all employees was in the company's best interest. She replied, "Anything I do is in the company's best interest." This is an example of circular reasoning.   [16f.5]

Multiple Choice Questions

6. What type of reasoning would you be using when your argument consists of combining a series of observations to lead to a probable conclusion?
   A. Causal reasoning
   B. Deductive reasoning
   *C. Inductive reasoning
   D. Reasoning by analogy
   E. None of the above   [16b]

7. One would be using a deductive pattern of reasoning when
   A. The argument consists of combining a series of observations to lead to a probable conclusion
   *B. The argument consists of demonstrating how the relationship of established premises lead to a necessary conclusion
   C. The argument consists of demonstrating how one event results from another
   D. The argument consists of drawing conclusions about unknown events based on what one knows about similar events
   E. Both B and D   [16c]

8. To say that the dockworkers' recent wage demands are the cause of inflation is to commit which sort of oversimplification?
   A. Ignoring multiple causation
   B. Overlooking cause and effect chaining
   C. Failing to distinguish between one-time causes and on-going causes

      *D. All of the above

      E. None of the above   [16d.2]

9.   To say that a proposed bill should be defeated because its sponsor has a drinking problem is an example of which fallacy?

      A. Setting up a straw figure

      B. Hasty generalization

      C. Extending an argument to the absurd

      D. Faulty reversal of an if-then statement

      *E. None of the above   [16f]

10.   "Your country, love it or leave it" is an example of

      A. Confusing sequence with cause

      *B. False dichotomy

      C. Circular reasoning

      D. Attacking the person rather than the argument

      E. None of the above   [16f.7]

11.   A speaker wants to challenge the statement that the social and intellectual development of children is harmed when both parents work outside the home. Which of the following would discredit that causal reasoning?

      A. Examples of children who are doing well overall while having working parents

      B. Examples of children who are having problems and have a parent at home full time

      C. Statistics that show no correlation between hours worked by parents and developmental level of children

      *D. All of the above

      E. None of the above   [16d]

Essay and Short Answer Questions

12.   Identify and explain the four different forms of reasoning. Give an example of how each type of reasoning might be used with health as the topic.   [16]

13.   Select a causal claim made by one of your classmates in the round of persuasive speeches. Analyze the validity of that claim using criteria from chapter **16**.   [16d.1]

14.   Identify and explain three reasoning fallacies. Use original examples (i.e., not from text, lectures, exams) to illustrate.   [16f]

15.   The following conclusions could have been reached inductively or deductively. Briefly lay out an inductive and deductive argument that leads to each.

      Children watch too much violence on television.

      The Catholic church should allow women to become priests.

      The United States should get out of the United Nations.   [16b,c]

16. Using the guidelines presented in your text, explain two ways you might disprove the following causal assertions.

    Students who attend class regularly receive better grades than students who don't.

    Lack of technology in classrooms has led to computer illiterate students. [16d]

17. Identify the fallacy or fallacies in each statement.

    All talk shows should be banned. Shortly after the airing of a show on surprises, one of the guests on the Jenny Jones talk shows killed another guest.

    Anyone who doesn't support gun control laws advocates violence. [16f.1–.10]

Chapter 17: Language and Style

True/False Questions

T   *F   1. Language comes into the speaking process after you have fully thought out your ideas and are ready to put them into an effective speech style. [17]

*T   F   2. Spoken language has features that make it more memorable than written language. [17a]

T   *F   3. Although what people think about and how they express their thoughts varies from culture to culture, the way people think appears to be universal. [17]

T   *F   4. Most nonstandard language is substandard and should be corrected to be in line with the dominant ways of speaking. [17c.3]

T*   F   5. The phrase, "If I've told you once, I've told you a million times," is an example of hyperbole. [17d.2]

T   F*   6. Because your listeners are a captive audience, it really doesn't matter if you have a tendency to be a bit wordy. [17b.3]

T*   F   7. There is no standard style to use in speaking. Different audiences and topics require different approaches. [17c]

T*   F   8. Oral style differs from written style in that it uses shorter sentences. [17a]

T*   F   9. There is no standard style to use in speaking; Thus, different audiences and topics require different approaches. [17c]

T   F*   10. It is never appropriate to use jargon or slang in a speech. [17c.2]

T*   F   11. Personification is a stylistic device which brings objects or ideas to life by imbuing them with qualities of human beings. [17d.2]

T*   F   12. A speaker is said to be using hyperbole when she deliberately overstates a point in a way that is more fanciful than misleading. [17d.2]

T   F* 13. The device of saying the same sound in a sustained sequence is called antithesis. [17d.2]

T   F* 14. There is no difference between oral and written style. [17a]

Multiple Choice Questions

15. Oral style differs from written style in that it
    A. Is less redundant
    *B. Uses shorter sentences
    C. Uses fewer personal pronouns
    D. Uses fewer contractions
    E. All of the above [17a]

16. "It has been argued that when we are in a crisis condition, we should bite the bullet and swallow our medicine." This sentence violates which principle of stylistic clarity?
    A. Be precise
    B. Be economical
    C. Keep figurative language unmuddled
    D. Use specific and concrete language
    *E. All of the above [17b]

17. The use of the generic "he" or "man"
    A. Is an example of inclusive language
    B. Is clearly understood by educated people to refer to all human beings
    *C. Runs the risk of being distracting or offensive to contemporary audiences
    D. Is recommended by your authors
    E. Is a definite sign of sexism in a speaker [17c.4]

18. The respectful and inclusive way to refer to members of non-dominant racial and ethnic groups is
    A. As people of color
    B. As minorities
    *C. To learn how they wish to be designated
    D. As multicultural
    E. By no title that sets them apart from European Americans [17c.4]

Essay and Short Answer Questions

19. Describe a serious social problem using at least four different stylistic devices. Label each in the margin. [17d.2]

20. Explain what is meant by the statement, "Language not only reflects culture but shapes society." Use specific examples to clarify your answer. [17]

21. List some of the positive features of oral expression that set it apart from written forms of expression. [17a]

22. As a public speaker how can you "strive for clarity in your language"? [17b.1–.3]

23. Briefly describe why it is so important to use "vivid and varied language". [17d]

24. Describe three ways a public speaker can make his/her language more vivid. [17d.1–.3]

25. Using your own example, illustrate the difference between the following stylistic devices: repetitive language and alliteration. [17d.2]

26. Use at least two difference stylistic devices to enliven each of the following phrases:
Attendance is required
Violence is a big problem [17d.2]

Chapter 18: Attention and Interest

True/False Questions

T   F*   1. Your text suggests that you should keep your audience involved, but not by using names of people in your audience. [18a.2]

T*   F   2. Incorporating techniques of effective storytelling is one way to convert momentary attention to a more sustained interest in your topic. [18b.2]

T*   F   3. A common misconception is that once you have grabbed your listeners' attention with a snappy introduction, it is yours until you relinquish it at the end of the speech. [18a]

T*   F   4. When integrating humor into your speech you should make sure it is appropriate to your personality and to the situation. [18a.4]

T*   F   5. Everyone can be funny, but not everyone should tell jokes. [18c.3]

Multiple Choice Questions

6. Which of the following is *not* an attention factor?
   A. Conflict
   B. The Vital
   C. Reality
   *D. Analogy
   E. Proximity [18a]

7. Being specific and concrete refers to which attention factor?
   A. The Vital
   *B. Reality
   C. Conflict
   D. Novelty
   E. Proximity [18a]

8. "Our teacher mentioned that she drives a Volvo. Mark says that he bought new French sunglasses, and Lakeisha always comes to class with a bottle of Perrier. Don't we believe in supporting our own US businesses?" This statement best illustrates
   *A. Proximity, reality, and conflict
   B. Novelty, reality, and humor
   C. Proximity, novelty, and The Vital
   D. Suspense, The Vital, and reality
   E. Activity, humor, and suspense   [18a]

Essay and Short Answer Questions

9. Write a paragraph discussing the general topic of art. Take any approach to this topic but make sure to integrate and label five different attention factors.   [18a]

10. A friend of yours has mentioned that she would like her speech to be really funny. Using the guidelines presented in your text, what suggestions would you offer your friend?   [18c.1–.4]

11. What is one way a speaker can convert attention to interest?   [18b.1&.2]

12. One way to maintain the attention and interest of your audience is to keep the energy level up throughout your speech. What are two ways you can keep the energy level up?   [18a.3]

Chapter 19: Credibility

True/False Questions

T*   F   1. Presenting a balanced view of pros and cons can add to your image of trustworthiness.   [19c.4]

T   F*   2. Some people have been blessed (i.e., born) with a high degree of credibility that allows them to be successful in any public speaking situation.   [19]

T   F*   3. Establishing credibility during your speech is more important than your perceived credibility prior to your speech.   [19b,c]

T   F*   4. Your text suggests that competency is the most important dimension of credibility.   [19]

T*   F   5. Speakers should not be reluctant to provide information about their qualifications in their speech.   [19c.1]

T*   F   6. Effective delivery during your speech can increase your credibility.   [19d]

T   F*   7. You can bolster your credibility on the dimension of competence by telling your listeners how much money you've donated to causes they support.   [19c.1]

T*   F   8. Credibility is that combination of perceived qualities that makes listeners predisposed to believe you.   [19]

Multiple Choice Questions

9. When you mention that you are a CPA in your speech on taxes, you are attempting to bolster your credibility on the dimension of
    *A. Competence
    B. Trustworthiness
    C. Concern
    D. Dynamism
    E. All of the above   [19c.1]

10. Being well-organized and composed during your speech refers to which dimension of credibility?
    A. Dynamism
    *B. Competence
    C. Trustworthiness
    D. Likeability
    E. Concern   [19a.1]

11. A speaker who does not acknowledge the limitations of her data and opinions lacks which dimension of credibility?
    A. Dynamism
    B. Competence
    *C. Trustworthiness
    D. Likeability
    E. Concern   [19a.3]

12. A speaker who stresses the audience's needs throughout his speech and whose delivery is warm and friendly, will most likely be perceived as a speaker with this quality:
    A. Dynamism
    B. Competence
    C. Trustworthiness
    D. Likeability
    *E. Concern   [19a.2]

13. A speaker can build credibility prior to her speech by:
    A. Helping the person introducing her to set a favorable tone
    B. Providing the contact person with adequate information about her qualifications
    C. Being aware of her image in all dealings with the group prior to the speech
    *D. All of the above are ways a speaker can build credibility   [19b]

Essay and Short Answer Questions

14. Discuss how you can enhance your credibility (indicate dimensions) through speech content and delivery.   [19]

15. Describe two topics on which you have a high degree of credibility and two topics on which you would have to work very hard to establish credibility.   [19a]

16.   How will you build your credibility prior to your informative and/or persuasive speeches?   [19b]

17.   Name three ways a speaker can bolster his/her credibility through speech content.   [19c]

18.   Evaluate President George W. Bush's credibility as high, medium or low on competence, concern, trustworthiness, and dynamism. Discuss your evaluation.   [19a]

19.   Describe a public figure who you believe is competent, concerned, and trustworthy, but whose image suffers due to lack of dynamism.   [19a]

21.   Name a public figure who you believe is dynamic, but whose image suffers due to lack of competence, concern, and trustworthiness.   [19a.1–.4]

Chapter 20: Motivational Appeals

True/False Questions

T   F*   1. Strong emotional appeals are usually more effective than moderate appeals.   [20a]

T   F*   2. Negative emotions, particularly fear appeals, are generally more effective than using positive emotions as motivators.   [20a]

T*   F   3. People will generally seek to satisfy their need for security before satisfying their need for status.   [20b]

T   F*   4. When any two values come into conflict, the one that is an authority value will take precedence.   [20c.2]

T*   F   5. Your text suggests that extreme emotional appeals can often be unethical as well as ineffective.   [20d]

T*   F   6. Culture has a strong influence, shaping values through families, schools, media and peers.   [20c.1]

T*   F   7. When adding emotion to your speech, remember the old adage, "although some is good, more is not always better."   [20a]

T*   F   8. It is important to identify and relate to the core values of your audience.   [20c.2]

T   F*   9. A personal belief that a particular thing is basically good or bad is called an opinion.   [20c]

Multiple Choice Questions

10.   Need for self-actualization refers to the following *except* for
        A. Personal growth
        *B. Status
        C. Self awareness
        D. Creativity

      E. Knowledge   [20b]

11. A personal belief that a particular thing is basically good or bad is called
    A. A need
    B. An emotion
    C. An opinion
    *D. A value
    E. A cultural creed   [20c]

12. Values that are influenced by and shared with groups and individuals most significant to a person are called
    A. Peripheral values
    B. Integral values
    *C. Authority values
    D. Core values
    E. None of the above   [20c.2]

13. The most useful information for a speaker to have about an audience member's values would be
    A. A list of that person's values
    *B. An understanding of that person's priorities among competing values
    C. A list of the dominant values of the culture as a whole
    D. A list of the groups the individual belongs to
    E. A list of the person's best friends and their core values   [20c.3]

14. Relate your speech to the values of your listeners by
    A. Incorporating appeals to the general values of the culture
    B. Identifying and relating to the core values of your audience
    C. Forging strong, logical links between the issues of your speech and the values of the audience
    D. Using motivational appeals to broaden your listeners' sense of history and community
    *E. All of the above   [20c.3]

Essay and Short Answer Questions

15. Assume that you are a president of a university and you are giving a speech to a group of high school students. How might you appeal to needs and values in order to persuade your audience to attend your university?   [20]

16. Under what conditions would motivational appeals be unethical, according to the text? List at least three of these conditions and provide original examples of how speakers might misuse appeals.   [20d]

17. List four of the values Ball-Rokeach *et al.* identified as dominant in contemporary US culture. Identify one controversial issue where two of these might come in direct conflict.   [20c.1]

18. What needs and values of the students in your speech class would you appeal to if you were trying to persuade them to advocate for gun control laws?   [20c]

19.   Describe the differences among the following terms: core values, authority values, peripheral values.

[20c.2]

20.   Which of Maslow's needs are appealed to in the following examples?
       Women should carry either a can of mace or a gun for protection
       All the popular students shop at Target
       Any employee who refuses to cross the picket line will be fired   [20b]

Chapter 21: Informative Strategies

True/False Questions

T*   F   1. To explain a concept clearly, begin with simple examples and move toward more complex ones.

[21a.3]

T   F*   2. The first thing listeners do when confronted with information overload is to tune out.   [21a.1]

T*   F   3. Our knowledge of information processing suggests that most people can comprehend between five and nine points in one session.   [21a.1]

T   F*   4. If a point is very important a speaker should use another channel instead of the spoken word to get it across.   [21b.5]

T*   F   5. A speaker's message will be more clear if he/she sends it through several channels.   [21b.5]

T   F*   6. According to the authors of your text, being repetitive and/or redundant will not help the audience remember what they hear, it will only aggravate them.   [21b.6]

T*   F   7. Signposts are an effective way to remind the audience of where you are going and where you have been.   [21b.1]

T   F*   8. Enumeration is a word formed from the first letters of a series of words, and that can be pronounced like the word.   [21b.1]

T*   F   9. A speaker's message will be more clear if she sends it through several channels.   [21b.4]

Multiple Choice Questions

10.   "So in looking at the A, B, Cs of CPR we've learned about clearing airways, and checking for breathing. That's A and B, now let's go on to C."
       This illustrates which principle(s) of clear explanation?
       A. Use emphasis cues
       *B. Use signposts
       C. Use examples
       D. Use analogies
       E. All of the above

[21b]

11. "Let me say this again. It's *so* important. First frame the shot, second, focus the camera, then and only then, snap the picture. Don't put the cart before the horse."
     Which principle(s) of clear explanation are present?
     A. Use enumeration
     B. Use analogies
     C. Use emphasis cues
     D. Use repetition
     *E. All of the above   [21b]

12. Which of the following does *not* serve as an organizer to enhance comprehension?
     A. Acronyms
     B. Previews
     C. Summaries
     *D. Extended exposition
     E. Slogans and catchwords   [21b]

13. Which of the following is *not* a way to make information more easily understood?
     A. Avoid information overload
     B. Move from the familiar to the unfamiliar
     C. Provide a conceptual framework
     *D. Use singular channels and modes
     E. Move from the simple to the complex   [21a]

14. "This is a very important point" is an example of
     *A. An emphasis cue
     B. An introduction
     C. Enumeration
     D. An attention getter
     E. A signpost   [21b]

Essay and Short Answer Questions

15. Choose one of these topics and explain it in a couple of paragraphs using at least five different techniques of clear explanation. Label each in parentheses.
     Cooking dinner for guests
     Changing the oil on a car
     Balancing a checkbook   [21b]

16. Why is it so important to "base your speech on an understanding of how people acquire, process, and retain information"? Provide three specific reasons to justify your response.   [21a]

17. Your instructor has warned you about overloading your audience with too much information. What are some ways you as a speaker can prevent this from happening during your speech?   [21a.1]

18. How might you link the familiar and the unfamiliar when speaking to a group of male politicians about increasing health care coverage to include birth control?   [21a.4]

19.   What role should repetition and redundancy play in informative speaking?   [21b.6]

Chapter 22: Persuasive Strategies

True/False Questions

T   F*   1. A persuasive speech has four possible goals: adoption, continuance, avoidance, and deterrence.

[22a]

T   F*   2. Drawing on stock issues tends to limit your ability to analyze a speech topic.   [22b.2]

T   F*   3. Arranging your arguments from strongest to weakest employs the primacy principle and is called the climax format.   [22e]

T*   F   4. To argue a proposition of policy, you will probably also have to argue propositions of fact and propositions of value.   [22b.1]

T   F*   5. It is best to begin a persuasive speech by addressing counter arguments.   [22f.2]

T*   F   6. The proposition, "The Roth IRA (individual retirement account) is not tax deductible" is an example of a proposition of fact.   [22b.1]

T   F*   7. The proposition, "Rap music promotes violence" is a proposition of policy.   [22b.1]

T*   F   8. The proposition, "'Reality TV' is a bad influence on teenagers" is a proposition of value. [22b.1]

T*   F   9. As a general rule, place your strongest points first or last.   [22e]

T*   F   10. Stressing common ground is especially important if you are speaking to an unfavorable audience.   [22c.3]

T   F*   11. Using stock issues will not help you analyze your persuasive topic.   [22b.2]

Multiple Choice Questions

12.   A thesis statement in a persuasive speech should take the form of a proposition that requires proof. All of the following are such propositions *except*
    A. Proposition of value
    B. Proposition of fact
    C. Proposition of policy
    *D. Proposition of inference
    E. None of the above   [22b.1]

13.   "The federal government should reduce spending for national defense" is an example of a proposition of
    A. Inference
    B. Value
    *C. Policy
    D. Fact

E. None of the above [22b.1]

14. Which of the following is a proposition of policy?
    A. It is unethical to advertise cigarettes on billboards within two miles of an elementary or junior high school
    *B. American College should lower fees for undergraduate students
    C. The death penalty is immoral
    D. Television violence leads to aggressive behavior in children
    E. All of the above are propositions of policy [22b.1]

15. Which of the following is *not* recommended for dealing with an unfavorable audience?
    A. Use plenty of evidence
    *B. Use plenty of emotional appeals
    C. Stress common ground
    D. Build your credibility
    E. Adjust your purpose to a moderate goal [22c.3]

16. If your audience is favorable, which of the following is *not* a persuasive strategy suggested by your text?
    *A. Use plenty of attention factors
    B. Use emotional appeals to strengthen your listeners' support
    C. Provide specific alternatives for action
    D. Prepare your audience to take your message to others
    E. Get your audience to make a public commitment [22c.1]

17. Which of the following is *not* recommended by your text for use when refuting opposing arguments?
    A. State the opposing view fairly and concisely
    B. State your position on that argument
    C. Document and develop your own position
    *D. Acknowledge the faults in your argument
    E. Summarize the impact of your argument and show how the two positions compare [22f.1]

18. The last step of the motivated sequence is:
    A. Need
    B. Satisfaction
    *C. Action
    D. Visualization
    E. Attention [22d.1]

19. When dealing with counter arguments, a speaker should *not:*
    A. Address the opposing arguments directly, using refutation techniques
    B. Answer counter arguments after developing his/her own position
    *C. Distort the opposing arguments
    D. All of the above should be avoided [22f.1]

Essay and Short Answer Questions

20. Suppose that your topic is the restructuring of educational financing in your county. Briefly explain how either the stock debate issues or the stock problem solving issues could direct your analysis of the topic.

[22b.2]

21. Suppose that you are speaking to a neutral, well-educated audience about a topic which will be very much in the news and upon which you have no special credibility. Outline your basic persuasive strategy and justify your choices.

[22c.2]

22. Write a proposition of fact, value and policy on each of the following general topics:
Lottery
Exercise
Marriage

[22b.1]

23. Provide two suggestions (each) on how to deal with a favorable, neutral, or unfavorable audience.

[22c]

24. Discuss the steps involved in Monroe's Motivated Sequence. Why is this pattern of organization so effective?

[22d.1]

25. Describe the best way(s) for a speaker to deal with opposing arguments.

[22f]

26. How would you change the proposition of policy "Men should be entitled to take 8 weeks of paternity leave" to a proposition of fact?

[22b.1]

Chapter 23: Adapting to Speaking Contexts

True/False Questions

T   F*   1. The same topic delivered in different contexts will elicit similar expectations.

[23a]

T   F*   2. All speaking contexts carry the expectations of a high level of formality.

[23a]

T*   F   3. In monologic situations, it is assumed that a primary speaker will take responsibility for what is talked about.

[23a]

T*   F   4. In dialogic situations, other participants can direct both the topic and form of interaction.

[23a]

T*   F   5. A PSR is a brief, memorable success story.

[23b]

T*   F   6. When participating in a panel or symposium, tailor your individual presentation to the group format.

[23c]

T*   F   7. Generally, an agenda for a meeting or banquet should follow a climactic order.

[23e]

T   F*   8. Acknowledging or celebrating the value of the one being eulogized will only make the family of
       the deceased feel sad.   [23d.2]

Multiple Choice Questions

9.   Which of the following is not one of the three kinds of contexts discussed in your text?
      A. business and professional
      B. civic and political
      C. social and ceremonial
      *D. monologic and dialogic   [23a]

10.   According to your text, a series of short speeches, usually informative, on various aspects of the same
      general topic is called a:
      *A. symposium
      B. panel
      C. forum
      D. debate   [23c]

11.   A _____ is defined, essentially, as a question and answer format.
      A. symposium
      B. panel
      *C. forum
      D. debate   [23c]

12.   A group of experts publicly discussing a topic is using which format?
      A. A symposium
      *B. A panel
      C. A forum
      D. A debate   [23c]

Essay and Short Answer

13.   What is a PSR statement and what is its purpose?   [23b]

14.   What considerations should a project manager make before organizing a group presentation? [23b.2]

15.   What are two typical speaking situations in the civic and political context?   [23c]

16.   Describe the difference between a symposium, a debate, and a forum.   [23c]

17.   You've been asked to present the speaker of the year award at the local toastmasters club. Describe what
      you might include in your speech.   [23d.4]

18.   List four guidelines for preparing a eulogy and briefly explain how you could apply each in a speech
      about your instructor.   [23d.2]

19.   Assume that you have just received a trophy for being voted the most improved speaker in your class.
      Write a one-paragraph acceptance speech that follows the guidelines in the text.   [23d.2]

20. You are hired as a consultant to a local candidate who will be participating in a public debate. List at least five pieces of advice that you would give the candidate. [23c.1]

21. Designate a job you might interview for and write a brief introductory statement that you could make to set the tone for a group interview. [23b.1]

22. Using the guidelines from your text, how should you prepare for a group interview? [23b.1]

Chapter 24: Modes of Delivery

True/False Questions

T   F*   1. When you are an inexperienced, nervous speaker, speaking from a manuscript is the easiest and most effective mode of delivery. [24a]

T*   F   2. Impromptu speaking, as in extemporaneous, manuscript, or memorized speeches, should utilize an organizational framework. [24b.3]

T*   F   3. For most speaking situations use the extemporaneous mode. [24a]

T*   F   4. When delivering a memorized speech the speaker should memorize the structure of the speech before memorizing the speech word for word. [24d.1]

T*   F   5. Speakers should be familiar enough with their manuscript to look and sound like they are speaking extemporaneously. [24c.2]

Multiple Choice Questions

6. Manuscript speaking is most appropriate
    A. For the average classroom speech
    B. For a debate in front of a mixed audience
    *C. When language must be precise or polished
    D. When time limits are flexible
    E. All of the above [24c]

7. When called upon to perform an unexpected speech, which of the following is *not* recommended?
    *A. Apologize for not being prepared
    B. Keep your composure
    C. Select a theme
    D. Select an organizational framework
    E. Plan your first and last sentences [24b]

8. When the President of the United States delivers his state of the union address, what mode of delivery is he most likely using?
    A. Impromptu
    *B. Manuscript
    C. Memorized
    D. Extemporaneous [24c]

9. You will be primarily using which mode of delivery for most of the speeches you will deliver in this speech class?
   A. Impromptu
   B. Manuscript
   C. Memorized
   *D. Extemporaneous   [24a]

10. You are at your best friend's wedding shower when you are asked to say a few words about the bride. What is your mode of delivery?
    *A. Impromptu
    B. Manuscript
    C. Memorized
    D. Extemporaneous   [24b]

11. When preparing for an extemporaneous speech you should first
    *A. Begin with a fully developed outline
    B. Convert your full-sentence outline to a key word or phrase outline
    C. Word the speech
    D. Covert your brief outline to speech notes   [24a]

12. When your instructor delivers a planned and practiced lecture on the importance of public speaking in an electronic age, he/she is most likely using which mode of delivery?
    A. Impromptu
    B. Manuscript
    C. Memorized
    *D. Extemporaneous   [24b]

Essay and Short Answer

13. You are in a department meeting when your boss surprises you by asking you to speak about the new internship program in the accounting department. Reflecting on the guidelines for impromptu speaking, what four steps should you take to cope with this situation?   [24b]

14. Describe the difference between the memorized and manuscript mode of delivery.   [24c,d]

15. Describe the steps you should take when preparing for an extemporaneous speech.   [24a]

16. What should a speaker do if she goes "blank" while delivering her memorized speech?   [24d.5]

Chapter 25: Practice Sessions

True/False Questions

T   F*   1. The final few practice sessions should be used for receiving feedback.   [25b.1–.3]

T   F*   2. Speech notes are essentially the same thing as your speech outline.   [25c]

T* F   3. Mental practice is not a substitute for practicing a speech aloud.   [25f.1]

T*   F   4. When offering a speaker feedback, start with positive comments.   [25a.1]

T*   F   5. Speech notes should consist of keywords and phrases and material that is to be cited directly.

                      [25c.1]

T*   F   6. It is possible for a speaker to over prepare.   [25f.3]

Multiple Choice Questions

7.   Lorena is supposed to deliver a 7-minute informative speech for her class in one week. Although she has researched her topic and practiced her speech, she can't seem to speak for more than 5 minutes. Lorena should probably
   A. Add a lengthy video clip
   B. Duplicate some of her evidence and/or examples
   *C. See if she can develop any of her ideas further
   D. Polish and tighten her language   [25d]

8.   If your speech is too short you should do all of the following except:
   A. Continue researching your topic
   B. Make sure you've proved your points
   *C. Accept the fact that your topic doesn't require a lengthy talk
   D. Check to make sure you aren't being too concise   [25d]

Essay and Short Answer Questions

9.   After practicing your speech several times, you realize that you your informative speech is two minutes too long. What should you do to fit your speech into the time limit?   [25d]

10.   Although you had planned on speaking for only 5 minutes, three of the other speakers haven't showed up and the moderator has asked you if you could extend your talk to 10 minutes. How will you adapt to this situation?   [25d]

11.   Suppose that you had prepared a half-hour speech to present at a business conference and the speaker before you went way overtime. The group still has to catch their planes, so you were left with 10 minutes to speak. What steps would you take?   [25d]

12.   Describe three of the four practice "pitfalls" speakers should avoid.   [25f]

Chapter 26: Vocal Delivery

True/False Questions

T   F*   1. It is essential to eliminate regional and non-native accents to be effective as a speaker.   [26a.4]

T   F*   2. A speaker is well advised to maintain steady rate and vocal pitch.   [26b]

T*   F   3. Vary your vocal delivery for interest and emphasis.   [26]

T   F*   4. Saying "uh," "um" and "err" during your speech is more effective than silently pausing.   [26d.3]

T*   F   5. Practice will make loud speaking more comfortable and natural.   [26a.3]

T*   F   6. Non native speakers of English can increase their intelligibility by prolonging their vowel sounds.   [26a.4]

Multiple Choice Questions

7. Which of the following is *not* a problem of voice quality?
   *A. Articulation
   B. Harshness
   C. Denasality
   D. Hoarseness
   E. Stridency   [26d.1]

8. Which of the following is caused by constriction of the throat, by tension, or by damage to the vocal cords?
   *A. Harshness
   B. Breathiness
   C. Weakness
   D. Nasality
   E. All of the above   [26d.1]

9. When you pronounce a word like "summer" as "thummer" or "this" as "dis" you have an articulation problem known as
   A. Distortion
   B. Addition
   C. Omission
   *D. Substitution
   E. Stuttering   [26d.2]

10. What is the average rate of speaking?
    A. 250 words per minute
    B. 200 words per minute
    C. 175 words per minute
    *D. 150 words per minute
    E. 100 words per minute   [26b.2]

11. To eliminate distracting habits of vocal quality a speaker should
    A. Assess his/her present behavior to quantify the exact frequency of the habit.
    B. Set a specific and realistic goal.
    C. Monitor his/her behavior for progress.
    *D. Do all of the above   [26d]

Essay and Short Answer Questions

12. Your authors say speakers should identify vocalized pauses and other irrelevant sounds/phrases. What do they mean by this, and what are three examples of irrelevant sounds and phrases? [26d.3]

13. How can you check your speaking rate? [26b]

14. The authors of your text offers three ways speakers can reinforce meaning and make their speeches more interesting through vocal variety. What are those three ways? [26b]

15. Explain what your authors mean when they say, "finding a voice is a powerful metaphor for social identity." [26]

16. Why should speakers be cautious of their speaking rate? [26b.2]

Chapter 27: Physical Delivery

True/False Questions

T*   F   1. It is effective to establish eye contact with individual audience members and to maintain it for at least three seconds. [27f]

T*   F   2. Your physical delivery creates a visual effect that compliments the content of your speech. [27]

T   F*   3. It really doesn't matter what you wear when you deliver a speech. [27a]

T*   F   4. Distracting mannerisms fall into two categories: those you have all of the time and those you have only when delivering a speech. [27b]

T*   F   5. Your facial expressions can add one more channel for effective communication. [27g]

T*   F   6. Physical movement during your speech works best during transition points. [27d]

Multiple Choice Questions

7. All of the following can be considered gesture-inhibiting stances *except* for
    A. The bear hug
    B. The flesh wound
    C. The fig leaf
    D. The supplicant
    *E. The golf swing [27e]

8. Tran didn't know what to do with his arms during his speech, so he kept them stiff, his wrist firmly nailed to his pelvis. Which gesture-inhibiting stance is Trang exhibiting?
    A. The bear hug
    B. The flesh wound
    C. The fig leaf

    D. The supplicant

 *E. The ten-hut!   [27e]

9.   Sheila was so nervous during her speech that she continuously wrung her hands. Which gesture-inhibiting stance is she exhibiting?

    A. Happy pockets

    B. The fig leaf

 *C. The Lady Macbeth

    D. The supplicant

    E. The bear hug   [27e]

Essay and Short Answer Questions

10.   Should a speaker be concerned about his/her appearance? Why/why not?   [27a]

11.   When is it advisable to keep movement during your speech to a minimum?   [27d]

12.   Describe three inhibiting stances speakers should avoid.   [27e]

13.   Sprague and Stuart say that distracting mannerisms fall into two categories. List those categories and provide a personal example of each.   [27b]

14.   Why is it important to maintain eye contact with the audience?   [27f]

15.   Your boss has asked you to train a new group of employees on effective presentation/delivery skills. What tips will you give to the new employees?   [27]

Chapter 28: Presentation Aids

True/False Questions

T   F*   1. If you wish to show proportional relationships visually, use line graphs.   [28a.3]

T*   F   2. There are places in a speech where a visual presentation aid can help you make a point more clearly and in a shorter time than if you were to use your spoken words alone.   [28a]

T*   F   3. A presentation aid is best used when you are attempting to explain a complex or technical idea, and when you want to reinforce a particular message.   [28a.1]

T   F*   4. Using clip art in presentation software slides is a simple and effective way to make your message unique.   [28d.3]

T   F*   5. It is not necessary to practice with your presentation aids, just incorporate them on the day of your speech.   [28c.1]

T   F*   6. You should stop talking when you are showing a visual aid.   [28c.4]

T   F*   7. A discrete presentation aid is one that does not challenge or offend your audience.   [28]

Multiple Choice Questions

8. Your text recommends the following when designing slides or transparencies.
   A. Use about three different typefaces for visual variety
   *B. Use lots of white space to keep information uncluttered
   C. Use uppercase titles for key ideas to make them clear
   D. Vary borders and formats to make each transparency distinctive
   E. Both C and D [28b.2]

9. Which of the following is *not* recommended by your text as a guideline for preparing your visual aids?
   A. Make your visual aids large enough to be seen by the entire audience
   B. Design your visual aids for maximum audience impact
   *C. Use all capital letters for headlines or titles to increase readability
   D. Keep visual aids simple and clear
   E. None, all are recommended [28b]

10. When using presentation software to accompany your speech, you should
   A. Keep your text slides simple
   B. Be judicious with clip art
   C. Maintain consistency
   D. Not become secondary to your slides
   *E. Follow all of the above [28d]

Essay and Short Answer Questions

11. How does a discrete presentation aid differ from a continuous aid? [28]

12. Describe two presentation aids you might incorporate into a speech on the topic of hybrid cars. [28a]

13. Describe two ways a speaker can incorporate and introduce presentation aids "so that they blend smoothly into the speech." [28c]

14. Describe two situations when a presentation aid could become a distraction. [28c.5]

15. What are some of the advantages and disadvantages to using presentation software? [28d]

16. Suggest two different presentation aids that might be used for speeches on each of these topics: Adoption, Pet Overpopulation, Increase in Gasoline Prices. [28a]

Chapter 29: Adapting to the Speech Situation

True/False Questions

T F* 1. When you discover your audience is more informed than you expected, your text suggests that you incorporate more definitions and examples. [29a]

T F* 2. If a verbal heckler attacks your character, it is a good idea to deny the accusations so that you do not lose your credibility. [29c.1]

T   F*   3. According to your text, the best strategy for dealing with a nonverbal heckler is to stop your speech and politely ask the person if he or she has a question or comment.   [29c.2]

T*   F   4. Fleeting or low-level distractions during your speech are best dealt with by not acknowledging them.   [29b.2]

T*   F   5. Sometimes distractions can be turned to your purpose by incorporating them into your speech.   [29b.3]

Multiple Choice Questions

6.   If your audience seems bored or restless, you should try to do which of the following?
    *A. Use more concrete examples
    B. Spend extra time on establishing credibility
    C. Insert more abstract materials from your research
    D. Appeal to fair play
    E. All of the above   [29a.1]

7.   If you are not getting the agreement you expected, you should try to do which of the following?
    A. Use more direct references to the audience
    B. Make your delivery more animated
    C. Condense your material and call it a review
    *D. Stress common ground
    E. All of the above   [29a.2]

8.   When your audience seems less informed than you expected, which of the following *is* recommended by your text?
    A. Stress common ground
    B. Use more humor or novelty
    C. Use direct references to the audience
    *D. Delete the more technical materials
    E. Shorten your speech by cutting out subpoints   [29a]

9.   You are speaking to a group of students in a room in the University Union. It is a cold day and you see several audience members shivering. The room temperature is clearly distracting your audience from your speech. There are no custodians in sight, but you know where the thermostat is located. What would your text suggest?
    A. Do not disrupt the flow of your speech! Continue your address and let the audience members be cold
    B. Make a joke out of the situation to bring the audience's attention back to you, then continue
    *C. Quickly ask an audience member to turn on the heat, remind the audience where you were, then continue
    D. Cut your speech short
    E. Have the audience take a ten minute break while you get the room heated   [29b.4]

10.   Which of these is *not* an effective technique to handle a heckler?
    *A. Invite the heckler up to the platform to express his or her position
    B. Build on common ground

    C. Appeal to fair play

    D. Establish a tone of reasonableness

    E. Close off discussion and continue your speech   [29c]

11. You are delivering your speech when you notice a student rolling his eyes, whispering to his neighbor, and fidgeting. What is the best way to deal with this non-verbal heckler?

    A. Appeal to fair play

    B. Establish an image or tone of fairness

   *C. Ignore him

    D. Ask him to leave the room

    E. Build on common ground   [29c.2]

Essay and Short Answer Questions

12. Describe several steps a speaker can take to prevent distractions during his/her speech.   [29b]

13. Provide three suggestions for dealing with verbal and non-verbal hecklers during a speech.   [29c.1&.2]

14. You've been speaking for 2 minutes when you realize your audience is bored and/or restless. Your speech is 15 minutes long. What considerations or adjustments should you make to your speech, if any? [29a.1]

Chapter 30: Answering Questions

True/False Questions

T   F*   1. When asked a direct question the speaker should always give a direct answer first and then proceed to elaborate on or qualify the answer.   [30b]

T*   F   2. Audience questions help a speaker determine what points were unclear.   [30]

T   F*   3. Delivery skills are not important during the question and answer period.   [30]

T*   F   4. Speakers should try to dignify bad questions and turn them into good ones.   [30c.3]

Multiple Choice Questions

5. After hearing Chong's speech on adding vegetarian options to the cafeteria, Marty, the line cook repeatedly asked questions and made irrelevant comments during the question and answer period. Chong is running out of time and needs feedback from other audience members. According to the book, what should he say to Marty?

    A. He should simply state the truth and sternly say that Marty is manipulating the question answer period and therefore needs to refrain from further comments

    B. To avoid appearing rude, he should engage in active listening and continue to focus on Marty

    C. He should ignore Marty and move on

   *D. He should say something like "Thank you. Those are some interesting insights. Maybe we can talk more about them later"

    E. He should just give yes or no answers until Marty stops asking questions.   [30c]

6. Speakers should be prepared to control the question and answer period by dealing with distracting questioners. All of the following are types of distracting questioners *except*
   A. The person who wants to give a speech
   B. The person who wants to have an extended dialogue
   C. The person who wants to pick a fight
   *E. The person who asks a difficult question   [30c]

Essay and Short Answer Questions

7. List and briefly explain three suggestions for managing the question-and-answer period of your speech effectively.   [30a,b,c]

8. Why is it important to come prepared for a question-and-answer period?   [30a]

9. What should you do if you don't know the answer to an audience's question?   [30b]

10. You've delivered a speech on the importance of educating teens about birth control. After your speech, one of your audience members becomes angry and begins attacking you on a personal level. What should you do?   [30c.3]

Rhetorical Analysis Essay Exam

The following is a popular way to have students synthesize their learning from a public speaking class. Select and duplicate a brief speech that illustrates a variety of rhetorical elements.

Rhetorical Analysis Essay Exam

Read the attached speech and respond to these questions. Be as specific as possible and use examples to support your answers.

1. What is the thesis of this speech?
2. What is the *general* purpose of this speech?
3. What is the speaker's *specific* purpose?
4. What is the *organizational pattern* that this speech follows?
5. If you were to outline this speech what would you designate as the *main* points?
6. Describe how the speaker fulfills the three functions of an introduction.
7. Describe how the speaker fulfills the three functions of a conclusion.
8. Identify three different kinds of reasoning found in the speech and lay out the basic structure of each.
9. Identify and briefly explain a fallacy of reasoning you find in the speech.
10. Identify at least two different forms of supporting material you find in the speech.
11. Identify and give examples of two transitional statements.
12. Identify and give examples of two methods this speaker uses to establish credibility.
13. Identify and give examples of three different motivational appeals.
14. Identify and give examples of two stylistic devices or effective techniques of language usage.
15. Identify and give examples of four different attention factors.

Part V
Resource Integration Guide

Handbook Part I: Foundation

Chapter 1: Understanding Speaking

Ideas for Instruction—Print	Ideas for Instruction—Electronic	Print Resources for Students	Electronic Resources for Students
Public Speaking Instructor's Guide to the Opposing Viewpoints Resource Center (OVRC) Includes chapters on Ways to Use OVRC in the Classroom, Suggested Activities, and Resources for Further Research. **The Teaching Assistant's Guide to the Basic Course** This guide covers general teaching and course management topics, as well as specific strategies for communication instruction. **Service Learning in Communication Studies: A Handbook** This book provides guidelines for connecting service-learning work with classroom concepts. **A Guide to the Basic Course for ESL Students** This guide assists the non-native speaker. Features FAQs, helpful URLs, and strategies for accent management and overcoming speech apprehension.	**The Speaker's Handbook Web site** http://communication.wadsworth.com/sprague7 Online access to: Instructor's Resource Manual with Test Bank Sample Speech Outlines InfoTrac® College Edition Resources **CNN Today® Videos: Public Speaking, Volumes I-V** Vol. 2: College and Radio Talk Shows **ExamView® Computerized Testing** Electronic version of the Test Bank. Questions for Chapter 1 can be used to create and deliver customized quizzes and tests, in print and online. **WebTutor™ Toolbox on WebCT and Blackboard** Online course management tool available on WebCT or Blackboard pre-loaded with text-specific content and resources.	**InfoTrac® College Edition Student Activities Workbook for Public Speaking 2.0** Research and critical thinking activities for students using the online InfoTrac library. 1.1 Importance of Public Speaking for Careers and Jobs 1.2 Public Speaking and Culture 1.3 The History and Tradition of Public Speaking in Education **Public Speaking Student Guide to the Opposing Viewpoints Resource Center (OVRC)** Includes Suggested Activities and Resources for Further Research using the OVRC online library.	**The Speaker's Handbook Web site** http://communication.wadsworth.com/sprague7 Online access to: Quizzes Interactive Activities Web links Sample Speech Outlines InfoTrac® College Edition activities **The Speaker's Handbook CD-ROM** Includes access to Speech Builder Express™, The Speaker's Handbook Web site, and InfoTrac®. The CD-ROM features *Speech Interactive*, a variety of sample student and professional speeches that can be watched, critiqued, and evaluated. 1. "Commencement Speech" by Richard Rodriguez 2. "All Hands" by Norman Mineta **InfoTrac® College Edition** An easy-to-use online database of reliable full-length articles from thousands of academic journals and popular periodicals. Keywords: *Public speaking* **Opposing Viewpoints Resource Center** Dynamic online database of articles and tools that allows students to analyze and think critically about the various sides of controversial issues.

Chapter 2: Listening

Ideas for Instruction—Print	Ideas for Instruction—Electronic	Print Resources for Students	Electronic Resources for Students
Public Speaking Instructor's Guide to the Opposing Viewpoints Resource Center (OVRC) Includes chapters on Ways to Use OVRC in the Classroom, Suggested Activities, and Resources for Further Research. **The Teaching Assistant's Guide to the Basic Course** This guide covers general teaching and course management topics, as well as specific strategies for communication instruction. **Service Learning in Communication Studies: A Handbook** This book provides guidelines for connecting service-learning work with classroom concepts. **A Guide to the Basic Course for ESL Students** This guide assists the non-native speaker. Features FAQs, helpful URLs, and strategies for accent management and overcoming speech apprehension.	**The Speaker's Handbook Web site** http://communication.wadsworth .com/sprague7 Online access to: Instructor's Resource Manual with Test Bank Sample Speech Outlines InfoTrac® College Edition Resources **CNN Today® Videos: Public Speaking, Volumes I-V** Vol. 2: Radio & Politics Vol. 5: Elizabeth Glaser, "Democratic National Convention Address" **ExamView® Computerized Testing** Electronic version of the Test Bank. Questions for Chapter 2 can be used to create and deliver customized quizzes and tests, in print and online. **WebTutor™ Toolbox on WebCT and Blackboard** Online course management tool available on WebCT or Blackboard pre-loaded with text-specific content and resources.	**InfoTrac® College Edition Student Activities Workbook for Public Speaking 2.0** Research and critical thinking activities for students using the online InfoTrac library. 4.1 Poor Listening Concerns, Practices, and Remedies 4.2 Background on Listening 4.3 Improving the Memory Element of Listening **Public Speaking Student Guide to the Opposing Viewpoints Resource Center (OVRC)** Includes Suggested Activities and Resources for Further Research using the OVRC online library.	**The Speaker's Handbook Web site** http://communication.wadsworth .com/sprague7 Online access to: Quizzes Interactive Activities Web links Sample Speech Outlines InfoTrac® College Edition activities **The Speaker's Handbook CD-ROM** Includes access to Speech Builder Express™, The Speaker's Handbook Web site, and InfoTrac®. The CD-ROM features *Speech Interactive*, a variety of sample student and professional speeches that can be watched, critiqued, and evaluated. **InfoTrac® College Edition** An easy-to-use online database of reliable full-length articles from thousands of academic journals and popular periodicals. Keywords: *Listening, Mental Distractions* **Opposing Viewpoints Resource Center** Dynamic online database of articles and tools that allows students to analyze and think critically about the various sides of controversial issues.

Chapter 3: Speaking Ethics

Ideas for Instruction—Print	Ideas for Instruction—Electronic	Print Resources for Students	Electronic Resources for Students
Public Speaking Instructor's Guide to the Opposing Viewpoints Resource Center (OVRC) Includes chapters on Ways to Use OVRC in the Classroom, Suggested Activities, and Resources for Further Research. **The Teaching Assistant's Guide to the Basic Course** This guide covers general teaching and course management topics, as well as specific strategies for communication instruction. **Service Learning in Communication Studies: A Handbook** This book provides guidelines for connecting service-learning work with classroom concepts. **A Guide to the Basic Course for ESL Students** This guide assists the non-native speaker. Features FAQs, helpful URLs, and strategies for accent management and overcoming speech apprehension.	**The Speaker's Handbook Web site** http://communication.wadsworth.com/sprague7 Online access to: Instructor's Resource Manual with Test Bank Sample Speech Outlines InfoTrac® College Edition Resources **CNN Today® Videos: Public Speaking, Volumes I-V** Vol. 2: Oprah vs. Beef **ExamView® Computerized Testing** Electronic version of the Test Bank. Questions for Chapter 3 can be used to create and deliver customized quizzes and tests, in print and online. **WebTutor™ Toolbox on WebCT and Blackboard** Online course management tool available on WebCT or Blackboard pre-loaded with text-specific content and resources.	**InfoTrac® College Edition Student Activities Workbook for Public Speaking 2.0** Research and critical thinking activities for students using the online InfoTrac library. 2.1 Analyzing Political Speaking for Exaggerations and Dishonesty 2.2 Personal Attacks and Ethics 2.3 Plagiarism From the World Wide Web **Public Speaking Student Guide to the Opposing Viewpoints Resource Center (OVRC)** Includes Suggested Activities and Resources for Further Research using the OVRC online library.	**The Speaker's Handbook Web site** http://communication.wadsworth.com/sprague7 Online access to: Quizzes Interactive Activities Web links Sample Speech Outlines InfoTrac® College Edition activities **The Speaker's Handbook CD-ROM** Includes access to Speech Builder Express™, The Speaker's Handbook Web site, and InfoTrac®. The CD-ROM features *Speech Interactive*, a variety of sample student and professional speeches that can be watched, critiqued, and evaluated. **InfoTrac® College Edition** An easy-to-use online database of reliable full-length articles from thousands of academic journals and popular periodicals. Keywords: *Cheating, Ethics, Plagiarism* **Opposing Viewpoints Resource Center** Dynamic online database of articles and tools that allows students to analyze and think critically about the various sides of controversial issues.

Chapter 4: Overcoming Fear of Speaking

Ideas for Instruction—Print	Ideas for Instruction—Electronic	Print Resources for Students	Electronic Resources for Students
Public Speaking Instructor's Guide to the Opposing Viewpoints Resource Center (OVRC) Includes chapters on Ways to Use OVRC in the Classroom, Suggested Activities, and Resources for Further Research.	**The Speaker's Handbook Web site** http://communication.wadsworth.com/sprague7 Online access to: Instructor's Resource Manual with Test Bank Sample Speech Outlines InfoTrac® College Edition Resources	**InfoTrac® College Edition Student Activities Workbook for Public Speaking 2.0** Research and critical thinking activities for students using the online InfoTrac library.	**The Speaker's Handbook Web site** http://communication.wadsworth.com/sprague7 Online access to: Quizzes Interactive Activities Web links Sample Speech Outlines InfoTrac® College Edition activities
The Teaching Assistant's Guide to the Basic Course This guide covers general teaching and course management topics, as well as specific strategies for communication instruction.	**CNN Today® Videos: Public Speaking, Volumes I-V** Vol. 2: Emigre Education **ExamView® Computerized Testing** Electronic version of the Test Bank. Questions for Chapter 4 can be used to create and deliver customized quizzes and tests, in print and online.	3.1 Coping with Public Speaking Anxiety in Real World Settings 3.2 Treatment of Severe Communication Apprehension 3.3 Using Visualization to Increase Performance Confidence	**The Speaker's Handbook CD-ROM** Includes access to Speech Builder Express™, The Speaker's Handbook Web site, and InfoTrac®. The CD-ROM features *Speech Interactive*, a variety of sample student and professional speeches that can be watched, critiqued, and evaluated.
Service Learning in Communication Studies: A Handbook This book provides guidelines for connecting service-learning work with classroom concepts.	**WebTutor™ Toolbox on WebCT and Blackboard** Online course management tool available on WebCT or Blackboard pre-loaded with text-specific content and resources.	**Public Speaking Student Guide to the Opposing Viewpoints Resource Center (OVRC)** Includes Suggested Activities and Resources for Further Research using the OVRC online library.	**InfoTrac® College Edition** An easy-to-use online database of reliable full-length articles from thousands of academic journals and popular periodicals. Keywords: *Communication apprehension, Stage fright*
A Guide to the Basic Course for ESL Students This guide assists the non-native speaker. Features FAQs, helpful URLs, and strategies for accent management and overcoming speech apprehension.			**Opposing Viewpoints Resource Center** Dynamic online database of articles and tools that allows students to analyze and think critically about the various sides of controversial issues.

Handbook Part II: Preparation

Chapter 5: Planning

Ideas for Instruction— Print	Ideas for Instruction— Electronic	Print Resources for Students	Electronic Resources for Students
Public Speaking Instructor's Guide to the Opposing Viewpoints Resource Center (OVRC) Includes chapters on Ways to Use OVRC in the Classroom, Suggested Activities, and Resources for Further Research. **The Teaching Assistant's Guide to the Basic Course** This guide covers general teaching and course management topics, as well as specific strategies for communication instruction. **Service Learning in Communication Studies: A Handbook** This book provides guidelines for connecting service-learning work with classroom concepts. **A Guide to the Basic Course for ESL Students** This guide assists the non-native speaker. Features FAQs, helpful URLs, and strategies for accent management and overcoming speech apprehension.	**The Speaker's Handbook Web site** http://communication.wadsworth .com/sprague7 Online access to: Instructor's Resource Manual with Test Bank Sample Speech Outlines InfoTrac® College Edition Resources **ExamView® Computerized Testing** Electronic version of the Test Bank. Questions for Chapter 5 can be used to create and deliver customized quizzes and tests, in print and online. **WebTutor™ Toolbox on WebCT and Blackboard** Online course management tool available on WebCT or Blackboard pre-loaded with text-specific content and resources.	**InfoTrac® College Edition Student Activities Workbook for Public Speaking 2.0** Research and critical thinking activities for students using the online InfoTrac library. **Public Speaking Student Guide to the Opposing Viewpoints Resource Center (OVRC)** Includes Suggested Activities and Resources for Further Research using the OVRC online library.	**The Speaker's Handbook Web site** http://communication.wadsworth .com/sprague7 Online access to: Quizzes Interactive Activities Web links Sample Speech Outlines InfoTrac® College Edition activities **The Speaker's Handbook CD-ROM** Includes access to Speech Builder Express™, The Speaker's Handbook Web site, and InfoTrac®. The CD-ROM features *Speech Interactive*, a variety of sample student and professional speeches that can be watched, critiqued, and evaluated. **InfoTrac® College Edition** An easy-to-use online database of reliable full-length articles from thousands of academic journals and popular periodicals. **Opposing Viewpoints Resource Center** Dynamic online database of articles and tools that allows students to analyze and think critically about the various sides of controversial issues.

Chapter 6: Topic Selection and Analysis

Ideas for Instruction—Print	Ideas for Instruction—Electronic	Print Resources for Students	Electronic Resources for Students
Public Speaking Instructor's Guide to the Opposing Viewpoints Resource Center (OVRC) Includes chapters on Ways to Use OVRC in the Classroom, Suggested Activities, and Resources for Further Research. **The Teaching Assistant's Guide to the Basic Course** This guide covers general teaching and course management topics, as well as specific strategies for communication instruction. **Service Learning in Communication Studies: A Handbook** This book provides guidelines for connecting service-learning work with classroom concepts. **A Guide to the Basic Course for ESL Students** This guide assists the non-native speaker. Features FAQs, helpful URLs, and strategies for accent management and overcoming speech apprehension.	**The Speaker's Handbook Web site** http://communication.wadsworth.com/sprague7 Online access to: Instructor's Resource Manual with Test Bank Sample Speech Outlines InfoTrac® College Edition Resources **CNN Today® Videos: Public Speaking, Volumes I-V** Vol. 4: Mary Fisher "A Whisper of AIDS" Vol. 5: Elizabeth Glaser "Democratic National Convention Address" **ExamView® Computerized Testing** Electronic version of the Test Bank. Questions for Chapter 6 can be used to create and deliver customized quizzes and tests, in print and online. **WebTutor™ Toolbox on WebCT and Blackboard** Online course management tool available on WebCT or Blackboard pre-loaded with text-specific content and resources.	**InfoTrac® College Edition Student Activities Workbook for Public Speaking 2.0** Research and critical thinking activities for students using the online InfoTrac library. 5.1 Identifying Speech Subjects, Topics, and Goals/Purposes 5.2 Selecting a Topic and Availability of Information 5.3 Browsing for Potential Speech Topics **Public Speaking Student Guide to the Opposing Viewpoints Resource Center (OVRC)** Includes Suggested Activities and Resources for Further Research using the OVRC online library.	**The Speaker's Handbook Web site** http://communication.wadsworth.com/sprague7 Online access to: Quizzes Interactive Activities Web links Sample Speech Outlines InfoTrac® College Edition activities **The Speaker's Handbook CD-ROM** Includes access to Speech Builder Express™, The Speaker's Handbook Web site, and InfoTrac®. The CD-ROM features *Speech Interactive*, a variety of sample student and professional speeches that can be watched, critiqued, and evaluated. **InfoTrac® College Edition** An easy-to-use online database of reliable full-length articles from thousands of academic journals and popular periodicals. Keywords: *Brainstorming, Thesis statement* **Opposing Viewpoints Resource Center** Dynamic online database of articles and tools that allows students to analyze and think critically about the various sides of controversial issues.

Chapter 7: Audience Analysis

Ideas for Instruction—Print	Ideas for Instruction—Electronic	Print Resources for Students	Electronic Resources for Students
Public Speaking Instructor's Guide to the Opposing Viewpoints Resource Center (OVRC) Includes chapters on Ways to Use OVRC in the Classroom, Suggested Activities, and Resources for Further Research. **The Teaching Assistant's Guide to the Basic Course** This guide covers general teaching and course management topics, as well as specific strategies for communication instruction. **Service Learning in Communication Studies: A Handbook** This book provides guidelines for connecting service-learning work with classroom concepts. **A Guide to the Basic Course for ESL Students** This guide assists the non-native speaker. Features FAQs, helpful URLs, and strategies for accent management and overcoming speech apprehension.	**The Speaker's Handbook Web site** http://communication.wadsworth.com/sprague7 Online access to: Instructor's Resource Manual with Test Bank Sample Speech Outlines InfoTrac® College Edition Resources **CNN Today® Videos: Public Speaking, Volumes I-V** Vol. 1: Million Man March Vol. 1: Trent Lott on Homosexuality Vol. 1: 1992 Reform Party Convention Vol. 2: "Hollywood" Gore Vol. 2: Democratic National Convention Vol. 3: Paddy Buchanan Vol. 3: Green Party Vol. 3: Women Voters in New York **ExamView® Computerized Testing** Electronic version of the Test Bank. Questions for Chapter 7 can be used to create and deliver customized quizzes and tests, in print and online. **WebTutor™ Toolbox on WebCT and Blackboard** Online course management tool available on WebCT or Blackboard pre-loaded with text-specific content and resources.	**InfoTrac® College Edition Student Activities Workbook for Public Speaking 2.0** Research and critical thinking activities for students using the online InfoTrac library. 8.1 Identifying Types of Audience 8.2 College Audience Makeup and Attitudes 8.3 Locating Information About College Audience Attitudes for Your Speech Topic 8.4 Analysis of Audience Adaptation Techniques **Public Speaking Student Guide to the Opposing Viewpoints Resource Center (OVRC)** Includes Suggested Activities and Resources for Further Research using the OVRC online library. *Audience Analysis:* Exercises 1-7	**The Speaker's Handbook Web site** http://communication.wadsworth.com/sprague7 Online access to: Quizzes Interactive Activities Web links Sample Speech Outlines InfoTrac® College Edition activities **The Speaker's Handbook CD-ROM** Includes access to Speech Builder Express™, The Speaker's Handbook Web site, and InfoTrac®. The CD-ROM features *Speech Interactive*, a variety of sample student and professional speeches that can be watched, critiqued, and evaluated. 1. "Eye Chip" by Vanessa Harikul 2. "No More Sugar" by Hans Erian **InfoTrac® College Edition** An easy-to-use online database of reliable full-length articles from thousands of academic journals and popular periodicals. Keywords: *Audience analysis, Demographics, Gender, Stereotypes* **Opposing Viewpoints Resource Center** Dynamic online database of articles and tools that allows students to analyze and think critically about the various sides of controversial issues.

Chapter 8: Research

Ideas for Instruction—Print	Ideas for Instruction—Electronic	Print Resources for Students	Electronic Resources for Students
Public Speaking Instructor's Guide to the Opposing Viewpoints Resource Center (OVRC) Includes chapters on Ways to Use OVRC in the Classroom, Suggested Activities, and Resources for Further Research. **The Teaching Assistant's Guide to the Basic Course** This guide covers general teaching and course management topics, as well as specific strategies for communication instruction. **Service Learning in Communication Studies: A Handbook** This book provides guidelines for connecting service-learning work with classroom concepts. **A Guide to the Basic Course for ESL Students** This guide assists the non-native speaker. Features FAQs, helpful URLs, and strategies for accent management and overcoming speech apprehension.	**The Speaker's Handbook Web site** http://communication.wadsworth .com/sprague7 Online access to: Instructor's Resource Manual with Test Bank Sample Speech Outlines InfoTrac® College Edition Resources **CNN Today® Videos: Public Speaking, Volumes I-V** Vol. 1: Library On-line Vol. 2: AFL-CIO Medicare Ads Vol. 3: Bush and Cheney **ExamView® Computerized Testing** Electronic version of the Test Bank. Questions for Chapter 8 can be used to create and deliver customized quizzes and tests, in print and online. **WebTutor™ Toolbox on WebCT and Blackboard** Online course management tool available on WebCT or Blackboard pre-loaded with text-specific content and resources.	**InfoTrac® College Edition Student Activities Workbook for Public Speaking 2.0** Research and critical thinking activities for students using the online InfoTrac library. 6.1 Practice Using InfoTrac to Research a Speech 6.2 Issues Related to Conducting E-mail Interviews 6.3 Guidelines for Reliable Internet Information 6.4 Researching Your Speech Topic **Public Speaking Student Guide to the Opposing Viewpoints Resource Center (OVRC)** Includes Suggested Activities and Resources for Further Research using the OVRC online library. *Source Credibility:* Exercises 1-7	**The Speaker's Handbook Web site** http://communication.wadsworth .com/sprague7 Online access to: Quizzes Interactive Activities Web links Sample Speech Outlines InfoTrac® College Edition activities **The Speaker's Handbook CD-ROM** Includes access to Speech Builder Express™, The Speaker's Handbook Web site, and InfoTrac®. The CD-ROM features *Speech Interactive*, a variety of sample student and professional speeches that can be watched, critiqued, and evaluated. **InfoTrac® College Edition** An easy-to-use online database of reliable full-length articles from thousands of academic journals and popular periodicals. Keywords: *Evidence, Search engine, Statistics, Testimony* **Opposing Viewpoints Resource Center** Dynamic online database of articles and tools that allows students to analyze and think critically about the various sides of controversial issues.

Handbook Part III: Organization

Chapter 9: Transforming Ideas Into Speech Points

Ideas for Instruction—Print	Ideas for Instruction—Electronic	Print Resources for Students	Electronic Resources for Students
Public Speaking Instructor's Guide to the Opposing Viewpoints Resource Center (OVRC) Includes chapters on Ways to Use OVRC in the Classroom, Suggested Activities, and Resources for Further Research. **The Teaching Assistant's Guide to the Basic Course** This guide covers general teaching and course management topics, as well as specific strategies for communication instruction. **Service Learning in Communication Studies: A Handbook** This book provides guidelines for connecting service-learning work with classroom concepts. **A Guide to the Basic Course for ESL Students** This guide assists the non-native speaker. Features FAQs, helpful URLs, and strategies for accent management and overcoming speech apprehension.	**The Speaker's Handbook Web site** http://communication.wadsworth .com/sprague7 Online access to: Instructor's Resource Manual with Test Bank Sample Speech Outlines InfoTrac® College Edition Resources **ExamView® Computerized Testing** Electronic version of the Test Bank. Questions for Chapter 9 can be used to create and deliver customized quizzes and tests, in print and online. **WebTutor™ Toolbox on WebCT and Blackboard** Online course management tool available on WebCT or Blackboard pre-loaded with text-specific content and resources.	**InfoTrac® College Edition Student Activities Workbook for Public Speaking 2.0** Research and critical thinking activities for students using the online InfoTrac library. 9.1 Identifying Traditional Speech Organizational Patterns **Public Speaking Student Guide to the Opposing Viewpoints Resource Center (OVRC)** Includes Suggested Activities and Resources for Further Research using the OVRC online library.	**The Speaker's Handbook Web site** http://communication.wadsworth .com/sprague7 Online access to: Quizzes Interactive Activities Web links Sample Speech Outlines InfoTrac® College Edition activities **The Speaker's Handbook CD-ROM** Includes access to Speech Builder Express™, The Speaker's Handbook Web site, and InfoTrac®. The CD-ROM features *Speech Interactive*, a variety of sample student and professional speeches that can be watched, critiqued, and evaluated. **InfoTrac® College Edition** An easy-to-use online database of reliable full-length articles from thousands of academic journals and popular periodicals. Keywords: *Concept mapping* **Opposing Viewpoints Resource Center** Dynamic online database of articles and tools that allows students to analyze and think critically about the various sides of controversial issues.

Chapter 10: Arranging Points

Ideas for Instruction—Print	Ideas for Instruction—Electronic	Print Resources for Students	Electronic Resources for Students
Public Speaking Instructor's Guide to the Opposing Viewpoints Resource Center (OVRC) Includes chapters on Ways to Use OVRC in the Classroom, Suggested Activities, and Resources for Further Research. **The Teaching Assistant's Guide to the Basic Course** This guide covers general teaching and course management topics, as well as specific strategies for communication instruction. **Service Learning In Communication Studies: A Handbook** This book provides guidelines for connecting service-learning work with classroom concepts. **A Guide to the Basic Course for ESL Students** This guide assists the non-native speaker. Features FAQs, helpful URLs, and strategies for accent management and overcoming speech apprehension.	**The Speaker's Handbook Web site** http://communication.wadsworth .com/sprague7 Online access to: Instructor's Resource Manual with Test Bank Sample Speech Outlines InfoTrac® College Edition Resources **CNN Today® Videos: Public Speaking, Volumes I-V** Vol. 3: Bush Acceptance Speech Vol. 3: Gore Concession Speech Vol. 4: Mary Fisher, "A Whisper of AIDS" Vol. 5: Elizabeth Glaser, "Democratic National Convention Address" **ExamView® Computerized Testing** Electronic version of the Test Bank. Questions for Chapter 10 can be used to create and deliver customized quizzes and tests, in print and online. **WebTutor™ Toolbox on WebCT and Blackboard** Online course management tool available on WebCT or Blackboard pre-loaded with text-specific content and resources.	**InfoTrac® College Edition Student Activities Workbook for Public Speaking 2.0** Research and critical thinking activities for students using the online InfoTrac library. 9.2 Speaker Signposting to Assist the Audience in Following the Speech Organization 9.3 Additional Organizational Tips **Public Speaking Student Guide to the Opposing Viewpoints Resource Center (OVRC)** Includes Suggested Activities and Resources for Further Research using the OVRC online library. *Organizing:* Exercises 1-8	**The Speaker's Handbook Web site** http://communication.wadsworth .com/sprague7 Online access to: Quizzes Interactive Activities Web links Sample Speech Outlines InfoTrac® College Edition activities **The Speaker's Handbook CD-ROM** Includes access to Speech Builder Express™, The Speaker's Handbook Web site, and InfoTrac®. The CD-ROM features *Speech Interactive*, a variety of sample student and professional speeches that can be watched, critiqued, and evaluated. 1. "No More Sugar" by Hans Erian 2. "Eye Chip" by Vanessa Harikul 3. "All Hands" by Norman Mineta **InfoTrac® College Edition** An easy-to-use online database of reliable full-length articles from thousands of academic journals and popular periodicals. **Opposing Viewpoints Resource Center** Dynamic online database of articles and tools that allows students to analyze and think critically about the various sides of controversial issues.

Chapter 11: Outlining

Ideas for Instruction— Print	Ideas for Instruction— Electronic	Print Resources for Students	Electronic Resources for Students
Public Speaking Instructor's Guide to the Opposing Viewpoints Resource Center (OVRC) Includes chapters on Ways to Use OVRC in the Classroom, Suggested Activities, and Resources for Further Research. **The Teaching Assistant's Guide to the Basic Course** This guide covers general teaching and course management topics, as well as specific strategies for communication instruction. **Service Learning in Communication Studies: A Handbook** This book provides guidelines for connecting service-learning work with classroom concepts. **A Guide to the Basic Course for ESL Students** This guide assists the non-native speaker. Features FAQs, helpful URLs, and strategies for accent management and overcoming speech apprehension.	**The Speaker's Handbook Web site** http://communication.wadsworth.com/sprague7 Online access to: Instructor's Resource Manual with Test Bank Sample Speech Outlines InfoTrac® College Edition Resources **ExamView® Computerized Testing** Electronic version of the Test Bank. Questions for Chapter 11 can be used to create and deliver customized quizzes and tests, in print and online. **WebTutor™ Toolbox on WebCT and Blackboard** Online course management tool available on WebCT or Blackboard pre-loaded with text-specific content and resources.	**InfoTrac® College Edition Student Activities Workbook for Public Speaking 2.0** Research and critical thinking activities for students using the online InfoTrac library. **Public Speaking Student Guide to the Opposing Viewpoints Resource Center (OVRC)** Includes Suggested Activities and Resources for Further Research using the OVRC online library.	**The Speaker's Handbook Web site** http://communication.wadsworth.com/sprague7 Online access to: Quizzes Interactive Activities Web links Sample Speech Outlines InfoTrac® College Edition activities **The Speaker's Handbook CD-ROM** Includes access to Speech Builder Express™, The Speaker's Handbook Web site, and InfoTrac®. The CD-ROM features *Speech Interactive*, a variety of sample student and professional speeches that can be watched, critiqued, and evaluated. 1. "Eye Chip" by Vanessa Harikul **InfoTrac® College Edition** An easy-to-use online database of reliable full-length articles from thousands of academic journals and popular periodicals. **Opposing Viewpoints Resource Center** Dynamic online database of articles and tools that allows students to analyze and think critically about the various sides of controversial issues.

Chapter 12: Transitions

Ideas for Instruction—Print	Ideas for Instruction—Electronic	Print Resources for Students	Electronic Resources for Students
Public Speaking Instructor's Guide to the Opposing Viewpoints Resource Center (OVRC) Includes chapters on Ways to Use OVRC in the Classroom, Suggested Activities, and Resources for Further Research. **The Teaching Assistant's Guide to the Basic Course** This guide covers general teaching and course management topics, as well as specific strategies for communication instruction. **Service Learning in Communication Studies: A Handbook** This book provides guidelines for connecting service-learning work with classroom concepts. **A Guide to the Basic Course for ESL Students** This guide assists the non-native speaker. Features FAQs, helpful URLs, and strategies for accent management and overcoming speech apprehension.	**The Speaker's Handbook Web site** http://communication.wadsworth.com/sprague7 Online access to: Instructor's Resource Manual with Test Bank Sample Speech Outlines InfoTrac® College Edition Resources **ExamView® Computerized Testing** Electronic version of the Test Bank. Questions for Chapter 12 can be used to create and deliver customized quizzes and tests, in print and online. **WebTutor™ Toolbox on WebCT and Blackboard** Online course management tool available on WebCT or Blackboard pre-loaded with text-specific content and resources.	**InfoTrac® College Edition Student Activities Workbook for Public Speaking 2.0** Research and critical thinking activities for students using the online InfoTrac library. **Public Speaking Student Guide to the Opposing Viewpoints Resource Center (OVRC)** Includes Suggested Activities and Resources for Further Research using the OVRC online library.	**The Speaker's Handbook Web site** http://communication.wadsworth.com/sprague7 Online access to: Quizzes Interactive Activities Web links Sample Speech Outlines InfoTrac® College Edition activities **The Speaker's Handbook CD-ROM** Includes access to Speech Builder Express™, The Speaker's Handbook Web site, and InfoTrac®. The CD-ROM features *Speech Interactive*, a variety of sample student and professional speeches that can be watched, critiqued, and evaluated. **InfoTrac® College Edition** An easy-to-use online database of reliable full-length articles from thousands of academic journals and popular periodicals. **Opposing Viewpoints Resource Center** Dynamic online database of articles and tools that allows students to analyze and think critically about the various sides of controversial issues.

Chapter 13: Introductions

Ideas for Instruction—Print	Ideas for Instruction—Electronic	Print Resources for Students	Electronic Resources for Students
Public Speaking Instructor's Guide to the Opposing Viewpoints Resource Center (OVRC) Includes chapters on Ways to Use OVRC in the Classroom, Suggested Activities, and Resources for Further Research. **The Teaching Assistant's Guide to the Basic Course** This guide covers general teaching and course management topics, as well as specific strategies for communication instruction. **Service Learning in Communication Studies: A Handbook** This book provides guidelines for connecting service-learning work with classroom concepts. **A Guide to the Basic Course for ESL Students** This guide assists the non-native speaker. Features FAQs, helpful URLs, and strategies for accent management and overcoming speech apprehension.	**The Speaker's Handbook Web site** http://communication.wadsworth .com/sprague7 Online access to: Instructor's Resource Manual with Test Bank Sample Speech Outlines InfoTrac® College Edition Resources **CNN Today® Videos: Public Speaking, Volumes I-V** Vol. 1: Effective Beginnings and Endings **ExamView® Computerized Testing** Electronic version of the Test Bank. Questions for Chapter 13 can be used to create and deliver customized quizzes and tests, in print and online. **WebTutor™ Toolbox on WebCT and Blackboard** Online course management tool available on WebCT or Blackboard pre-loaded with text-specific content and resources.	**InfoTrac® College Edition Student Activities Workbook for Public Speaking 2.0** Research and critical thinking activities for students using the online InfoTrac library. 10.1 Analysis of Introductions 10.3 Motivating the Audience to Listen Because of Relevancy Presented in Introductions 10.4 Practice Speech Introductions **Public Speaking Student Guide to the Opposing Viewpoints Resource Center (OVRC)** Includes Suggested Activities and Resources for Further Research using the OVRC online library. *Introductions and Conclusions:* Exercises 1-8	**The Speaker's Handbook Web site** http://communication.wadsworth .com/sprague7 Online access to: Quizzes Interactive Activities Web links Sample Speech Outlines InfoTrac® College Edition activities **The Speaker's Handbook CD-ROM** Includes access to Speech Builder Express™, The Speaker's Handbook Web site, and InfoTrac®. The CD-ROM features *Speech Interactive*, a variety of sample student and professional speeches that can be watched, critiqued, and evaluated. 1. "Eye Chip" by Vanessa Harikul 2. "No More Sugar" by Hans Erian 3. "Commencement Speech" by Richard Rodriguez 4. "All Hands" by Norman Mineta **InfoTrac® College Edition** An easy-to-use online database of reliable full-length articles from thousands of academic journals and popular periodicals. **Opposing Viewpoints Resource Center** Dynamic online database of articles and tools that allows students to analyze and think critically about the various sides of controversial issues.

Chapter 14: Conclusions

Ideas for Instruction—Print	Ideas for Instruction—Electronic	Print Resources for Students	Electronic Resources for Students
Public Speaking Instructor's Guide to the Opposing Viewpoints Resource Center (OVRC) Includes chapters on Ways to Use OVRC in the Classroom, Suggested Activities, and Resources for Further Research. **The Teaching Assistant's Guide to the Basic Course** This guide covers general teaching and course management topics, as well as specific strategies for communication instruction. **Service Learning in Communication Studies: A Handbook** This book provides guidelines for connecting service-learning work with classroom concepts. **A Guide to the Basic Course for ESL Students** This guide assists the non-native speaker. Features FAQs, helpful URLs, and strategies for accent management and overcoming speech apprehension.	**The Speaker's Handbook Web site** http://communication.wadsworth.com/sprague7 Online access to: Instructor's Resource Manual with Test Bank Sample Speech Outlines InfoTrac® College Edition Resources **CNN Today® Videos: Public Speaking, Volumes I-V** Vol. 1: Effective Beginnings and Endings **ExamView® Computerized Testing** Electronic version of the Test Bank. Questions for Chapter 14 can be used to create and deliver customized quizzes and tests, in print and online. **WebTutor™ Toolbox on WebCT and Blackboard** Online course management tool available on WebCT or Blackboard pre-loaded with text-specific content and resources.	**InfoTrac® College Edition Student Activities Workbook for Public Speaking 2.0** Research and critical thinking activities for students using the online InfoTrac library. 10.2 Analysis of Conclusions **Public Speaking Student Guide to the Opposing Viewpoints Resource Center (OVRC)** Includes Suggested Activities and Resources for Further Research using the OVRC online library. *Introductions and Conclusions:* Exercises 1-8	**The Speaker's Handbook Web site** http://communication.wadsworth.com/sprague7 Online access to: Quizzes Interactive Activities Web links Sample Speech Outlines InfoTrac® College Edition activities **The Speaker's Handbook CD-ROM** Includes access to Speech Builder Express™, The Speaker's Handbook Web site, and InfoTrac®. The CD-ROM features *Speech Interactive*, a variety of sample student and professional speeches that can be watched, critiqued, and evaluated. 1. "Endings" **InfoTrac® College Edition** An easy-to-use online database of reliable full-length articles from thousands of academic journals and popular periodicals. **Opposing Viewpoints Resource Center** Dynamic online database of articles and tools that allows students to analyze and think critically about the various sides of controversial issues.

Handbook Part IV: Development

Chapter 15: Supporting Materials

Ideas for Instruction—Print	Ideas for Instruction—Electronic	Print Resources for Students	Electronic Resources for Students
Public Speaking Instructor's Guide to the Opposing Viewpoints Resource Center (OVRC) Includes chapters on Ways to Use OVRC in the Classroom, Suggested Activities, and Resources for Further Research. **The Teaching Assistant's Guide to the Basic Course** This guide covers general teaching and course management topics, as well as specific strategies for communication instruction. **Service Learning in Communication Studies: A Handbook** This book provides guidelines for connecting service-learning work with classroom concepts. **A Guide to the Basic Course for ESL Students** This guide assists the non-native speaker. Features FAQs, helpful URLs, and strategies for accent management and overcoming speech apprehension.	**The Speaker's Handbook Web site** http://communication.wadsworth.com/sprague7 Online access to: Instructor's Resource Manual with Test Bank Sample Speech Outlines InfoTrac® College Edition Resources **ExamView® Computerized Testing** Electronic version of the Test Bank. Questions for Chapter 15 can be used to create and deliver customized quizzes and tests, in print and online. **WebTutor™ Toolbox on WebCT and Blackboard** Online course management tool available on WebCT or Blackboard pre-loaded with text-specific content and resources.	**InfoTrac® College Edition Student Activities Workbook for Public Speaking 2.0** Research and critical thinking activities for students using the online InfoTrac library. 7.1 Identifying Types of Support Materials 7.2 Testing Support Materials 7.3 Making Numbers and Statistics Accessible and Meaningful to the Audience **Public Speaking Student Guide to the Opposing Viewpoints Resource Center (OVRC)** Includes Suggested Activities and Resources for Further Research using the OVRC online library. *Supporting Material:* Exercises 1-8	**The Speaker's Handbook Web site** http://communication.wadsworth.com/sprague7 Online access to: Quizzes Interactive Activities Web links Sample Speech Outlines InfoTrac® College Edition activities **The Speaker's Handbook CD-ROM** Includes access to Speech Builder Express™, The Speaker's Handbook Web site, and InfoTrac®. The CD-ROM features *Speech Interactive*, a variety of sample student and professional speeches that can be watched, critiqued, and evaluated. 1. "Eye Chip" by Vanessa Harikul 2. "Electoral College" by Robert McDermott 3. "Celebrating Women in Business" by Carly Fiorina 4. "All Hands" by Norman Mineta 5. "No More Sugar" by Hans Erian 6. "Trucks" by Charon Frankel **InfoTrac® College Edition** An easy-to-use online database of reliable full-length articles from thousands of academic journals and popular periodicals.

Chapter 16: Reasoning

Ideas for Instruction—Print	Ideas for Instruction—Electronic	Print Resources for Students	Electronic Resources for Students
Public Speaking Instructor's Guide to the Opposing Viewpoints Resource Center (OVRC) Includes chapters on Ways to Use OVRC in the Classroom, Suggested Activities, and Resources for Further Research. **The Teaching Assistant's Guide to the Basic Course** This guide covers general teaching and course management topics, as well as specific strategies for communication instruction. **Service Learning in Communication Studies: A Handbook** This book provides guidelines for connecting service-learning work with classroom concepts. **A Guide to the Basic Course for ESL Students** This guide assists the non-native speaker. Features FAQs, helpful URLs, and strategies for accent management and overcoming speech apprehension.	**The Speaker's Handbook Web site** http://communication.wadsworth.com/sprague7 Online access to: Instructor's Resource Manual with Test Bank Sample Speech Outlines InfoTrac® College Edition Resources **CNN Today® Videos: Public Speaking, Volumes I-V** Vol. 2: Littleton Vol. 4: Mary Fisher, "A Whisper of Aids" Vol. 4: President George W. Bush, "Address to a Joint Session of Congress and the American People, September 20, 2001" Vol. 5: President George W. Bush, "National Day of Prayer and Remembrance" Vol. 5: Elizabeth Glaser, "Democratic National Convention Address" **ExamView® Computerized Testing** Electronic version of the Test Bank. Questions for Chapter 16 can be used to create and deliver customized quizzes and tests, in print and online. **WebTutor™ Toolbox on WebCT and Blackboard** Online course management tool available on WebCT or Blackboard pre-loaded with text-specific content and resources.	**InfoTrac® College Edition Student Activities Workbook for Public Speaking 2.0** Research and critical thinking activities for students using the online InfoTrac library. 15.3 Modeling Arguments **Public Speaking Student Guide to the Opposing Viewpoints Resource Center (OVRC)** Includes Suggested Activities and Resources for Further Research using the OVRC online library.	**The Speaker's Handbook Web site** http://communication.wadsworth.com/sprague7 Online access to: Quizzes Interactive Activities Web links Sample Speech Outlines InfoTrac® College Edition activities **The Speaker's Handbook CD-ROM** Includes access to Speech Builder Express™, The Speaker's Handbook Web site, and InfoTrac®. The CD-ROM features *Speech Interactive*, a variety of sample student and professional speeches that can be watched, critiqued, and evaluated. 1. "No More Sugar" by Hans Erian 2. "Trucks" by Charon Frankel 3. "All Hands" by Norman Mineta **InfoTrac® College Edition** An easy-to-use online database of reliable full-length articles from thousands of academic journals and popular periodicals. Keywords: *Deductive reasoning, Inductive reasoning* **Opposing Viewpoints Resource Center** Dynamic online database of articles and tools that allows students to analyze and think critically about the various sides of controversial issues.

Chapter 17: Language and Style

Ideas for Instruction— Print	Ideas for Instruction— Electronic	Print Resources for Students	Electronic Resources for Students
Public Speaking Instructor's Guide to the Opposing Viewpoints Resource Center (OVRC) Includes chapters on Ways to Use OVRC in the Classroom, Suggested Activities, and Resources for Further Research. **The Teaching Assistant's Guide to the Basic Course** This guide covers general teaching and course management topics, as well as specific strategies for communication instruction. **Service Learning in Communication Studies: A Handbook** This book provides guidelines for connecting service-learning work with classroom concepts. **A Guide to the Basic Course for ESL Students** This guide assists the non-native speaker. Features FAQs, helpful URLs, and strategies for accent management and overcoming speech apprehension.	**The Speaker's Handbook Web site** http://communication.wadsworth .com/sprague7 Online access to: Instructor's Resource Manual with Test Bank Sample Speech Outlines InfoTrac® College Edition Resources **CNN Today® Videos: Public Speaking, Volumes I–V** Vol. 1: Great Speeches Vol. 1: Fuzzy Fallout Vol. 2: The Ebonics Controversy Vol. 3: The Also Rans: Bradley Vol. 5: George W. Bush, "National Day of Prayer and Remembrance" Vol. 5: Rep. Richard Gephardt, "Special Session of Congress Commemorating September 11th" **ExamView® Computerized Testing** Electronic version of the Test Bank. Questions for Chapter 17 can be used to create and deliver customized quizzes and tests, in print and online. **WebTutor™ Toolbox on WebCT and Blackboard** Online course management tool available on WebCT or Blackboard pre-loaded with text-specific content and resources.	**InfoTrac® College Edition Student Activities Workbook for Public Speaking 2.0** Research and critical thinking activities for students using the online InfoTrac library. 12.1 Language, Culture, and Identity 12.2 Avoiding Sexist Language 12.3 Identifying Effective Language Strategies **Public Speaking Student Guide to the Opposing Viewpoints Resource Center (OVRC)** Includes Suggested Activities and Resources for Further Research using the OVRC online library. *Language and Delivery:* Exercises 1-8	**The Speaker's Handbook Web site** http://communication.wadsworth .com/sprague7 Online access to: Quizzes Interactive Activities Web links Sample Speech Outlines InfoTrac® College Edition activities **The Speaker's Handbook CD-ROM** Includes access to Speech Builder Express™, The Speaker's Handbook Web site, and InfoTrac®. The CD-ROM features *Speech Interactive*, a variety of sample student and professional speeches that can be watched, critiqued, and evaluated. 1. "All Hands" by Norman Mineta **InfoTrac® College Edition** An easy-to-use online database of reliable full-length articles from thousands of academic journals and popular periodicals. Keywords: *Analogy, Connotation, Denotation, Jargon, Metaphor, Slang* **Opposing Viewpoints Resource Center** Dynamic online database of articles and tools that allows students to analyze and think critically about the various sides of controversial issues.

Chapter 18: Attention and Interest

Ideas for Instruction—Print	Ideas for Instruction—Electronic	Print Resources for Students	Electronic Resources for Students
Public Speaking Instructor's Guide to the Opposing Viewpoints Resource Center (OVRC) Includes chapters on Ways to Use OVRC in the Classroom, Suggested Activities, and Resources for Further Research. **The Teaching Assistant's Guide to the Basic Course** This guide covers general teaching and course management topics, as well as specific strategies for communication instruction. **Service Learning in Communication Studies: A Handbook** This book provides guidelines for connecting service-learning work with classroom concepts. **A Guide to the Basic Course for ESL Students** This guide assists the non-native speaker. Features FAQs, helpful URLs, and strategies for accent management and overcoming speech apprehension.	**The Speaker's Handbook Web site** http://communication.wadsworth.com/sprague7 Online access to: Instructor's Resource Manual with Test Bank Sample Speech Outlines InfoTrac® College Edition Resources **CNN Today® Videos: Public Speaking, Volumes I-V** Vol. 4: Mary Fisher, "A Whisper of Aids" Vol. 4: Nelson Mandela, "Glory and Hope: Let There be Work, Bread, Water, and Salt For All" **ExamView® Computerized Testing** Electronic version of the Test Bank. Questions for Chapter 18 can be used to create and deliver customized quizzes and tests, in print and online. **WebTutor™ Toolbox on WebCT and Blackboard** Online course management tool available on WebCT or Blackboard pre-loaded with text-specific content and resources.	**InfoTrac® College Edition Student Activities Workbook for Public Speaking 2.0** Research and critical thinking activities for students using the online InfoTrac library. **Public Speaking Student Guide to the Opposing Viewpoints Resource Center (OVRC)** Includes Suggested Activities and Resources for Further Research using the OVRC online library.	**The Speaker's Handbook Web site** http://communication.wadsworth.com/sprague7 Online access to: Quizzes Interactive Activities Web links Sample Speech Outlines InfoTrac® College Edition activities **The Speaker's Handbook CD-ROM** Includes access to Speech Builder Express™, The Speaker's Handbook Web site, and InfoTrac®. The CD-ROM features *Speech Interactive*, a variety of sample student and professional speeches that can be watched, critiqued, and evaluated. 1. "DeAnza College Keynote Address" by Lance Dawson 2. "Reentry Student" by Mona Brasher **InfoTrac® College Edition** An easy-to-use online database of reliable full-length articles from thousands of academic journals and popular periodicals. **Opposing Viewpoints Resource Center** Dynamic online database of articles and tools that allows students to analyze and think critically about the various sides of controversial issues.

Chapter 19: Credibility

Ideas for Instruction—Print	Ideas for Instruction—Electronic	Print Resources for Students	Electronic Resources for Students
Public Speaking Instructor's Guide to the Opposing Viewpoints Resource Center (OVRC) Includes chapters on Ways to Use OVRC in the Classroom, Suggested Activities, and Resources for Further Research. **The Teaching Assistant's Guide to the Basic Course** This guide covers general teaching and course management topics, as well as specific strategies for communication instruction. **Service Learning in Communication Studies: A Handbook** This book provides guidelines for connecting service-learning work with classroom concepts. **A Guide to the Basic Course for ESL Students** This guide assists the non-native speaker. Features FAQs, helpful URLs, and strategies for accent management and overcoming speech apprehension.	**The Speaker's Handbook Web site** http://communication.wadsworth.com/sprague7 Online access to: Instructor's Resource Manual with Test Bank Sample Speech Outlines InfoTrac® College Edition Resources **CNN Today® Videos: Public Speaking, Volumes I-V** Vol. 1: Queen Elizabeth II Speaks on Princess Diana's Death Vol. 3: Who are the Candidates? Vol. 3: Paddy Buchanan Vol. 3: McCain Apologizes Vol. 3: Lazio Campaign Tour Vol. 3: Hillary Wins Primary Vol. 4: Mary Fisher, "A Whisper of Aids" Vol. 4: President George W. Bush, "Address to a Joint Session of Congress and the American People, September 20, 2001" Vol. 5: Elizabeth Glaser, "Democratic National Convention Address" **ExamView® Computerized Testing** Electronic version of the Test Bank. Questions for Chapter 19 can be used to create and deliver customized quizzes and tests, in print and online. **WebTutor™ Toolbox on WebCT and Blackboard** Online course management tool available on WebCT or Blackboard pre-loaded with text-specific content and resources.	**InfoTrac® College Edition Student Activities Workbook for Public Speaking 2.0** Research and critical thinking activities for students using the online InfoTrac library. **Public Speaking Student Guide to the Opposing Viewpoints Resource Center (OVRC)** Includes Suggested Activities and Resources for Further Research using the OVRC online library.	**The Speaker's Handbook Web site** http://communication.wadsworth.com/sprague7 Online access to: Quizzes Interactive Activities Web links Sample Speech Outlines InfoTrac® College Edition activities **The Speaker's Handbook CD-ROM** Includes access to Speech Builder Express™, The Speaker's Handbook Web site, and InfoTrac®. The CD-ROM features *Speech Interactive*, a variety of sample student and professional speeches that can be watched, critiqued, and evaluated. 1. "Celebrating Women in Business" by Carly Fiorina **InfoTrac® College Edition** An easy-to-use online database of reliable full-length articles from thousands of academic journals and popular periodicals. **pposing Viewpoints Resource Center** Dynamic online database of articles and tools that allows students to analyze and think critically about the various sides of controversial issues.

Chapter 20: Motivational Appeals

Ideas for Instruction— Print	Ideas for Instruction— Electronic	Print Resources for Students	Electronic Resources for Students
Public Speaking Instructor's Guide to the Opposing Viewpoints Resource Center (OVRC) Includes chapters on Ways to Use OVRC in the Classroom, Suggested Activities, and Resources for Further Research. **The Teaching Assistant's Guide to the Basic Course** This guide covers general teaching and course management topics, as well as specific strategies for communication instruction. **Service Learning in Communication Studies: A Handbook** This book provides guidelines for connecting service-learning work with classroom concepts. **A Guide to the Basic Course for ESL Students** This guide assists the non-native speaker. Features FAQs, helpful URLs, and strategies for accent management and overcoming speech apprehension.	**The Speaker's Handbook Web site** http://communication.wadsworth .com/sprague7 Online access to: Instructor's Resource Manual with Test Bank Sample Speech Outlines InfoTrac® College Edition Resources **CNN Today® Videos: Public Speaking, Volumes I-V** Vol. 1: Farrakhan Motivates a Million Men Vol. 1: Million Man March Vol. 4: Mary Fisher, "A Whisper of Aids" Vol. 4: Nelson Mandela, "Glory and Hope: Let There be Work, Bread, Water, and Salt For All" Vol. 4: President George W. Bush, "Address to a Joint Session of Congress and the American People, September 20, 2001" Vol. 5: President George W. Bush, "National Day of Prayer and Remembrance" **ExamView® Computerized Testing** Electronic version of the Test Bank. Questions for Chapter 20 can be used to create and deliver customized quizzes and tests, in print and online. **WebTutor™ Toolbox on WebCT and Blackboard** Online course management tool available on WebCT or Blackboard pre-loaded with text-specific content and resources.	**InfoTrac® College Edition Student Activities Workbook for Public Speaking 2.0** Research and critical thinking activities for students using the online InfoTrac library. **Public Speaking Student Guide to the Opposing Viewpoints Resource Center (OVRC)** Includes Suggested Activities and Resources for Further Research using the OVRC online library.	**The Speaker's Handbook Web site** http://communication.wadsworth .com/sprague7 Online access to: Quizzes Interactive Activities Web links Sample Speech Outlines InfoTrac® College Edition activities **The Speaker's Handbook CD-ROM** Includes access to Speech Builder Express™, The Speaker's Handbook Web site, and InfoTrac®. The CD-ROM features *Speech Interactive*, a variety of sample student and professional speeches that can be watched, critiqued, and evaluated. 1. "DeAnza College Keynote Address" by Lance Dawson 2. "Commencement Speech" by Richard Rodriguez **InfoTrac® College Edition** An easy-to-use online database of reliable full-length articles from thousands of academic journals and popular periodicals. Keywords: *Core values* **Opposing Viewpoints Resource Center** Dynamic online database of articles and tools that allows students to analyze and think critically about the various sides of controversial issues.

Chapter 21: Informative Strategies

Ideas for Instruction—Print	Ideas for Instruction—Electronic	Print Resources for Students	Electronic Resources for Students
Public Speaking Instructor's Guide to the Opposing Viewpoints Resource Center (OVRC) Includes chapters on Ways to Use OVRC in the Classroom, Suggested Activities, and Resources for Further Research. **The Teaching Assistant's Guide to the Basic Course** This guide covers general teaching and course management topics, as well as specific strategies for communication instruction. **Service Learning in Communication Studies: A Handbook** This book provides guidelines for connecting service-learning work with classroom concepts. **A Guide to the Basic Course for ESL Students** This guide assists the non-native speaker. Features FAQs, helpful URLs, and strategies for accent management and overcoming speech apprehension.	**The Speaker's Handbook Web site** http://communication.wadsworth.com/sprague7 Online access to: Instructor's Resource Manual with Test Bank Sample Speech Outlines InfoTrac® College Edition Resources **CNN Today® Videos: Public Speaking, Volumes I-V** Vol. 1: A Motivational Marketing Presentation Vol. 3: Bush and Cheney **ExamView® Computerized Testing** Electronic version of the Test Bank. Questions for Chapter 21 can be used to create and deliver customized quizzes and tests, in print and online. **WebTutor™ Toolbox on WebCT and Blackboard** Online course management tool available on WebCT or Blackboard pre-loaded with text-specific content and resources.	**InfoTrac® College Edition Student Activities Workbook for Public Speaking 2.0** Research and critical thinking activities for students using the online InfoTrac library. 14.1 Informative Speaking in the "Information Age" 14.2 Identifying Informative Speeches 14.3 Analyzing Informative Approaches and Strategies 14.4 Informative Speaking to Counter Misinformation **Public Speaking Student Guide to the Opposing Viewpoints Resource Center (OVRC)** Includes Suggested Activities and Resources for Further Research using the OVRC online library. *Informing:* Exercises 1-8	**The Speaker's Handbook Web site** http://communication.wadsworth.com/sprague7 Online access to: Quizzes Interactive Activities Web links Sample Speech Outlines InfoTrac® College Edition activities **The Speaker's Handbook CD-ROM** Includes access to Speech Builder Express™, The Speaker's Handbook Web site, and InfoTrac®. The CD-ROM features *Speech Interactive*, a variety of sample student and professional speeches that can be watched, critiqued, and evaluated. 1. "Eye Chip" by Vanessa Harikul 2. "Electoral College" by Robert McDermott **nfoTrac® College Edition** An easy-to-use online database of reliable full-length articles from thousands of academic journals and popular periodicals. **Opposing Viewpoints Resource Center** Dynamic online database of articles and tools that allows students to analyze and think critically about the various sides of controversial issues.

Chapter 22: Persuasive Strategies

Ideas for Instruction—Print	Ideas for Instruction—Electronic	Print Resources for Students	Electronic Resources for Students
Public Speaking Instructor's Guide to the Opposing Viewpoints Resource Center (OVRC) Includes chapters on Ways to Use OVRC in the Classroom, Suggested Activities, and Resources for Further Research. **The Teaching Assistant's Guide to the Basic Course** This guide covers general teaching and course management topics, as well as specific strategies for communication instruction. **Service Learning in Communication Studies: A Handbook** This book provides guidelines for connecting service-learning work with classroom concepts. **A Guide to the Basic Course for ESL Students** This guide assists the non-native speaker. Features FAQs, helpful URLs, and strategies for accent management and overcoming speech apprehension.	**The Speaker's Handbook Web site** http://communication.wadsworth .com/sprague7 Online access to: Instructor's Resource Manual with Test Bank Sample Speech Outlines InfoTrac® College Edition Resources **CNN Today® Videos: Public Speaking, Volumes I-V** Vol. 1: Verbal Judo Vol. 1: Clinton Speaks Vol. 2: Marion Barry Vol. 2: Littleton Vol. 3: Who Are the Candidates? Vol. 3: Lazio Campaign Tour Vol. 4: Mary Fisher, "A Whisper of Aids" Vol. 4: Nelson Mandela, "Glory and Hope: Let There be Work, Bread, Water, and Salt For All" Vol. 4: President George W. Bush, "Address to a Joint Session of Congress and the American People, September 20, 2001" Vol. 5: Rep. Richard Gephardt, "Special Session of Congress Commemorating September 11th" Vol. 5: Elizabeth Glaser, "Democratic National Convention Address" **ExamView® Computerized Testing** Electronic version of the Test Bank. Questions for Chapter 22 can be used to create and deliver customized quizzes and tests, in print and online. **WebTutor™ Toolbox on WebCT and Blackboard** Online course management tool available on WebCT or Blackboard pre-loaded with text-specific content and resources.	**InfoTrac® College Edition Student Activities Workbook for Public Speaking 2.0** Research and critical thinking activities for students using the online InfoTrac library. 15.1 Identifying the Steps of Monroe's Motivated Sequence in a Speech 15.2 Identifying and Analyzing Problem/Solution Organization in a Speech **Public Speaking Student Guide to the Opposing Viewpoints Resource Center (OVRC)** Includes Suggested Activities and Resources for Further Research using the OVRC online library. *Persuading:* Exercises 1-8	**The Speaker's Handbook Web site** http://communication.wadsworth .com/sprague7 Online access to: Quizzes Interactive Activities Web links Sample Speech Outlines InfoTrac® College Edition activities **The Speaker's Handbook CD-ROM** Includes access to Speech Builder Express™, The Speaker's Handbook Web site, and InfoTrac®. The CD-ROM features *Speech Interactive*, a variety of sample student and professional speeches that can be watched, critiqued, and evaluated. 1. "All Hands" by Norman Mineta 2. "Online Pharmacies" by Sabrina Worsham **InfoTrac® College Edition** An easy-to-use online database of reliable full-length articles from thousands of academic journals and popular periodicals. Keywords: *Persuasive speaking* **Opposing Viewpoints Resource Center** Dynamic online database of articles and tools that allows students to analyze and think critically about the various sides of controversial issues.

Chapter 23: Adapting To Speaking Contexts

Ideas for Instruction— Print	Ideas for Instruction— Electronic	Print Resources for Students	Electronic Resources for Students
Public Speaking Instructor's Guide to the Opposing Viewpoints Resource Center (OVRC) Includes chapters on Ways to Use OVRC in the Classroom, Suggested Activities, and Resources for Further Research. **The Teaching Assistant's Guide to the Basic Course** This guide covers general teaching and course management topics, as well as specific strategies for communication instruction. **Service Learning in Communication Studies: A Handbook** This book provides guidelines for connecting service-learning work with classroom concepts. **A Guide to the Basic Course for ESL Students** This guide assists the non-native speaker. Features FAQs, helpful URLs, and strategies for accent management and overcoming speech apprehension.	**The Speaker's Handbook Web site** http://communication.wadsworth .com/sprague7 Online access to: Instructor's Resource Manual with Test Bank Sample Speech Outlines InfoTrac® College Edition Resources **CNN Today® Videos: Public Speaking, Volumes I-V** Vol. 1: Queen Elizabeth II, Speaks on Princess Diana's Death Vol. 2: "Hollywood" Gore Vol. 3: Paddy Buchanan Vol. 3: Bush Acceptance Speech Vol. 3: Gore Concession Speech Vol. 4: President George W. Bush, "Address to a Joint Session of Congress and the American People, September 20, 2001" Vol. 5: President Ronald Reagan, "Space Shuttle Challenger Tragedy" Vol. 5: President George W. Bush, "Space Shuttle Columbia Tragedy" Vol. 5: Senator Tom Harkin, "Memorial for Senator Paul Wellstone" **ExamView® Computerized Testing** Electronic version of the Test Bank. Questions for Chapter 23 can be used to create and deliver customized quizzes and tests, in print and online. **WebTutor™ Toolbox on WebCT and Blackboard** Online course management tool available on WebCT or Blackboard pre-loaded with text-specific content and resources.	**InfoTrac® College Edition Student Activities Workbook for Public Speaking 2.0** Research and critical thinking activities for students using the online InfoTrac library. 16.1 Analyzing Commemorative Speeches 16.2 Analyzing Speeches of Tribute 16.3 Analyzing Speeches of Acceptance 17.1 Importance of Small Group Communication in the Professional World **Public Speaking Student Guide to the Opposing Viewpoints Resource Center (OVRC)** Includes Suggested Activities and Resources for Further Research using the OVRC online library.	**The Speaker's Handbook Web site** http://communication.wadsworth .com/sprague7 Online access to: Quizzes Interactive Activities Web links Sample Speech Outlines InfoTrac® College Edition activities **The Speaker's Handbook CD-ROM** Includes access to Speech Builder Express™, The Speaker's Handbook Web site, and InfoTrac®. The CD-ROM features *Speech Interactive*, a variety of sample student and professional speeches that can be watched, critiqued, and evaluated. **InfoTrac® College Edition** An easy-to-use online database of reliable full-length articles from thousands of academic journals and popular periodicals. Keywords: *Commencement address, Dedication, Eulogy, Speech of acceptance, Speech of nomination, Speech of presentation, Speech of tribute, Speech of welcome* **Opposing Viewpoints Resource Center** Dynamic online database of articles and tools that allows students to analyze and think critically about the various sides of controversial issues.

Handbook Part V: Presentation

Chapter 24: Modes of Delivery

Ideas for Instruction—Print	Ideas for Instruction—Electronic	Print Resources for Students	Electronic Resources for Students
Public Speaking Instructor's Guide to the Opposing Viewpoints Resource Center (OVRC) Includes chapters on Ways to Use OVRC in the Classroom, Suggested Activities, and Resources for Further Research. **The Teaching Assistant's Guide to the Basic Course** This guide covers general teaching and course management topics, as well as specific strategies for communication instruction. **Service Learning in Communication Studies: A Handbook** This book provides guidelines for connecting service-learning work with classroom concepts. **A Guide to the Basic Course for ESL Students** This guide assists the non-native speaker. Features FAQs, helpful URLs, and strategies for accent management and overcoming speech apprehension.	**The Speaker's Handbook Web site** http://communication.wadsworth.com/sprague7 Online access to: Instructor's Resource Manual with Test Bank Sample Speech Outlines InfoTrac® College Edition Resources **CNN Today® Videos: Public Speaking, Volumes I-V** Vol. 1: Million Man March Vol. 2: Governor Jesse Ventura Vol. 2: Maya Angelou Vol. 3: Hillary Wins Primary Vol. 5: President George W. Bush, "National Day of Prayer and Remembrance" Vol. 5: Rep. Richard Gephardt, "Special Session of Congress Commemorating September 11th" **ExamView® Computerized Testing** Electronic version of the Test Bank. Questions for Chapter 24 can be used to create and deliver customized quizzes and tests, in print and online. **WebTutor™ Toolbox on WebCT and Blackboard** Online course management tool available on WebCT or Blackboard pre-loaded with text-specific content and resources.	**InfoTrac® College Edition Student Activities Workbook for Public Speaking 2.0** Research and critical thinking activities for students using the online InfoTrac library. **Public Speaking Student Guide to the Opposing Viewpoints Resource Center (OVRC)** Includes Suggested Activities and Resources for Further Research using the OVRC online library.	**The Speaker's Handbook Web site** http://communication.wadsworth.com/sprague7 Online access to: Quizzes Interactive Activities Web links Sample Speech Outlines InfoTrac® College Edition activities **The Speaker's Handbook CD-ROM** Includes access to Speech Builder Express™, The Speaker's Handbook Web site, and InfoTrac®. The CD-ROM features *Speech Interactive*, a variety of sample student and professional speeches that can be watched, critiqued, and evaluated. 1. "DeAnza College Keynote Address" by Lance Dawson 2. "Celebrating Women in Business" by Carly Fiorina 3. "All Hands" by Norman Mineta 4. "College Voters" by Amy Wood **InfoTrac® College Edition** An easy-to-use online database of reliable full-length articles from thousands of academic journals and popular periodicals. **Opposing Viewpoints Resource Center** Dynamic online database of articles and tools that allows students to analyze and think critically about the various sides of controversial issues.

Chapter 25: Practice Sessions

Ideas for Instruction— Print	Ideas for Instruction— Electronic	Print Resources for Students	Electronic Resources for Students
Public Speaking Instructor's Guide to the Opposing Viewpoints Resource Center (OVRC) Includes chapters on Ways to Use OVRC in the Classroom, Suggested Activities, and Resources for Further Research. **The Teaching Assistant's Guide to the Basic Course** This guide covers general teaching and course management topics, as well as specific strategies for communication instruction. **Service Learning in Communication Studies: A Handbook** This book provides guidelines for connecting service-learning work with classroom concepts. **A Guide to the Basic Course for ESL Students** This guide assists the non-native speaker. Features FAQs, helpful URLs, and strategies for accent management and overcoming speech apprehension.	**The Speaker's Handbook Web site** http://communication.wadsworth .com/sprague7 Online access to: Instructor's Resource Manual with Test Bank Sample Speech Outlines InfoTrac® College Edition Resources **ExamView® Computerized Testing** Electronic version of the Test Bank. Questions for Chapter 25 can be used to create and deliver customized quizzes and tests, in print and online. **WebTutor™ Toolbox on WebCT and Blackboard** Online course management tool available on WebCT or Blackboard pre-loaded with text-specific content and resources.	**InfoTrac® College Edition Student Activities Workbook for Public Speaking 2.0** Research and critical thinking activities for students using the online InfoTrac library. **Public Speaking Student Guide to the Opposing Viewpoints Resource Center (OVRC)** Includes Suggested Activities and Resources for Further Research using the OVRC online library.	**The Speaker's Handbook Web site** http://communication.wadsworth .com/sprague7 Online access to: Quizzes Interactive Activities Web links Sample Speech Outlines InfoTrac® College Edition activities **The Speaker's Handbook CD-ROM** Includes access to Speech Builder Express™, The Speaker's Handbook Web site, and InfoTrac®. The CD-ROM features *Speech Interactive*, a variety of sample student and professional speeches that can be watched, critiqued, and evaluated. **InfoTrac® College Edition** An easy-to-use online database of reliable full-length articles from thousands of academic journals and popular periodicals. **Opposing Viewpoints Resource Center** Dynamic online database of articles and tools that allows students to analyze and think critically about the various sides of controversial issues.

Chapter 26: Vocal Delivery

Ideas for Instruction—Print	Ideas for Instruction—Electronic	Print Resources for Students	Electronic Resources for Students
Public Speaking Instructor's Guide to the Opposing Viewpoints Resource Center (OVRC) Includes chapters on Ways to Use OVRC in the Classroom, Suggested Activities, and Resources for Further Research. **The Teaching Assistant's Guide to the Basic Course** This guide covers general teaching and course management topics, as well as specific strategies for communication instruction. **Service Learning in Communication Studies: A Handbook** This book provides guidelines for connecting service-learning work with classroom concepts. **A Guide to the Basic Course for ESL Students** This guide assists the non-native speaker. Features FAQs, helpful URLs, and strategies for accent management and overcoming speech apprehension.	**The Speaker's Handbook Web site** http://communication.wadsworth .com/sprague7 Online access to: Instructor's Resource Manual with Test Bank Sample Speech Outlines InfoTrac® College Edition Resources **CNN Today® Videos: Public Speaking, Volumes I–V** Vol. 1: Million Man March Vol. 2: Governor Jesse Ventura Vol. 2: Maya Angelou Vol. 3: Hillary Wins Primary Vol. 3: The Also Rans: Bradley Vol. 4: Mary Fisher, "A Whisper of AIDS" Vol. 4: President George W. Bush, "Address to a Joint Session of Congress and the American People, September 20, 2001" **ExamView® Computerized Testing** Electronic version of the Test Bank. Questions for Chapter 26 can be used to create and deliver customized quizzes and tests, in print and online. **WebTutor™ Toolbox on WebCT and Blackboard** Online course management tool available on WebCT or Blackboard pre-loaded with text-specific content and resources.	**InfoTrac® College Edition Student Activities Workbook for Public Speaking 2.0** Research and critical thinking activities for students using the online InfoTrac library. 13.1 Regional Pronunciation in Speaking **Public Speaking Student Guide to the Opposing Viewpoints Resource Center (OVRC)** Includes Suggested Activities and Resources for Further Research using the OVRC online library.	**The Speaker's Handbook Web site** http://communication.wadsworth .com/sprague7 Online access to: Quizzes Interactive Activities Web links Sample Speech Outlines InfoTrac® College Edition activities **The Speaker's Handbook CD-ROM** Includes access to Speech Builder Express™, The Speaker's Handbook Web site, and InfoTrac®. The CD-ROM features _Speech Interactive_, a variety of sample student and professional speeches that can be watched, critiqued, and evaluated. 1. "Study Abroad" by Anna Luebbering 2. "Eye Chip" by Vanessa Harikul 3. "Celebrating Women in Business" by Carly Fiorina 4. "Electoral College" by Robert McDermott **InfoTrac® College Edition** An easy-to-use online database of reliable full-length articles from thousands of academic journals and popular periodicals. Keywords: _Enunciation, Pronunciation, Vocal quality_ **Opposing Viewpoints Resource Center** Dynamic online database of articles and tools that allows students to analyze and think critically about the various sides of controversial issues.

Chapter 27: Physical Delivery

Ideas for Instruction— Print	Ideas for Instruction— Electronic	Print Resources for Students	Electronic Resources for Students
Public Speaking Instructor's Guide to the Opposing Viewpoints Resource Center (OVRC) Includes chapters on Ways to Use OVRC in the Classroom, Suggested Activities, and Resources for Further Research. **The Teaching Assistant's Guide to the Basic Course** This guide covers general teaching and course management topics, as well as specific strategies for communication instruction. **Service Learning in Communication Studies: A Handbook** This book provides guidelines for connecting service-learning work with classroom concepts. **A Guide to the Basic Course for ESL Students** This guide assists the non-native speaker. Features FAQs, helpful URLs, and strategies for accent management and overcoming speech apprehension.	**The Speaker's Handbook Web site** http://communication.wadsworth .com/sprague7 Online access to: Instructor's Resource Manual with Test Bank Sample Speech Outlines InfoTrac® College Edition Resources **CNN Today® Videos: Public Speaking, Volumes I-V** Vol. 1: Million Man March Vol. 2: Governor Jesse Ventura Vol. 2: Maya Angelou Vol. 3: Hillary Wins Primary **ExamView® Computerized Testing** Electronic version of the Test Bank. Questions for Chapter 27 can be used to create and deliver customized quizzes and tests, in print and online. **WebTutor™ Toolbox on WebCT and Blackboard** Online course management tool available on WebCT or Blackboard pre-loaded with text-specific content and resources.	**InfoTrac® College Edition Student Activities Workbook for Public Speaking 2.0** Research and critical thinking activities for students using the online InfoTrac library. 13.2 Using the Body to Communicate Confidence and Power 13.3 Natural Gestures in Public Speaking **Public Speaking Student Guide to the Opposing Viewpoints Resource Center (OVRC)** Includes Suggested Activities and Resources for Further Research using the OVRC online library.	**The Speaker's Handbook Web site** http://communication.wadsworth .com/sprague7 Online access to: Quizzes Interactive Activities Web links Sample Speech Outlines InfoTrac® College Edition activities **The Speaker's Handbook CD-ROM** Includes access to Speech Builder Express™, The Speaker's Handbook Web site, and InfoTrac®. The CD-ROM features *Speech Interactive*, a variety of sample student and professional speeches that can be watched, critiqued, and evaluated. 1. "Reentry Student" by Mona Brasher 2. "No More Sugar" by Hans Erian 3. "Eye Chip" by Vanessa Harikul **InfoTrac® College Edition** An easy-to-use online database of reliable full-length articles from thousands of academic journals and popular periodicals. Keywords: *Facial expressions, Nonverbal communication* **Opposing Viewpoints Resource Center** Dynamic online database of articles and tools that allows students to analyze and think critically about the various sides of controversial issues.

Chapter 28: Presentation Aids

Ideas for Instruction—Print	Ideas for Instruction—Electronic	Print Resources for Students	Electronic Resources for Students
Public Speaking Instructor's Guide to the Opposing Viewpoints Resource Center (OVRC) Includes chapters on Ways to Use OVRC in the Classroom, Suggested Activities, and Resources for Further Research. **The Teaching Assistant's Guide to the Basic Course** This guide covers general teaching and course management topics, as well as specific strategies for communication instruction. **Service Learning in Communication Studies: A Handbook** This book provides guidelines for connecting service-learning work with classroom concepts. **A Guide to the Basic Course for ESL Students** This guide assists the non-native speaker. Features FAQs, helpful URLs, and strategies for accent management and overcoming speech apprehension.	**The Speaker's Handbook Web site** http://communication.wadsworth.com/sprague7 Online access to: Instructor's Resource Manual with Test Bank Sample Speech Outlines InfoTrac® College Edition Resources **CNN Today® Videos: Public Speaking, Volumes I-V** Vol. 1: A Motivational Marketing Presentation **ExamView® Computerized Testing** Electronic version of the Test Bank. Questions for Chapter 28 can be used to create and deliver customized quizzes and tests, in print and online. **WebTutor™ Toolbox on WebCT and Blackboard** Online course management tool available on WebCT or Blackboard pre-loaded with text-specific content and resources.	**InfoTrac® College Edition Student Activities Workbook for Public Speaking 2.0** Research and critical thinking activities for students using the online InfoTrac library. 11.1 Creating Visual Aids for Statistical/Numerical Data 11.2 Issues About the Use of Computer-generated Visual Aids 11.3 Information About Technology Used in Creating and Showing Visual Aids 11.4 Advanced Techniques for Computer Software Slide Shows **Public Speaking Student Guide to the Opposing Viewpoints Resource Center (OVRC)** Includes Suggested Activities and Resources for Further Research using the OVRC online library.	**The Speaker's Handbook Web site** http://communication.wadsworth.com/sprague7 Online access to: Quizzes Interactive Activities Web links Sample Speech Outlines InfoTrac® College Edition activities **The Speaker's Handbook CD-ROM** Includes access to Speech Builder Express™, The Speaker's Handbook Web site, and InfoTrac®. The CD-ROM features *Speech Interactive*, a variety of sample student and professional speeches that can be watched, critiqued, and evaluated. 1. "Eye Chip" by Vanessa Harikul 2. "No More Sugar" by Hans Erian **InfoTrac® College Edition** An easy-to-use online database of reliable full-length articles from thousands of academic journals and popular periodicals. Keywords: *Audiovisual aids, Flowcharts, Graphs, LCD projector, Organizational charts, Visual aids* **Opposing Viewpoints Resource Center** Dynamic online database of articles and tools that allows students to analyze and think critically about the various sides of controversial issues.

Chapter 29: Adapting To The Speech Situation

Ideas for Instruction—Print	Ideas for Instruction—Electronic	Print Resources for Students	Electronic Resources for Students
Public Speaking Instructor's Guide to the Opposing Viewpoints Resource Center (OVRC) Includes chapters on Ways to Use OVRC in the Classroom, Suggested Activities, and Resources for Further Research. **The Teaching Assistant's Guide to the Basic Course** This guide covers general teaching and course management topics, as well as specific strategies for communication instruction. **Service Learning in Communication Studies: A Handbook** This book provides guidelines for connecting service-learning work with classroom concepts. **A Guide to the Basic Course for ESL Students** This guide assists the non-native speaker. Features FAQs, helpful URLs, and strategies for accent management and overcoming speech apprehension.	**The Speaker's Handbook Web site** http://communication.wadsworth.com/sprague7 Online access to: Instructor's Resource Manual with Test Bank Sample Speech Outlines InfoTrac® College Edition Resources **CNN Today® Videos: Public Speaking, Volumes I-V** Vol. 2: "Hollywood" Gore Vol. 2: Littleton Vol. 3: Paddy Buchanan Vol. 3: Women Voters in New York **ExamView® Computerized Testing** Electronic version of the Test Bank. Questions for Chapter 29 can be used to create and deliver customized quizzes and tests, in print and online. **WebTutor™ Toolbox on WebCT and Blackboard** Online course management tool available on WebCT or Blackboard pre-loaded with text-specific content and resources.	**InfoTrac® College Edition Student Activities Workbook for Public Speaking 2.0** Research and critical thinking activities for students using the online InfoTrac library. 18.1 Handling Difficult Audience Members Invitationally **Public Speaking Student Guide to the Opposing Viewpoints Resource Center (OVRC)** Includes Suggested Activities and Resources for Further Research using the OVRC online library.	**The Speaker's Handbook Web site** http://communication.wadsworth.com/sprague7 Online access to: Quizzes Interactive Activities Web links Sample Speech Outlines InfoTrac® College Edition activities **The Speaker's Handbook CD-ROM** Includes access to Speech Builder Express™, The Speaker's Handbook Web site, and InfoTrac®. The CD-ROM features *Speech Interactive*, a variety of sample student and professional speeches that can be watched, critiqued, and evaluated. 1. "All Hands" by Norman Mineta **InfoTrac® College Edition** An easy-to-use online database of reliable full-length articles from thousands of academic journals and popular periodicals. **Opposing Viewpoints Resource Center** Dynamic online database of articles and tools that allows students to analyze and think critically about the various sides of controversial issues.

Chapter 30: Answering Questions

Ideas for Instruction—Print	Ideas for Instruction—Electronic	Print Resources for Students	Electronic Resources for Students
Public Speaking Instructor's Guide to the Opposing Viewpoints Resource Center (OVRC) Includes chapters on Ways to Use OVRC in the Classroom, Suggested Activities, and Resources for Further Research. **The Teaching Assistant's Guide to the Basic Course** This guide covers general teaching and course management topics, as well as specific strategies for communication instruction. **Service Learning in Communication Studies: A Handbook** This book provides guidelines for connecting service-learning work with classroom concepts. **A Guide to the Basic Course for ESL Students** This guide assists the non-native speaker. Features FAQs, helpful URLs, and strategies for accent management and overcoming speech apprehension.	**The Speaker's Handbook Web site** http://communication.wadsworth.com/sprague7 Online access to: Instructor's Resource Manual with Test Bank Sample Speech Outlines InfoTrac® College Edition Resources **ExamView® Computerized Testing** Electronic version of the Test Bank. Questions for Chapter 30 can be used to create and deliver customized quizzes and tests, in print and online. **WebTutor™ Toolbox on WebCT and Blackboard** Online course management tool available on WebCT or Blackboard pre-loaded with text-specific content and resources.	**InfoTrac® College Edition Student Activities Workbook for Public Speaking 2.0** Research and critical thinking activities for students using the online InfoTrac library. **Public Speaking Student Guide to the Opposing Viewpoints Resource Center (OVRC)** Includes Suggested Activities and Resources for Further Research using the OVRC online library.	**The Speaker's Handbook Web site** http://communication.wadsworth.com/sprague7 Online access to: Quizzes Interactive Activities Web links Sample Speech Outlines InfoTrac® College Edition activities **The Speaker's Handbook CD-ROM** Includes access to Speech Builder Express™, The Speaker's Handbook Web site, and InfoTrac®. The CD-ROM features *Speech Interactive*, a variety of sample student and professional speeches that can be watched, critiqued, and evaluated. **InfoTrac® College Edition** An easy-to-use online database of reliable full-length articles from thousands of academic journals and popular periodicals. **Opposing Viewpoints Resource Center** Dynamic online database of articles and tools that allows students to analyze and think critically about the various sides of controversial issues.